We Soviet Women

By

Tatiana Tchernavin

Author of "ESCAPE FROM THE SOVIETS."

Translated by N. ALEXANDER

When the giant tidal wave of the Russian Revolution had spent its force, the world saw many of the lowest people in Russian life appearing on the top, and many that were fine, especially women, submerged into depths. Mme. Tchernavin was one of these women.

In her new book, she tells the story of 15 Russian women living under Soviet conditions. It is all actual, personal experiences told in the first person; and they are of women that Mme. Tchernavin herself came into touch with, or whose story she came to know.

Read about "Vera," the girl who committed suicide when she was rejected as a school-teacher — — "The Wife of a Soviet Official," showing the amount of power that was given to totally inefficient women, merely because they were the wives of Officials — - — "G. P. U. Official," an account of a cruel, frightful creature, "A Peasant Woman," showing the agricultural plight of the people — — "The Girl Student," the pitiful disillusionment of an idealistic girl who believed in Utopia.

Forceful and dramatic — — portraying the conditions in the life of the women in Soviet Russia — — those who are its favorites and those whom it regards as its traditional enemies.

The author has seen much, has felt deeply. That she can convey these sights and feelings to others was attested by the instant success of her former book. Her new volume — eagerly awaited by thousands of readers of "Escape from the Soviets" — is not merely corroboration of her former book; it has power, humanity, interest and rich substance of its own.

WE SOVIET WOMEN

TATIANA TCHERNAVIN

(*Photo by Harris & Ewing*)

WE SOVIET WOMEN

BY

TATIANA TCHERNAVIN

Author of *Escape from the Soviets*

TRANSLATED BY

N. ALEXANDER

1936

NEW YORK

E. P. DUTTON & CO., INC.

CONTENTS

VERA

AFTER the revolution many aspects of life in old Russia were summed up for political purposes under simplified formulae which entirely misrepresent the truth. Thus, for instance, types of landowner, bourgeois and priest were created for the benefit of the young and for foreign propaganda. All these typical figures were such hideous caricatures that in talking to young people I sometimes wondered whether it would not be easier to reconstruct an image of an ancient Roman or Egyptian than that of an ordinary Russian tradesman or landowner. These men, many of whom were still alive, had all been declared "class enemies," which simplified the situation and gave the Soviet Government a free hand in dealing with them. To kill a man, for instance, is not quite the thing, but "to liquidate" a bourgeois, a *kulak* or a priest is quite natural, since they are class enemies. What sort of people they were, good or bad, in sympathy with the revolution or really hostile to it—nobody cared to know.

In 1931 a questionnaire was put to the students of the Leningrad University to find out what knowledge they had of history. The enormous majority answered that all they knew about European history was the 'Industrial Revolution' in England and the 'Paris Commune' which they dated back to the French revolution of 1789, and that of Russian history they knew nothing. Others wrote, "I know that there was Bloody Nicolas," meaning Nicolas II. The offensive nickname, which, by the way, was rarely used, was intended to show their contempt for monarchy. I do not know whether things are any better now in this respect: two or three years ago when the study of the past was neglected to a perfectly ridiculous extent, and only the greyheaded figure of Karl Marx lit up the darkness of unknown centuries, the Commissariat of Public Education made the astonishing discovery that knowledge of history was not counter-revolutionary, provided the facts were interpreted on Marx-Leninist lines. And so the past is coming into its own once more. But, judging from the newspapers and Soviet literature, the established 'class types' have remained untouched, that of priest being painted in particularly lurid colours. He has been turned into such a red-nosed, fat-bellied monster of drunkenness and profligacy that there is obviously no place for him in real life and he can only exist on anti-religious posters. It is hard to say whether anyone believes this propaganda, but since the young generation knows nothing about the past, the Government thinks it will pass muster and to some extent prevent people from understanding that the clergy are human after all.

We of the old generation were ashamed of all this vulgar and ridiculous nonsense, but we could do nothing. The least interference on our part would have led to an accusation of 'furthering religious prejudices'— i.e. to prison and exile. It seemed incredible to recall what indifferent, callous atheists most of the 'intelligentsia' had been under the old régime—and now it was dangerous to behave with ordinary decency towards the pitiful remains of the church and the clergy!

The Government 'campaign' against the church is both disgusting in itself and utterly unprovoked. During the whole of the revolution the Russian church has not once risen as a body against the Soviet Government, has not organised a popular rebellion or done anything illegal. It has not opposed 'militant churchmen' to 'militant atheists.' Its downfall has been tragic and complete. But it must be said that in spite of the Government's attempts to rob the clergy of all human dignity, making them into repulsive scarecrows, a great many of them rose to wonderful heroism and sanctity. The Government declared them to be 'social parasites,' deprived them of the right to earn their living, of the right to be citizens of their own country, placed them in conditions in which any social group was bound to perish—to say nothing of the thousands that have been shot or sent into exile; yet in spite of all this priests manage to exist and to be a support to others. All religious education is forbidden, and yet they succeed in training young priests, ready to face terrible hardships and inevitable persecution. What is the source of their strength? What will be left of the Russian church when the Government is able at any moment 'to liquidate' all its representatives? When these years of persecution have become history, someone will write the heroic epic of the Church. For my part, I was only a casual outside observer.

The beginning of this story dates many years back. Long before the war, when I was a little girl, my mother decided to spend the summer in the country. I was born in Moscow, but when I was four we moved to

Siberia which I considered my real native land. After
the freedom and broad expanse of Siberia and the
huge park on the banks of a full, wide river, the prospect of life in a hired cottage in a Russian village did
not seem at all alluring. But in those days my wishes
were not consulted.

The first thing to comfort me was that the place
turned out to be remarkably beautiful. A lovely
white church stood at the top of a high, steep hill. A
river flowed at the bottom. According to Siberian
standards it was a poor little stream, but in Russia it
passed for a real river. It wound its way through the
plain between wide green banks, birch copses and
thickets of birdcherry in the ravines. Behind the
church, which could be seen for miles around, stood
the priest's cottage, closely surrounded by lime-trees.
The house we lived in was not far from it. Ours was a
fine house, but the priest's cottage struck me as very
peculiar. It had three windows in front, tiny as in the
peasants' huts, the only difference being that it had
white curtains and pots of fuchsias and geraniums on
the window-sills. On one side it had no windows at all
and at the back only one window which obviously
belonged to the kitchen. There was an upper storey
with one window in it, probably the bedroom. What
puzzled me most was that the cottage seemed to have
no doors; there was only a plain wooden gate leading
into the covered courtyard. I could not imagine how
one entered the place, until my mother sent me there
to buy some eggs.

"Eggs? from the priest?" I asked in surprise. The
only priest I had seen so far at close quarters was the
University chaplain. The chapel was inside the

University building, opposite the entrance hall. It was closed during the week, and all day long the noisy crowd of students hurried past it along the corridor, coming and going. On Saturday evenings and Sunday mornings the chapel door was opened, on solemn occasions a red velvet carpet was spread before it and two laurel bushes in tubs were placed at the sides. The priest was an important looking man with grave, slow movements. He was Professor of Divinity and Canonical Law and usually wore a purple silk cassock, a golden cross on a chain round his neck, and gold spectacles. So far as I remember scarcely any students came to the services. The families of the staff attended regularly. The professors came from time to time so as not to be too conspicuous by their absence. As I was the eldest and could be trusted to behave myself, I was sometimes sent to church, to keep up appearances for the family. I went with our governess, a young and pretty French girl. I did not know the service at all, and she was a Catholic and did not understand a word of Russian. The beginning of the service was fairly interesting, because we inspected the congregation's Sunday clothes, but afterwards we grew very tired and bored. We both tried to catch signs by which we could tell whether the service would soon be over. This was all that my impressions of the church amounted to. There were several churches in the town where we lived, and a monastery close by, but I thought that only tradesmen and working people went there—and I knew nothing about them in those days.

And now, in the country, the idea of going to the priest to buy eggs seemed to me simply preposterous.

"What gentility!" my mother remarked sarcastically as though I were to blame for my bringing up. "If you went to church you would see that peasant women pay for requiems and special services with eggs instead of money. Some give one egg, others two. An egg is worth one copeck. This is a poor parish."

I went reluctantly. The gate into the yard opened when I pulled the string hanging at the top of it, and immediately shut behind me with a loud bang. The courtyard seemed dark, though it was midday, and I could not understand where the voice came from asking: "Who is there?"

"Mother sent me for eggs," I answered into space.

Gradually I began to distinguish that there was a cow at the other end of the courtyard and that a woman in a white kerchief sat almost under it, milking.

"Step into the kitchen," she said.

I went in with some hesitation. The kitchen was clean and cosy and smelt of black bread. The window and the shelves of the dresser were hung with homespun linen. A plain deal table stood in the middle, and along the walls there were two settles and a stool. On the table there were two earthenware plates and two wooden spoons.

I felt rather uncomfortable but it was interesting to look round.

"Is the table set for dinner?" I wondered. "But why do they eat in the kitchen? Why have they only one plate each? Why are there no forks and knives? Will they eat nothing but soup? And who is the woman in the yard, milking? She must be their servant. Where is the priest's wife, then?"

I could hear that the woman had finished milking. She came into the kitchen.

"Well, good morning. Let us have a look at you," she said good-naturedly, turning me round to the light. "Do you like being in the country?"

"Yes," I answered, trying to make up my mind whether she was the servant or the priest's wife.

"How many eggs would you like?"

"Mother said as many as you could spare."

She went out of the room and came back with a basket.

"It isn't two dozen. Take all there are. They are new-laid, the women gave us them yesterday. We don't want any for ourselves just now, it's St. Peter's fast, you know."

I did not know. So she was the priest's wife! I thought I ought to say something out of politeness, but the only thing that occurred to me was to ask

"You have a cow?"

"We have two. The other one is out with the village herd, but I don't let this one out, she has just calved. Come in the evening, I will show you both cows and the calf."

"Thank you," I said undecidedly. I was not interested in cows, and in the open I was frankly afraid of them.

I had nothing more to say. I took leave of her awkwardly and went away. Lost in thought, I brought the basket of eggs straight into the drawing room.

"What are you doing?" my mother cried in surprise.

"You can't think how poor they are! The priest's wife milks the cow. They eat in the kitchen, off earthenware plates and with wooden spoons!"

"They aren't likely to use silver ones in the country!" my mother laughed.

"But we have silver!" I retorted.

"We are on a holiday and are not used to country ways. But the clergy here live very simply, little better than peasants, and are sometimes even poorer."

This did not make matters clearer to me, and the priest on acquaintance turned out to be even more peculiar than his wife.

He was very tall, pale and thin, with one shoulder higher than the other. He had black eyebrows, a clipped moustache and long black hair, which was pushed behind his ears, and lay on either side of his face reaching to his narrow black beard. His grey cassock was worn almost threadbare and the coarse leather of his Russian boots, patched in several places, was rusty with age.

Peasant women who brought butter, curds, cream, chickens, and strawberries to sell to my mother said:

"Our priest looks like a gipsy, but he is a good man. He takes what you give him for a service and never asks to be paid. And if anyone is dying he doesn't mind going in the middle of the night to them. Once he was nearly drowned during the spring floods—an old woman on the other side of the river sent for him. And the woman was a beggar, too, not worth a farthing, body and soul."

The priest used to come to tea with us and 'to have a talk,' as he put it. Seeing that I did not quite know what to do with myself he said to me once:

"You wait, when the fast is over, we'll go mowing."

"Do you do the mowing yourself?" I asked in surprise.

"Why, who is to do it for me?" he laughed. "My wife's cows want a lot of fodder. And without cows we should be done for—a tall fellow like me can't live on potatoes and black bread, you know."

"And when will the fast be over?" I asked, having no idea what fast he meant.

"On the day of St. Peter and St. Paul, June 29. We'll have a special service after Mass, and next day, with God's blessing, I'll go mowing. Have you seen my meadow? The first you come to on the river bank, on the way to the forest, is the peasants'. It's fine grass there, tall and luscious. And further along is the church meadow—the sexton's and mine. It's dry there and the grass isn't so good, but God willing, we'll get enough hay for our cows."

I did not see what cows and meadows had to do with me. The priest carefully took a little jam on his spoon, drank some tea, and wiping his moustache with a huge checked handkerchief, went on.

"When hay is made, I must earth the potatoes, weed the kitchen garden once more, and then it will be time for mushrooms. And meanwhile, as you run about the woods picking flowers, keep your eyes open! As soon as mushrooms appear we'll go off on a mushrooming expedition, you and I. We'll go a long way, to the forest. You can't go there alone, you would lose your way, but we'll go together if you care to."

The summer months were busy and peaceful. Hay was made, the women were out in the fields with the sickles and corn ricks rose above the yellow stubble. It was then that mushrooms* appeared.

"Good news!" said the priest gaily when I told him of my discovery. "Get ready early to-morrow morning and bring some lunch with you; it will be a long day."

* Edible fungi are meant.—TRANSLATOR'S NOTE.

I no longer felt shy as I trotted beside him, taking two or three steps to his one. I had grown used to meeting the priest constantly in the village street, in the fields, in the meadow, in the by-roads. In addition to doing ordinary peasant's work he walked miles almost every day on parish duties. One village wanted to pray for rain, another for fair weather; an old woman who had lost count of her years and need not have hurried to depart this life chose the busiest season to do so; a baby happened to be born just at hay-making time. Apples ripened and had to be blessed; honey was taken from the hives and also required blessing. In all this there was more of pious tradition than of religious faith, but somehow it seemed appropriate and gave form and colour to the peasants' hard life.

Mushrooms were an important item of housekeeping; old women and children were sent to gather them. The priest had no children; his wife had the house and the cows and the kitchen garden to look after, and could do no more than pickle and dry the mushrooms which he brought her. And so for him mushrooming was a duty as well as a favourite sport.

We went to the forest almost every day. When we came to the edge of it the priest pointed out to me the direction which I was to follow, said warningly, "mind you keep your eyes open!" and we parted. But we did not go far from each other, and I could hear him singing some holy words in his soft baritone and talking to the mushrooms at the same time.

"Lord, I cry unto Thee, hear me... Ah, you wretched slug, you've got no business here, you've gnawed all round the stem. . . . Give ear unto my voice when I cry unto Thee."

"What are you singing, Father?" I asked ironically.
"Psalms."

"How does the slug come in?"

"What slug?" he asked absent-mindedly. "Ah, you little mischief, you've caught me! Sharp little thing that you are! You sing yourself; we'll see if you do it better."

"I can't sing Psalms."

"Sing anything you like. Psalms are in my line."

And so we walked along, he singing sacred songs and I—airs from my favourite operas, *Russlan* and *Tcherevichki*. About midday we sat down to rest and 'fortify ourselves' as he called it. I ate egg sandwiches and he—black bread and onion. I imagined that his lunch tasted much nicer than mine, but I did not like to ask for a bite, because he always brought only one onion with him. I offered him my sandwiches but he refused.

"You eat it, your delicacies aren't in my line. And I mayn't have eggs now, it is the Assumption fast."

"What fast?"

"The fast before the Assumption of Our Lady, the Mother of God."

During one of our last expeditions I ventured at last to ask him a question that had long been on my mind:

"Tell me, please, why have you no children?"

"God does not give me any," he answered simply. "I should love to have a child, a snub-nosed little girl like you, you know. We'd go mushrooming together, read books in winter, have long talks . . . " he said wistfully.

. . . . . .

Soon after this we left the place. Fifteen years passed, there was the war and the revolution. I felt like a weary old woman: one year of the revolution is as good as five. I was in charge of one of the palaces outside Petersburg, all of which had been converted into museums. In winter I had sometimes to travel on behalf of the Society for the Preservation of Art Treasures and Antiquities, to inspect derelict country houses, to rescue the remaining pictures, statues and furniture. On one occasion I was sent to an estate the former owners of which had played an important part in the history of eighteenth-century Russia. The house was reported to contain a collection of family portraits, but no one knew in what condition it was, for the estate lay at some distance from the railway and it was difficult to reach.

The station proved to be the very one to which we had travelled that summer fifteen years before. I was met there by a young boy from the Komsomol who had been sent by the local Executive Committee to drive me to the estate and act as my guide and assistant.

We crawled along in our sledge, diving from one snowdrift into another. The boy was sorry for me.

"Fancy sending a little thing like you in such a frost! Why, you haven't any felt boots even," he grumbled good-naturedly. "And much good it is, going there! Everything's been wrecked long ago. Old portraits, indeed! Who ever wants to look at them? They were gentry and rich, bourgeois element, class enemies, and none of them are living now—as though anyone would care to see their faces!"

"It isn't their faces that one cares about, but the work of the artists who gave their labour to paint them," I tried to explain. "One may paint a rich man so that it will be a work of art, an historical treasure, and make such a portrait of a poor labourer that it would be a bore to look at it."

"You're right there," he agreed readily. "It's no pleasure to look at the poor, there are quite enough of them about. But all the same, it's galling to look at the gentry who battened on our labour. It's sheer waste your travelling in this frost."

"I have an order, I've been told to go," I said instructively.

"Oh well, if it's an order, that's different. There's no gainsaying that," he answered and urged on his nag.

The road seemed to be the very one that led to the village where my old friend the priest used to live. I wanted to know what had happened to him, but I did not like to ask the young Communist: it might lead to no end of trouble and mean explaining 'on what basis' I had met 'a servitor of the cult.'

We turned off before we came to the hill with the church and slowly made our way along a deserted road buried in snowdrifts to an old, weather-beaten but still beautiful house. There was hardly a pane to be seen in the windows and many of the frames were missing too; there were no porches or balconies. All that could be used for fuel had been taken away, though one would have thought there was enough wood all round. The front door was ajar, snow had drifted in and it was frozen so hard that we could not push it open. Wind was blowing through the house, stirring the remains of silken hangings on the walls. There was not a table or chair left in any of the rooms and not a single bolt or door handle—nothing!

"That's neatly done!" my companion said in surprise. "I wonder they had time to clear it all out! Only last summer there was a school camping here. It's a fine house, strongly built. It might be put to good use, but by the spring it will be pulled to pieces," he said with conviction.

I quickly passed from room to room.

"There's nothing to look at here. Why, it's as though mice had been gnawing at it! Come away," he grumbled.

"I must inspect everything and draw up a report," I answered sternly.

"Oh well, if you must make a report, there's nothing for it," he agreed obediently.

Everywhere there was the eerie emptiness peculiar to houses that have been plundered. But in the last room to which we came, a corner room on the first floor which must have been used as a study, the two inner walls were covered with eighteenth-century portraits. The family was obviously not renowned for beauty, and it was rather a formidable display of ugly faces, many of them painted in old age. The colours were faded; on some of the portraits the varnish had turned white and the surface seemed covered with a film. It was evidently the unattractiveness of the portraits that had saved them from being stolen.

I found it difficult to tell at the first glance whether they were valuable, but as they obviously dated back to the eighteenth century, they had to be taken to the museum.

"The older, the uglier—and the uglier the better!" said my guide with a comic sigh. "I see you'll order me to take them down."

"I will," I answered laughing. "I've scored, you

see." It was jolly to save something that had been doomed.

"Where am I to get the steps? I can't reach the top layer." He tried to make difficulties.

"Go and fetch the watchman. We must tell him that we have an order for removing the pictures."

"The watchman, indeed!" he whistled. "We'll remove them in accordance with the revolutionary law," and he began taking down the portraits.

"Go and find the watchman," I insisted sternly.

He went away rather annoyed, leaving me in the freezing room alone with the dry, aristocratic yellow faces that looked at me haughtily as though displeased at being saved from destruction.

He returned, bringing with him a squat little woman in huge felt boots, short jacket and a big shawl worn threadbare.

"Here is the watchwoman," he said.

"That's what I am, though I don't know what I am watching over," she began in a quick patter. "Last year I took care of the school, and now I live in the bath-house waiting for the summer."

I briefly explained my business to her, wrote down my name on a piece of paper and repeated it to her twice so that she would remember it and be able to say who took away the pictures, in case she were asked. But instead of listening she kept staring at me and suddenly broke out into exclamations, sighs and questions.

"Why, it's you, miss! Madam, I mean! That is, citizen, I should say, idiot that I am. It's a silly old habit, saying 'miss'. Don't you remember me? You spent a summer here once. Is madam your mother

still living? She was not strong. My mother used to
say 'that lady is not for long in this world, that's why
she is so kind'. Don't you remember Agashka?
Agashka was my mother, she did your washing for
you."

I remembered neither Agashka nor her daughter
who must have been at the time a child like me and
was now a woman who had evidently been through a
good deal. But she reminded me of that summer, of
the forest, of the peaceful Russian country in which
everything seemed centuries old and likely to go on
for ever.

"Is your priest still living?" I asked while the
Communist was busy carrying out the portraits.

"Yes. He is an old man now. He is as thin as ever,
but strong, only his back is bent. His wife is dead.
When the revolution began we, women, came to take
away her cows. It couldn't be helped, you know. . . .
They said priests sowed religious opium. We knew
nothing about that, our priest did not sow anything,
he had only a meadow. And his wife had two cows and
a heifer; fine cows they were and she was ever so fond
of them. Well, so we came to their gate and tried to
force our way in, but she bolted it and wouldn't let
us in. 'Open the gate!' we shouted. 'Open at once,
or we'll burn down the house! It's the revolution, the
orders are to kill priests and bourgeois! Open while
you can. We've come for your cows.'

"We shouted and banged on the gate with our fists
and boots, and we heard her saying from the other
side ever so pitifully, 'Go away, I beg you, go away for
the dear Lord's sake! Just think what you are doing!
As though I had ever done you any wrong! I won't

give you my cows. You'll destroy them. Do be sensible. Is it right to take away one's last? How shall I feed my little girl? You have children, too, have pity on mine, don't take this sin on your conscience!'

"But the women were angry and went on clamouring for the cows. 'We peasants are masters now,' we said; 'the village has decided to take away your cows!'

"And then all of a sudden we heard Father Alexey come up to her. We were frightened. We were fond of him—you know yourself, we had seen nothing but kindness from him. And besides, he was a priest, it's a holy office, so we felt a bit uneasy and stopped shouting. He opened the gate, drew his wife aside and said to her 'you go indoors,' and told us to come into the yard and take the cows. Some of the women set up a wail and fell at his feet, saying 'forgive us, foolish sinful creatures that we are,' and others, rowdy ones, shouted at them 'what are you snivelling about? A priest is no better than a peasant, nothing to fuss over.' And the girls—the bad ones, of course—began singing:

> 'Priest Sergey, hey, hey,
> Pair of boots grey, grey.'

A silly song, and, besides, our priest was Alexey—not Sergey."

"Well, did you take the cows away?" I asked.

"We did. They mooed something dreadful, poor beasts! It sounded like a human voice."

"Who got them?"

"Why, no one. There were two cows and a heifer, and there are nineteen families in our village. And women from other villages ran up too—'It's our parish,' they said, 'the priest is for us all and so are his cows, so you must share them.' All are poor, you know, all want to have more. But of course every family had a cow of their own and some had two—not like nowadays when a cow is a marvel. So while we were quarrelling and fighting, the men came up. They joined in also and it was decided to kill the cows and cut them up into portions—so that all could have a good feed of meat, anyway. Some of the women wept; they were dreadfully sorry for the cows—such fine beasts and good milkers, too. And others kept egging the men on, 'Kill them quick,' they said, 'no good can come of a priest's belongings.' So they killed the cows, shared the meat and that was the end of it."

"Weren't you sorry to destroy the cows?"

"Ever so sorry! But, you see, we couldn't share them, so there was nothing for it."

"And when did the priest's wife die?"

"Soon after that. She fretted. It was hard on her, you know. It isn't as though she were a stranger; she was born in our village, her father was priest here, and a very nice man he was. Not so kind as Father Alexey—this one is really too kind—but still he was a good priest."

"When was their daughter born? They had no children when I was here."

"No, they hadn't, that's true. They hadn't any for years. We thought they'd never have any. And then, just fancy, a year or two before the war a daughter was born to them. Such a pretty little thing. Her hair was black like her father's, but she was nice and plump like her mamma. A regular little flower she was—straight and fair skinned and pretty red lips. Her

father simply doted on her. He christened her Vera.*
I always believed that I would have a daughter, he
said, so I'll call her Faith. He does love her! He'd
die a thousand deaths for her."

"Where is she now?"

"At home in the village. Their house is on its last
legs; the roof of the yard has fallen in—though indeed
what's the use of a yard when there is no cattle. You'd
better go and see them, they would be delighted.
Father Alexey was very fond of you. People used to
laugh at the way he took you mushrooming with him—
a tall, thin, black-haired man like him with a little
dot for a companion. It's because he so wanted a
daughter."

"Haven't they closed your church?"

"They wanted to. It's the only one left in our
neighbourhood; all the others are closed. We manage
to keep up this one. People are afraid to die without a
priest. About marriage, now, they no longer mind—
they just go to a registry office. Girls, of course, prefer
a church marriage, it is more secure somehow, but the
young men are chary of it. They can't get a job if
they go to church; it's downright persecution, I call
it."

"The nonsense you talk! Persecution, indeed!" the
Communist youth interrupted her. He had finished
with the portraits and came to fetch me. "You have
no sense, you silly women, you don't know yourselves
what you want. When you had churches, there was
no getting you there; now we close the churches, you
call it persecution. Marriage in the registry office isn't
secure enough, if you please! It would be securer if

* Faith.—TRANSLATOR'S NOTE.

you didn't go trapseing about after other people's husbands. We've come on business, and here you are with your church propaganda."

"Anything else! You must have gone off your chump, you silly," she snapped back, knowing from Soviet experience that in such cases abuse is the best answer. "You've picked up a nice selection of ancient gentlemen, so take them home and admire them. You be thankful I didn't heat the stove with them! That old witch in a bonnet frightened me. You go and kiss the beauty," she taunted him.

He laughed, gave her a slap on the back, and crying "so long!" ran down the stairs. Settling me in the sledge he urged on the horse, cold and tired of standing still.

On the way back, dozing in the railway carriage with cold and weariness, I was conscious of some pleasant thought at the back of my mind. What was it? Ah, yes, Vera. What sort of life did she lead, poor child? 'Social parasites' like them are allowed neither bread nor medical help nor relief in old age. Father Alexey might be happy because he had his heart's desire at last, but she must have found things difficult. If she was born in 1912 she was six in 1918. The first thing she had to learn as she began to grow up was that she was 'a noxious element' by birth, the daughter of a 'servitor of the cult' and therefore 'a class enemy.' There was nothing for her in life so far as I could see.

·   ·   ·   ·   ·

Another five years passed. It was the dreadful autumn of 1930. At the end of September 'the 48' were shot and in November the 'Industrial Party'

case began.   New mass shootings were expected in
connection with it; people told one another in whispers
about the treachery of Ramzin who made out that
2,000 persons belonged to his 'organisation.'   A search
for them was being made and many were said to have
been shot.   Moreover, there were many sudden deaths
among those who were still 'free.'   It was forbidden to
publish news of suicides, and when some Communist
or official person killed himself there was simply a
notice of his 'untimely death.'   Many died a natural
death because they had not the strength to resist the
most trifling illness. In the course of one month I had
attended three funerals. This time we were burying a
young girl who died of consumption that suddenly
took an acute form. In the spring she was still able to
keep the disease at bay, but with the increase of
political terror and general depression, she looked in
the autumn both spiritually and physically exhausted.
She died within a month and we, her colleagues, had
to see about her funeral.

She had no relatives or intimate friends and the
burial was badly managed, though indeed this was
always the case with 'civic' funerals. Somehow it did
not seem right simply to carry the coffin out into the
street, take it to the cemetery and lower it into a pit
in the ground—and nothing more. When Communists,
military men or important industrial workers were
buried, the Local Committee sent an orchestra which,
throughout the journey to the cemetery, played
atrociously several bars of Chopin's funeral march
over and over again. When it was a private funeral,
the undertakers' bureau sent a coffin and two or three
roughish young men to carry it out of the house. They

hurried one rather rudely, for others were waiting their turn. It was painful both for believers and for unbelievers, but there was nothing for it—the funeral had to be over by a certain hour. This time we succeeded in getting the hearse by the evening of the fourth day. The corpse had been waiting for its turn in the hideous hospital mortuary. It was dusk when we drew near the cemetery, tramping wearily over the uneven cobblestones and hardly able to keep pace with the coffin.

"We must hurry! . . ."

"It's getting dark."

"They close the gates at six," the mourners whispered to one another.

We walked quickly past the old women at the entrance selling wreaths of pine branches adorned with a few paper flowers, and passed through the dilapidated gates. The hearse jogged along the deep muddy ruts of the central avenue. Almost all the old graves had been destroyed: the railings were broken down and piled up in untidy heaps. About a year before an order had been issued to collect old iron and take away iron railings round the graves as well as iron crosses, seats, etc. But as 'the means of transport' were lacking, the stuff was simply thrown on the ground on the spot or dragged as far as the cemetery gates. New graves were crowded in among the old. For the most part they had no crosses on them and were not even covered with turf; in the damp autumn, the clay mounds were shapeless masses of mud.

As we slowly moved forward, strange figures rose from the grave-stones or from behind the monuments and came to the side of the road. Only after we had

passed them I made out that one was a monk in a black
cap and a rusty black cassock belted with a still more
rusty leather strap. Another, a bent old man with a
stick in one hand and a censer in the other, came right
into the road, as though looking for something.

"Who are they?" I whispered to an elderly woman
walking beside me.

"Priests from the closed churches. This is their last
refuge: they wait for funerals to see if anyone will ask
them to bless a grave. Hardly anyone dares to call
them to the house, but here it is not so noticeable.
If a red coffin is brought along, they hide behind the
graves, but if an ordinary one, they come out into the
road. If a service is not wanted, they may get something by way of alms."

The hearse turned into a side alley, so narrow that
the wheels kept catching at the tumbledown crosses of
the old graves or at the fresh mounds of the new.

"Dreadful!" the old lady said irritably.

"I wish it were over, I can't stand it" I kept
thinking.

"She was such a frail little thing. . . . To think of
her on that horrible hearse," whispered a friend of the
dead girl.

When we came to the grave with wet slippery lumps
of clay piled up at the sides, the grave-digger scanned
us ill-humouredly, and failing to find the chief mourner,
asked crossly of no one in particular:

"Shall I lower the coffin?"

"Do," someone answered irresolutely.

Two long white strips of linen appeared from somewhere, two grave-diggers cleverly slipped them under
the coffin and rapidly slid it on them into the grave.

They looked at us expectantly once more. Someone remembered in time to throw a handful of earth into the grave, and in the awkward silence that followed all that was heard was the swish of spades cutting into the damp soil and the lumps of clay resounding against the coffin-lid and then falling into the half-filled pit with a dull thud.

I turned and walked away. I could not endure any more of it. The clouds lifted in the distance, leaving a pale streak of clear sky; an old birch stood out clearly against the yellow sunset, and by the tree trunk I saw a tall priest, thin as a post, with one shoulder higher than the other. His lips were moving without making a sound; from time to time he raised his head as though to intone a prayer, and with an habitual gesture swayed the censer that had neither incense nor embers in it. Why, it was he! the village priest! How had he come here? His church must have been closed. And where was Vera? How dreadful he looked!

His face was so thin that the skin was drawn tight over the cheekbones and the bridge of the long sharp nose. His long straight hair was a dead white except for a few remaining streaks of black. There was an intent, far-off look in his black sunken eyes.

Should I speak to him? I wondered. Would it be any good reminding him about myself? But perhaps he and Vera were in such straits now that even I could help them, though after my husband's arrest I too was in a desperate plight.

I went up to him.

"How do you do!"

He looked at me in surprise.

"Do you remember, years ago, my mother and I

spent a summer in your village? You taught me to gather mushrooms."

"So I did," he said, "I recall it now. I used to go in to your mother's to have a chat and drink a cup of tea." He spoke in a strained, far-away voice.

"I have heard you had a daughter, Vera," said I, to bring pleasant memories into his mind.

"Vera is no more. She is dead," he said shortly.

"Vera dead?" I repeated horrified. "When did she die?"

"Six weeks yesterday."

"What did she die of?" I asked sorrowfully. I had never met Vera, but I felt as though I had watched her in the woods I knew so well and in the little old house by the church.

"She laid her hands on herself, foolish child." His voice failed him.

I stood there feeling that I hadn't the strength either to speak or to go away.

All my companions had gone. The grave-diggers were shaping the fresh mound with no cross on it, but only a solitary wreath of pine branches that looked black in the dusk.

"It's time for you to go," the priest said kindly.

"Come to my flat," I said, feeling that it would be unthinkable, inhuman, to leave him alone in the cemetery when perhaps he had had nothing to eat all day. "Impossible. I see you buried your friend without religious rites. . . . I did bless her grave, though, when they had dug it. I secretly said a requiem for her, too—for the rest of Thy departed servant, O Lord, whose name Thou knowest."

"She had no family, no one belonging to her. Her friends at the office saw to the funeral," I said—just to say something.

"I don't blame you. These are hard times. God will forgive. You go home now."

"I should like to know about Vera," I said, feeling that he was not repulsing me.

He looked at me closely once more. Going up to an old tombstone he brushed off the dead leaves from it and sat down, making room for me. I sat down beside him.

"Vera was born before the war," he began in a calm, low voice, as though it were a tale he had often told before—perhaps to himself. "It was a great joy. It had been my secret dream for years. God gave me a daughter because of my faith, and I called her Faith—Vera. She was Faith and Hope and Love to me. I ponder and ponder and cannot make out whether there was any sin in my joy, for it knew no bounds. War came, I was singing requiems for those who fell on the battlefield, comforting mothers and widows, but though I grieved in my mind, there was joy in my heart. I used to hurry home from my parishioners with one anxious thought—was my child alive and well? Bright happiness was given me, sinner, and I haven't been able to keep it."

He spoke with his eyes on the ground or on the fresh grave mound close by.

"Trouble came when my wife died. Persecution was too much for her. I did my best to comfort her; I reminded her that bitter trials were sent to everyone. Worse than cold and hunger—though we were in dire need, our cows were taken and the meadow also—

worse than any hardship is human hatred. People
were embittered by poverty, privations, anarchy . . ."

His way of speaking bore the stamp of his forty
years of priesthood, but behind the bookish words I
could sense a simple and hopeless tragedy. All his
life had passed in the country, all his existence had
been bound up with the church, and now he was
torn up by the roots and there was nothing before
him.

"My wife could put up with a great deal, but what she
could not get over was that our own villagers slaughtered
her cows," he went on in a softened voice. "She was
born in the village, she and those very women had
played together as little girls, bathed in the river,
gone looking for berries and mushrooms. And she did
so much for their children, gave them medicine against
stomache-ache, made little shirts for them out of old
clothes. But they had no pity on our Vera—it was
during the famine year they took away our cows.
How were we to feed our child? Both she and her
mother had a dreadful time."

Then followed an indescribably touching tale of
how he was left alone with the seven year old Vera.
In the early spring they collected and burnt last year's
dry leaves for manure and dug over their kitchen
garden; in winter he taught her reading and arithmetic;
before the holy days they cleaned the church together
with two or three women who came secretly to help
them.

"Thank God they left us the house," he said, though
all this was now in the dead past. "It was not likely
to tempt anyone, certainly, but many priests were
turned out of their homes, parted from their families,

put in prison, sent into exile into Polar regions and
the frozen marshes of the North. We kept our church
. . ." he paused. "We kept it for many years. The
people knew that they needed God though they might
not think of Him till their last hour. They knew to
Whom to come in trouble and illness. In earthly
sorrow man seeks comfort from above and now he
has nowhere to find it. His last refuge has been taken
away from him. It may be different in towns. In the
country man is weighed down by the earth and his
spirit sinks if he does not hear God's Word, has no
holy days, does not know how to bring beauty into
his life. I had a small flock left, but a faithful one.
The authorities did not like this. They decided to
liquidate the church."

He pronounced the word 'liquidate' in a clear, loud
voice. Yes, that word means a great deal in Soviet
Russia. And the saddest part of it is, it has no effect
upon undesirable facts. For instance, an order is
issued 'to liquidate illiteracy,' but the result is that
people hastily taught to read and write soon forget
what they have learned and are as illiterate as before.
Or there is an order 'to liquidate arrears in wages':
special sums are raised to pay two or three months'
arrears to one group of factory hands or office workers,
but more arrears accumulate elsewhere. Or, an order
is made 'to liquidate hooliganism': there are two or
three round-ups by the militia, some two hundred
citizens, often absolutely innocent, are sent into exile,
and then everything goes on as before.

But an order to liquidate a church, a museum, a
learned society or books disapproved by the Government, is carried out with the utmost thoroughness and

efficiency. It is simplest of all 'to liquidate class enemies'
—they are shot, and that's the end of them.

"How did you live after that?" I asked with appre-
hension. He made a hopeless gesture and bowed his
head. We sat in silence. It had grown quite dark.
Lights flickered in the distance; life in the town was
going on as usual, and the cemetery lay in a pool of
darkness. There was something reassuring in this:
no one could overhear us now, no one cared what we
were talking about as we sat on the tombstone, or
asked what had brought together this village priest
and me. He had lost all he had and it was a mystery
where he found the strength to go on living; I had
had my friends shot and my husband arrested and all
that was left me was my son for whose sake I had to
carry on.

"I sent Vera to school in town," he went on, not
answering my question. "I thought, as one does, you
know, that she would have no one to look after her
when I die and that if she received an education she
could earn her living. But God judged otherwise,
and it is she who was the first to go. Yes. I sent her
to town so that she could go to school—the Soviet
school, open to all workers. I remained in the village,
near my church. In winter I used to sit with a sanctuary
lamp so as not to spend money on paraffin or walked
up and down my room in the dark, singing psalms.
I saved every potato to send to her and her aunt.
'She is growing,' I thought, 'she wants plenty of
nourishment, and they are not allowed ration cards
and cannot buy either bread or potatoes.' Her aunt
too had nothing to live on, except what good people
gave her for baking the bread of offering.

"She had finished school the year before we were turned out of our house. She would have been top of the school if she hadn't been a priest's daughter. How many tears she shed because the boys taunted her with it! And the school authorities were unfair to her. Other children used to get praised and to receive prizes, but she never had any encouragement.

"Just before she finished school she came to stay with me for the 'spring vacation' in Lent. They do not let the children off for Easter for fear they might go to church. It was warm and sunny, birds were singing, all nature was rejoicing. We walked about in the fields and talked. I said to her, 'You are a clever girl, my dear, you ought to go to the University.' And she just said quietly, 'They won't let me.'—'Give me up,' I said. 'I read in the paper the other day that a son renounced his father, a priest, and asked his name to be changed from Theophilov to Luxemburgsky, in honour of Rosa Luxemburg. I take it that he simply wanted to go on with his education. I do not know this young man, but I prayed for him, and I understood that it was not his fault. I gave him my blessing in my mind and I'll bless you, too. I will take your sin upon myself. And it is not your sin, for it is I who am leading you into temptation. It is my idea, so the sin is mine. Give me up!'

"She looked quite angry; I had never seen such an expression in her face before. 'Never!' she said. 'I don't want education that means giving up my own father. I recognise the Soviet power, I want to serve it, but I am not going to give you up. It's dishonourable.'

"That was her last word. She went away leaving

me to my thoughts.   I began going to the village
reading room to read the newspapers.   That year the
newspapers would not accept the clergy as subscribers,
and anyway it was beyond my means.   I kept reading
the papers to see if some explanation would be given
about the children of the clergy.   In many Government
speeches and articles it said clearly that the proletarian
State did not consider it necessary to put 'the weapon
of education into the hands of class enemies—priests,
landowners and bourgeois.'   But I couldn't grasp that
my Vera was 'a class enemy.'   Why, she wouldn't hurt
a fly!   And I thought about myself, too—what harm
had I done, a poor village priest?   And how could I
free Vera from me?   Even my death would not free
her—she would always be the daughter of a 'servitor
of the cult.'

    "Vera finished school," he went on, treasuring
every memory.   "She came home cheerful.   She told
me they had a party—dancing, singing, talking of
what each would do.   Vera said she wanted to go on
studying and be a teacher, and the headmaster replied
'You might get a job in a kindergarten or an elementary school, they are forty per cent short of teachers
there.   I'll give you a testimonial.   Only you wouldn't
be able to go to church then.'   All the others laughed,
and she said 'religion is my own affair,' but the headmaster would not allow them to argue.   She told me
this and suddenly gave me such an earnest, questioning
look.   And I, sinner, said to her, 'I agree and give you
my blessing.   God knows and sees our persecutions.
You will pray to Him in your heart, and I will pray
for you in church.'   She made no answer—perhaps
because she did not want to condemn me for my weak-

ness. She had pity on me. She was wonderfully up-
right, but she had a loving heart.

"That was our last summer at home together. She
was very sweet and kind to me. When I asked her,
'What about your plans, Vera?' she replied, 'I'll stay
with you in the village. One can be of use to people
here also.' But how can one be of use if we are not
allowed to do anything? Even the dead I have to
approach by stealth, and for the living we are worse
than the plague. It was hard for me, an old man, and
what it must have been for Vera! Forgive her, O Lord,
and give rest to her poor soul in Thy Kingdom'"

He crossed himself and sank into silence, not
noticing the cold and the damp.

"When they drove us out of the house," he went on
after a while, "she collected our belongings and tied
them up into bundles. We had no home, no shelter,
nothing to live on. My courage failed me in my old
age. I walked along not knowing which way to turn.
It happened last autumn. Mud, wet snow, wind
howling. . . . I dreaded to think what would become
of us, where I could take my child now that we had
no roof over our heads. And she, clever girl, said
to me, 'Let us go to the station, daddy, and take the
train to town. Auntie will let us stay with her. I'll
find work there; we'll manage right enough.' And my
heart felt so light when she said that. 'Vera, my
darling child,' I said, 'you are my only hope.' "

Then followed a terrible account of how Vera sought
work or some place in life. She made the round of all
the University Schools and Technical Institutes with
her excellent school diploma. As soon as she had filled
in the inquiry form and answered the question as to

her social origin, "a priest's daughter," she was rudely refused admission. Then she went to factories, workrooms, hospitals; to get work anywhere it was necessary to belong to a trade union, but when she applied for admission to one, they simply laughed at her and turned her out to the accompaniment of loud guffaws and indecent couplets from anti-religious songs. In the course of that year she took in needlework, washed clothes, laid out the dead—did anything she could to earn enough for bread, or rather, enough to buy vegetable refuse since bread was beyond their means. While he was hiding in the cemetery waiting for funerals, she tramped about the town seeking work. When they met in the evening he produced his miserable coppers and they both felt like weeping. And suddenly she had a gleam of hope. Reduced to despair, Vera went to see the head of her former school which now seemed to her the one bright spot in her past—the only place where, strangely enough, they allowed her to work like everyone else before closing every door to her and turning her into a pariah.

The headmaster was shocked by her story and her appearance. He dictated to her a letter to Krupskaya, a statement for the Education Department, Pedagogical Institute and something else. He wrote such a testimonial to her that his typist sighed as she copied it out, fearing he would get into trouble for it. Everyone at the school liked Vera, but it was not a reason for risking one's position—after all, she was a priest's daughter.

The headmaster, who must have been a kind man and a dreamer, inspired her with such confidence that she forgot all her troubles. Of course the school which had taught her was sure to save her! She ought to have thought of it before!

The headmaster had promised to speak about her the following day to a friend of his at the Education Department, a nice man and not a formalist, and told her to go straight to the Education Office and apply for the post of a village school mistress. Half the schools were short of teachers, he said, some were hastily appointed to make up for deficiencies during the summer, but proved to be half-illiterate themselves. And she had really been the top girl in the school and done excellent work.

During the two days that she had to wait till the headmaster had spoken to the right people, Vera could speak of nothing but him: the head had said, the head had promised, the head had explained. On the third day she went to the Education Office. Her father blessed her, gave her his last twenty copecks for the tram, and after he had seen her off stood in the road making the sign of the cross in the direction she had gone. Then he waited. He waited for what seemed an endless time. She never came back.

In the evening a militioner came, summoning him to the militia station; from there he was sent to the hospital, and from the hospital to the mortuary. The sister who took him there told him how it had all happened.

The typist saw how Vera had gone in to the inspector and heard his loud voice as he curtly said, "Unfortunately, citizen, children of the servitors of the cult cannot be admitted anywhere as teachers." Then she heard Vera's low, timid voice, "Here is my testimonial, here is a letter of introduction. I did well at school.

I do so want to work, and teachers are badly needed."
"The matter is clear, citizen, don't waste my time and
yours," was the answer. Vera came out of the room
apparently calm. No one took any notice of her. She
returned an hour later. The clerk had gone out to
lunch, and the secretary said to her that the inspector
was busy. "I must see him, I'll wait" said Vera. "Wait
if you like, but it's not the slightest use," replied the
secretary, and went in into the inspector's. At that
moment a shot rang out. The secretary rushed back
into the room, the inspector after her. Vera lay on
the floor. She had shot herself through the heart.
Other officials ran in. They telephoned for the militia
and for an ambulance. She was still living. As they
lifted her on to the stretcher she said to the sister
"a letter, for the inspector." The sister noticed there
was a piece of paper in the collar of her blouse, so
she gave it to the inspector. He was annoyed—why
should she write to him? How did he come in? "If
I am not allowed to study or to work I cannot live a
human life and I had better die. This was my last
hope. Perhaps my death may draw attention to the
fate of others," he read, hostile and embarrassed,
without taking in the meaning of the words. Then a
G.P.U. agent appeared and asked for the note which
he said had to be included in the protocol. He also
took the revolver, for, he said, he must find out where
'those decadent elements' get hold of firearms.

"I was arrested and cross-examined," the priest went
on. "I was nearly out of my mind with grief. I could
not think where she could have got the revolver.
After a few days they told me I could go. I begged
them to tell me where did the revolver come from,

who had led her into the sin. 'Go,' they said, 'the matter is clear.' So I went away."

I looked at him questioningly.

"My sister-in-law found out—they took pity on her at the militia and told her. Vera got the revolver from their school instructor in military science. She went to him from the Education Office. He wasn't at home. His landlady told Vera he had gone to the bath-house. Vera asked if she might go into his room, to write a note. She soon came out again. And when the instructor came home he rushed straight to his landlady, shouting 'Who's been in my room? My service revolver has been stolen.' The landlady knew nothing and only said a pretty girl had called. He went to the militia, but it was in another part of the town, so it took them some time to find out."

We sat in silence again for a few minutes. Then he said:

"The sister, a kind woman, told me, when they had put Vera into the ambulance she came to herself and opened her eyes. The sister began talking to her and pitying her, saying 'How could you do it.' Vera looked at her as though suddenly remembering the one thing that mattered, and cried out with all the strength she had left, 'Daddy darling, forgive me!' And she passed away."

"God has forgiven her," he added in a voice so low that I scarcely heard him. "But He does not forgive me, He does not send me death and rest."

He relapsed into silence. The censer which he held in his folded hands jingled faintly because he was trembling all over. Suddenly he stood up, drew himself to his full height and raising his arms as though

in invocation, called out, "Send me death, O Lord!"
Then he turned and walked away without looking,
stepping over the graves in the dark, dodging between
the crosses and steering his way in the opposite direction
to the gate.

I walked behind him as one walks in sleep when
all rational considerations are in abeyance. At some
point he turned sharply to the right and coming up
to a broken-down portion of the wall looked back at
me.

"Goodbye! Go that way." He pointed to the lights
in a side street and disappeared through the gap in
the wall.

THE WIFE OF A SOVIET OFFICIAL

In 1924 I was appointed curator of the Peterhof Palace Museums. I had so far succeeded in doing purely academic work and avoiding administrative posts which require constantly adjusting one's activities to the 'line of the Party.' But in 1924 it occurred to one of the Communists that I was just the right person for the job, so I had to accept it.

My duties included transforming ten different palaces into museums, having charge of three huge parks in which restoration of the fountains was going on, planning the work of my five assistants, training fifteen students and supervising their work, taking part in organising lectures and excursions, and a great deal besides. One of my duties proved rather unexpected.

In Tsarist times a wing had been added to the Peterhof Palace. It consisted of a number of small but beautifully decorated furnished apartments, assigned to members of the Imperial household. After the revolution it was solemnly decided that in place of the 'toadies of the Tsars,' these apartments should be given to members of the museum staff occupied in research work. As a matter of fact, however, the rooms were constantly crowded with important Communists and their families, especially at week-ends. On Fridays the Communist in charge of the Palace began ringing me up on the telephone:

"Keep No. 15 for X, his wife is coming."

"Keep No. 12 for our friends from the Finance Department. Two of them will come with their children, so what about beds? Perhaps you can put in a sofa of some sort."

On Saturday morning I had to answer, just as though I were an hotel keeper, "No rooms available."

"How do you mean? What about No. 19?"

"No. 19 is reserved for a museum worker, an expert on textiles. We sent for her specially to inspect the stuffs."

"But it's a woman! Don't you try to throw dust in my eyes, comrade. A woman can sleep in your room; you'll be a bit crowded for a time, that's all."

One of the most frequent and most objectionable visitors was a certain squint-eyed little man called Vassilyev. Before the revolution he had been a lackey at the Winter Palace and after the revolution he remained there as a commissar. He chattered incessantly and was a bore; his wife, a distinctly unattractive, middle-aged woman, was spiteful and a fearful gossip. They made trouble wherever they went: they interfered with everything, set people against one another and then carried 'the news' all over the place.

"Here we are!" they announced almost every Saturday. "It's all my wife, you know," he explained playfully. "She simply adores Peterhof. I believe she'd like never to leave it."

"The lovely air . . ." she began languidly, but immediately broke into a quick patter: "What's the use of sticking in Leningrad, I say? I've been telling him over and over again; 'give it up.' Much good it is! We lived at the Winter Palace under the Tsars, and now the revolution has come and we are still there! One may well get tired of it. I am not one to envy people, but I do envy you."

I smiled, recalling that the evening before at eleven o'clock just as I had taken off my dress they rang me up from Leningrad: a party of Communists after a good late dinner had decided to go for a drive and see Peterhof by moonlight. One of the museum chiefs insisted that I should take them round the Big Palace —he thought it would be very interesting. I did not think so, but I knew that if I refused I should have no end of trouble afterwards. So I had to dress, find the watchman on duty, get the keys, sign in a book and go through a number of formalities required in order to open the palace at the wrong time, knowing that after the visitors had gone I should have to go through it all in the reverse order, so as not to overlook any of the precautionary details intended for the protection of the palace. And all that takes time.

They drove up in a car about midnight, fortunately considerably sobered by the fresh air. They slouched about the palace, made jokes about the pleasant life the Tsars had led, said playfully that it would be nice to take away a few mementoes and drove off. I did not get to bed till one o'clock and was wakened at seven by the telephone: there had been much rain in the night, the tanks were overflowing and it was essential to let off some of the fountains, but it was the men's day off and the architect did not know how to get at them or what amends to make to them for calling them to work.

I certainly was to be envied!

"There's something I wanted to ask you," the Commissar's wife went on. "I should like to have a nice little glass dish for jam, half a dozen or so of pretty wine glasses, a few small plates, and two or three dainty little tea cups: we may be having some visitors to-morrow."

She was very genteel and liked to speak in diminutives, but that did not make it any easier to provide her with the things she wanted: there was a very limited supply of crockery for the visitors' use, and her demands were always excessive.

As soon as I managed to get rid of her I went to the park to have a final look at a recently restored curious fountain of the time of the Empress Elizabeth: a shepherd in the centre of a wheel and round him three ducks and a dog, supposed to be pursuing them. The inscription underneath said: "You may pursue, but catch you mayn't." The fountain had been put into working order the evening before: the wheel turned, the ducks quacked, and the audience was as delighted as in the eighteenth century. I had to see for the last time that all was in order, draw up an official statement to that effect and give orders to set the fountain going on the Sunday.

I came up to the fountain and saw that the shepherd had a red Komsomol necktie painted round his neck and instead of a staff held a small red flag in his hand! "Who's done it?" I asked the watchman indignantly.

"Commissar's orders. He said the public would find it more amusing."

While a telephone message was sent to the Commissar his wife came up to the fountain. I noticed from a distance that she had a new dress on—an unusual thing in U.S.S.R.—but curiously enough it looked

familiar to me. What did it remind me of? I knew!
The curtains in the Queen of Würtemberg's rooms.
Another complication!

At last the Commissar was found; he had to climb
down and give orders there and then for the red paint
to be washed off the shepherd and the red flag taken
away. When this was settled, I had to tackle the private
matter of his wife's new dress.

"Tell me, what is your wife's new dress made of?"
I asked angrily.

"What business is it of yours?" he asked defiantly.

"It's my business because the curtains from the
Queen of Würtemberg's bedroom are missing."

"What do I care about your 'queen'?" he snorted.

"I don't care about that queen either, but I want
to know what has become of the curtains."

"Well, I took them and gave them to my wife.
Hang it all, this isn't the old régime! Why should
we keep the Tsar's old rubbish when we've got no
clothes to our backs? Curtains, indeed! What does
it matter?"

"You'll have to give me a written statement about
the use you've made of those curtains" I said.

As I walked away I heard him quarrelling with his
wife and when I came back to my study at the museum
I found Vassilyev's wife still there.

She was firmly and comfortably settled beside my
writing table on which the telephone was ringing
continually as it usually did on Saturdays.

"Can you receive five excursion parties from the
'Electro-force' at ten in the morning?" I heard on the
telephone with my left ear.

"The flowers in your park are simply lovely," she

was saying into my right ear. What was she after, I
wondered.

"No, I can't. At ten o'clock we have parties from
The Red Nail and the March Factory. Send them
at eleven-thirty."

"I looked in at the hot-house—roses, stocks, carnations. The smell is perfectly delicious . . ."

"Hulloa!" I answered another call.

"Four hundred Red Army soldiers will arrive at
five-twenty; provide them with guides."

"The guides are all engaged, apply to the Education
Department." I put down the receiver to stop the
useless conversation: the whole day from 10 till 7 had
been booked up.

"And so I said to the gardener 'what lovely flowers
you've got. Are the roses left from the Tsar's times?'
The Empress was very fond of roses," she explained
to me. "She used to have roses everywhere in baskets.
They were brought in first thing in the morning," she
recalled with some emotion.

Another telephone call.

"Comrade, I'll complain of your undermining
educational work in the Red Army . . ."

"Do," I answered calmly and put down the receiver.

"All kinds of roses," the Commissar's wife went on
with feeling, "summer and winter. And now, just
think of it," she passed to her own grievances, "that
gardener of yours grudges me one little rose! He said
so rudely that you've given orders to keep all the
flowers for the palaces. Surely you don't put flowers
into empty palaces? What's the good?"

"We do," I answered. "You go and see how nice
the rooms look: there are flowers in the vases, creepers

on the trellises, all the clocks are wound up regularly
and are ticking."

"Yes, I think I will," she agreed out of curiosity.
"I'll come and tell you in the evening whether it's
all as it used to be in the old days."

"Do, certainly." I supported her idea so as to get
rid of her and distract her from the idea of appropriating
a few roses, every one of which the gardener had to
account for.

"I wonder why the lower classes are so acquisitive?"
I reflected, but at that moment another telephone call
interrupted me.

"Will you allow me to cut the hedge roses by the
Big Palace?" asked the gardener.

"It seems a pity," I protested. "They've only just
come out. They look so pretty."

"If we don't cut them the sightseers to-morrow will
ruin the bushes picking the flowers. I'll tell the men
to cut them off on the outside and leave a few on the
inside," he said to comfort me.

"Very well," I agreed, recalling the Commissar's
wife who had her eye on the roses, and the incident
with the curtains.

· · · · ·

During the summer we had two big scandals: two
Communists, one after the other, proved to be thieves.
On the first occasion the whole staff drew a sigh of
relief—it is not pleasant to have to deal with a thief—
but the second left them unmoved: "The next man
is sure to be a thief, too," they said. "The post here
is a profitable one. A man may perhaps hold himself
in check in the winter, but is sure to break out in the
summer."

Our museum, one of the most popular, was becoming a profitable concern. A restaurant with wine and music was opened in the former 'Maids of Honour House'; flowers from the palace hot-houses were sold, only a few being left for decoration; the lawns were let out for hay-making; ice-cream sellers had to pay a tax on their takings, and some were allowed, for special payment, to sell their goods in park pavilions; the landing-stage by Nicolas II's Palace was hired out to some fishermen; palace offices and parts of the actual palaces were let as summer residences and rest homes to various institutions for big sums of money. This of course ruined the historical character of the place, but was exhibited to foreigners as an achievement of the revolution—"palaces put to the service of the masses." An entrance fee to all the palace-museums was introduced and there were no free days. One project for making money followed another, while the needs of the museum were relegated to the background.

It was natural that such 'economic prosperity' attracted Communists who had their eye on the main chance and could not resist helping themselves to 'socialistic revenues.' We, non-Party workers, watched with helpless anger our Communist chiefs pilfering all that we had guarded so jealously and meticulously. We prevented them from plundering wholesale, but could not alter the system.

This time, however, I was solemnly promised that my next Communist superintendent would be absolutely honest. He must have been difficult to find, for we were left to ourselves for a whole week. Everything went on smoothly and quietly. But one day we were

alarmed by a telephone call: Vassilyev requested a
carriage to be sent to the railway station. Could they
have appointed him? that horrid, interfering, petty,
unendurable creature? His honesty would be small
comfort to us!

Alas, it was so.

We did have a time of it! First thing in the morning
he wanted the carriage to drive him from his flat to
the office—it was a five minutes' walk. Then his wife
wanted the carriage to drive her to the town—it was
less than ten minutes' walk, but she kept the carriage
for over an hour. Meanwhile he disconnected all
the telephones and asked for the carriage to drive him
to the museum which was within three minutes' walk.

"He can wait, what's the hurry?" his wife said to
the staff servant who had been running after her in the
town.

Returning from her shopping she walked into my
study.

"Tell that stuck-up girl of yours to heat the stove
for me. I'll do my cooking in your kitchen for the
present. I'll keep my name-day in town, and after
that I'll settle here properly. You help me, and I'll
help you. My man is *erengetic* enough but he can't
see to everything. If you want something, you just
whisper to me, and I'll give him no peace till he does
it."

It was a bright look out! To begin with, there
were tragedies in the kitchen because my servant was
an independent character and accustomed to be
treated politely. Secondly, there was every promise
of unpleasant complications: people would 'whisper'
to her and she would worry 'her man,' and quarrels

would be sure to follow. The thievish Communists were bad enough, but at any rate their wives did not interfere with our work.

Meanwhile her husband was showing his 'erengy' as they both pronounced the word: in the course of two days he had called three meetings, made several official reprimands and dismissed one of the staff.

"You see!" his wife said delightedly, "I told you he'll do wonders. We had a good look in the summer at the way you run things here. What he failed to notice I pointed out to him. And so he swooped down on the place like a hawk. We'll put everything in order, you may be quite sure of that. And I'll remember that gardener who grudged me a rose that day."

It was apropos of the gardener that we had the final flare up.

On September 17th the Church commemorates the saints Vera, Nadezhda, Lubov and Sofya, and it is the name-day of all who bear those names. The bolsheviks do not recognise name-days but they are quite ready to make use of 'prejudices' which may be of advantage to them. And so Vassilyev gave orders 'to mobilize' all the flowers for sale to the local population. His wife was called Ludmilla, and her name-day was on September 16th; he ordered for her a bouquet which the gardener was to bring him at six o'clock on the evening of September 15th. She had already gone to Leningrad to bake pies for the feast, and he dashed about like mad letting off a two days' supply of energy, for he was having a day off on the 16th.

I had decided to take advantage of that day and go to the Museum Department to resign my job:

much as I liked my work at Peterhof I could not go on doing it in the Vassilyevs' company. But about 7 o'clock on the evening of the 15th the watchman on duty came running to my flat to call me to the office.

There was a regular pandemonium going on there. Vassilyev stood in the middle of the room shouting so that he could be heard all over the building. The gardener and the staff servants were arguing with him and trying to shout him down. When I came in they subsided and Vassilyev pounced upon me:

"Nice sort of staff you have! Regular slackers! That's what you've made of them! It's shocking. They can't look after a trifle like a bouquet and you trust the museum to them, the people's property! It's sheer anarchy! *Chavos*, I call it!"

"What's the matter, comrade?" I asked to cool him down a little.

"What's the matter? Why, I have told the gardener to bring the bouquet at six o'clock. My wife asked me to bring her some flowers for her name-day. But you can't do us a favour! You've let them all get out of hand! What's the good of keeping you at your post?"

"We'll discuss that at the Museum Department to-morrow," I answered drily, "and meanwhile . . ."

But at that moment the old coachman thrust in his head at the door.

"You've missed two trains already. If you want to sleep here I'll unharness the horse. He's had nothing to eat all day and no more have I," he grumbled, exasperated by weariness and senseless waiting.

"I'm coming," cried Vassilyev. "Drive as fast as you can! But I shan't forget it," he added turning to us. "I'll look into it! I'll clear out the lot of you! Couldn't do one a favour . . . flowers for the name-day . . ." his voice came to us from the steps.

All was quiet at last. The men felt awkward. They had always been obliging and well-behaved; we got on admirably but had never gone beyond purely formal, business relations.

"He'll catch it from her for that bouquet," said one of the men, but stopped in confusion under the disapproving glances of the others.

"Sit down, please," I said. "We must be clear as to what has happened. What do you say?" I asked the gardener.

"I brought the bouquet in here myself at six o'clock precisely. Would you believe it, I've been on my feet since early morning preparing flowers and button-holes for to-morrow's sale . . ."

"Very well." I interrupted the tale of his grievances and turned to the man on duty. "Where were you at six o'clock?"

"I didn't leave the place," he answered with vexation.

"To whom did you give the bouquet?" I asked the gardener.

"I left it on the table . . . the man on duty wasn't in the room," he added reluctantly, in answer to my questioning look.

"Where were you at six o'clock?" I repeated my question to the man on duty.

"I went to light the lamps in the corridor. I wasn't away five minutes. I didn't leave the building."

Two small breaches of the museum rules thus came to light: the gardener had failed to give the bouquet personally to the man on duty, and the man on duty had gone out of the room without locking it. Ordinarily, this would have led at most to a remark, but the angry Communist might use it as a pretext for dismissing both men who, by the way, were excellent workers.

I can speak about them without fear of harming them for neither of them is living now, though they were both younger than I. One died of consumption, the other of a cold caught while at work.

"Now we must find out who came into the room between six o'clock and six-five."

All sat in silence, exchanging glances, whispering to one another, shrugging shoulders. It was clear that no one knew.

"Let us put it off till the morning," I decided. "We'll meet here at nine o'clock to-morrow and perhaps we shall have found out something between now and then."

Reluctantly they went away, one after the other. It was disturbing to feel that all of us, honest people and devoted to our work, were in the hands of a capricious Communist. But there was nothing for it. Almost all had gone out when there were footsteps outside and the whole crowd hastened back into the room again, jostling one another and talking.

"It's been found! He's found it! Wait a minute! Where?" excited exclamations were heard.

One of the men walked in front carrying the name-day bouquet—but in what a state! The flowers were crushed, wire was showing in between, the feathery green stuff round the bouquet was covered with mud and hung in wet patches.

We could not help laughing at the sight of this name-day present. Only the gardener felt insulted.

"Where did you find the bouquet?" I asked.

"In the ditch," answered the hero of the occasion. "Just as I came out and walked along looking down I suddenly saw it in the ditch by the lamp post."

"Who could have done it?" I wondered.

"A dog must have taken it," somebody said confidently.

"A dog! What next! Why should a dog take it? It isn't food," another man laughed.

"I tell you it's a dog! It's Druzhok, he is a naughty dog and wanders all over the place. Couldn't be anyone else," he added with less conviction.

"But why should he break the flowers?"

"No, it's a man," the gardener said decisively. "It's a man, and he's done it out of spite."

All were silent and began to think. The gardener had evidently made the right suggestion.

"Mishka, run along and call Ivan," the senior watchman said to one of the lads.

All sat down again, looking expectantly at the door. Ivan had quarrelled with Vassilyev that morning. Vassilyev told the coachman to drive through the Upper Garden where horses were not allowed. Ivan was on duty at the gates and stopped them saying that driving was forbidden in the garden and they would have to go round. Vassilyev shouted at him, "You fool! you have no business to listen to stupid orders!" Ivan was angry that a mere peasant like himself should swear at him, so he swore too and turned the horses round. Then Vassilyev yelled, "I dismiss you from your post, clear out!" But Ivan would not go away until the enraged Communist sent a senior watchman from the office with another man who was to take Ivan's place.

Everyone was indignant about it. The annoying thing was that Ivan had used bad language—Vassilyev would be sure to make capital out of that.

Mishka returned looking uncomfortable.

"Ivan won't come."

"Why?" the senior watchman asked sternly.

"He is very drunk," Mishka answered in a low voice. Again there was an awkward silence.

"You go and question him," I said to the senior watchman. I thought that probably Ivan refused to come not because he was drunk but because he was shy of facing me. The gardener went too.

We waited. Many of us had not been home since morning or had any dinner, and it was close on nine o'clock in the evening. But we all felt that this absurd affair disturbed our work, and were waiting for some solution. I felt as helpless as they did: we were the non-Party mass, at the mercy of our Party chiefs.

The senior watchman came back distressed.

"Yes, it was Ivan did it. He told us how it happened. When he was dismissed he went straight to the palace restaurant and asked for a bottle of vodka. He hadn't had anything to eat all day but he did not ask for any food—it's too expensive, he just nibbled a crust of bread. He started for home at six o'clock as he would have done in the ordinary way—he thought his wife would not know what had happened. On the way he peeped in at the Office window. There was no one in the room and a bouquet lay on the table. This was more than he could stand, drunk and miserable as he was: a bouquet for Vassilyev's wife, and nothing but wretchedness for his own! So he stepped into the office, seized the bouquet, pulled it to pieces in his spite, and threw it in the ditch."

We were all anxious and depressed. At bottom it was all Vassilyev's fault, but we should have to answer for it. Ivan certainly would lose his post, the man on duty might lose his, and the gardener was threatened with an official reprimand.

"Look here," I said, trying to think of the most reasonable line for them to take. "When the case is brought up before the Local Committee, I advise the gardener to say that he brought the bouquet at the time requested, although it was a private order—to prepare a bouquet in his off-time and without payment."

"I see," the gardener acquiesced. "A private order, in my off-time, without payment."

"The man on duty must say, 'I am to blame for failing to lock the office, but I only left it for five minutes, on a business errand—to light the lamps in the corridor. I am sorry for what has happened, but according to my instructions I am not obliged to look after private belongings, and comrade Vassilyev's bouquet is his private affair which does not concern my official duties.' "

"Quite so," he said, having heard me out attentively and taken it all in.

I sent them all home, but as I closed the office door I heard their excited voices downstairs discussing the events of the day.

"The chief thing is, we must rub it in about that name-day present," one of the men kept repeating.

"It's all her doing, his good lady's! She's at the bottom of it," another one insisted.

The only hope for us all, I thought, was that his good lady should be angry with us and refuse to come back to Peterhof.

As luck would have it, this was precisely what happened.

LADIES IN AUTHORITY

I. MADAME TROTSKY

NATALYA IVANOVNA TROTSKY may be quite a different woman from what I took her to be. Neither she nor I is to blame for the misapprehension: it is the fault of the distance which separated us. She was at that time the Head of the Museum Department and I an ordinary assistant in one of the museums.

At the beginning of the revolution, when the slogan "down with the old régime distinctions of rank" was still popular, the intellectuals were prone to regard their Communist chiefs as their equals. But the slogan went out of fashion very quickly, and we soon discovered that the difference between the 'Tsarist' and the Socialist chiefs was not in favour of the latter. The high officials of the old régime, though by no means always cultured, had, so to speak, cultured habits and behaved decently in most circumstances; the new, even when they happened to be fairly cultured people, were ostentatiously rude, for to be so was considered 'revolutionary.' They often shouted, used obscene swearwords, interrupted at every moment with the curt exclamation 'the matter is clear!' The Tsarist officials were used to power and often 'unbent'; they regarded it as the correct thing to point out that 'we were all doing our best to serve our country,' etc., even though in truth our aims might be very different. The Com-

63

munist officials could not resist the temptation to show off their power. Besides, Lenin said "It would be childish to think that we, Communists, can build up a communistic society. We are a drop in the ocean. We must learn to rule and to build by means of others." Many Communists understood this literally: "we must govern and you obey and work."

Madame Trotsky does not seem to have been different from other Soviet officials. Our colleagues in Moscow said, it is true, that she was exceptionally capricious and arbitrary, but we in Petersburg had nothing to boast of either: our chief, a former stage decorator, was remarkably rude and stupid. Moreover, her position must have been a very awkward one, for she knew nothing about art and occupied her high post simply because she was Trotsky's wife.

But we did not see much of our superiors. They sat in their offices, and we had plenty of work which went on more or less smoothly so long as they did not interfere. I saw Madame Trotsky only in 1921, after I had been at my post for four years.

It happened in winter. A group of Petersburg museum assistants was urgently requested to go to Moscow to make a report on their activities. There was a terrible frost, the carriages were not heated, the train from Petersburg to Moscow was twelve hours late, i.e. took twice as long as it should have done. In Moscow we had to walk from the station through snowdrifts and find shelter with friends, most of whom lived the whole family together in one room because of the shortage of fuel. I remember I arrived so stiff with cold that I could not move my hands and had to be helped to undress.

The following day the eventful meeting with Madame
Trotsky was to take place. We all came. At first we
sat patiently, though the room was very cold; then we
began walking about, stamping and moving our arms
up and down to get warm, as cab-drivers used to do in
the old days in winter.

"Is she always late?" the Petersburg visitors asked
their Moscow colleagues.

"Always," they answered sadly. "She may not turn
up at all."

"Couldn't we ring her up and remind her?" we
asked. "After all, it was she who sent for us, and we
have to go back by the evening train."

"It's no good. She might be angry, and then it will
go badly with our work."

"Is it the same with you in Petersburg?" they asked
us.

"Just the same," we answered dolefully, remembering the hours spent waiting at our chief's door, only
to be told by his secretary that he was too busy to see
us that day.

At last we heard the whirr of a motor car at the
front door. She arrived—only an hour and a quarter
late.

I cannot say that we thought her particularly
attractive, but she certainly was coquettishly dressed.
Beside our shivering figures in shabby overcoats and
battered hats she looked like a lady patroness graciously
visiting some strange gathering.

Archly turning her little head to right and to left, she
shook hands with some, but not with others, and
declared that she could not take the chair, for she was
busy and in a hurry. One of the Moscow museum

workers who generally acted as chairman got up and
began a short opening speech:

"Our meeting to-day is not an ordinary business
meeting but quite an exceptional one, for we have the
pleasure of welcoming here . . . "

"Oh, don't! . . . " Madame Trotsky interrupted him
with a playful sigh and a coquettish wave of her gloved
hand.

" . . . a group of our Petersburg colleagues," the
chairman went on imperturbably.

But indeed Madame Trotsky had every right to
expect a complimentary reference to herself: she seldom
came to meetings of this kind and was of course of more
importance than plain workers like us. She probably
thought it very tactless of us not to show proper respect
to her.

.   .   .   .   .

The second time I saw her was at Peterhof in the
autumn of 1925 if I remember rightly.

"Comrade Trotskaya is coming to us to-morrow,"
the Communist superintendent of the palace-museum
announced solemnly. He was not a bad sort, but he had
a strong feeling of respect for rank and office.

"Are you arranging a triumphal entry?" I could not
resist asking.

"No," he answered shamefacedly. "She will come
to see Peterhof in her private capacity."

"I wonder he did not say *incognito!*" I thought crossly.
Like most Russian intellectuals, I had been brought up
to scoff at those in high places, and under the 'Socialist'
régime this was growing increasingly awkward.

"Do you think we could have the fountains playing,
perhaps just the 'big cascade' only?" the superintendent

asked me timidly. I must confess he was rather afraid
of my temper.

"Can't be done," I answered curtly. "You know very
well that the pipes have to be emptied by 1st September
for fear they may burst with the early frosts. There is
no water in any of the fountains."

I went to my work. During the seven years of the
revolution I had grasped thoroughly that conversations
with one's chiefs were sheer waste of time.

The head gardener stopped me.

"I've been ordered to make a bouquet for comrade
Trotskaya and there are no flowers. The roses are over.
I can't use asters, it would look too crude."

He was obviously annoyed and wanted sympathy.

"There must be some carnations," I observed.

"The scent is too strong."

"Oh, it will do."

He was a Pole who had been exiled to Siberia in the
days of Tsardom. After the revolution he resumed his
work as gardener which he loved with a jealous love;
it galled him to give away flowers that he grew for the
adornment of the museum park.

"I'll make it up in red, then," he said with a grin.

"Red, certainly," I agreed.

He went to his work and I to mine.

I had not been at it for many minutes before the
clerk on duty came to call me to the office.

"The chief superintendent has come and asks for
you."

I went to the office.

"Help me with your advice," the chief superintendent
said to me amiably. "Comrade Trotskaya is coming
here to-morrow. Do you happen to have a small tea-

service? Perhaps you have one that isn't registered in the inventory."

"Everything is registered," I answered gloomily, thinking to myself, "wouldn't there be a row if someone reported that my things weren't registered! Last year a committee of inquiry looked at every thermometer and spittoon to see if it was numbered and now they would like to sneak something away!"

"You might have a tea-service not belonging to the palace collection. A nice one, but without the coat of arms," the zealous Communist went on.

"Everything is marked in the inventory," I persisted.

"Have you no private collections—some of those that we had in store and entered on special lists?"

"No."

"Is there anything belonging to the Museum Fund?"

"China from the palace of the Grand Duke Nicolas at Znamenka."

"Excellent! Show us the inventory."

Angry but powerless to refuse, I produced the inventory.

The two Communists studied it and picked out a tea-service. "Send us this one from the store-room."

"Which of you will sign the order?" I asked, glad to put a spoke in their wheel, though I knew it would serve no useful purpose.

They exchanged glances. Neither wanted to sign, but both knew that I would not give the tea-service without the necessary formalities.

"Make a note in the inventory that the service was taken out at my request, I'll sign it," said the chief superintendent after some thought.

"A clever dodge!" I thought. In this way he avoided making out an order which would have to go to the main office where someone might discover it and denounce him. "They have brains enough for tricks of this sort!"

The following day a carriage—a relic of the old régime—was sent to the station for Madame Trotsky. She arrived at the museum carrying a bouquet of red carnations, which had already been presented to her. I do not know what she saw in Peterhof or what she thought of it, for she did not say a word to the keepers of the museum. She merely nodded to us as she passed us, accompanied by her two Communist comrades. Nor did I see them present her with the Grand Duke's tea-service, carefully packed in a basket, and I cannot say whether she was pleased with it.

A year or two passed. Trotsky fell into disfavour. Madame Trotsky was immediately dismissed from her post. The amiable Communist found himself in a very unpleasant position. He was not a dishonest man at bottom, but he fell in with his comrades' love for gifts. He was threatened with prosecution and exile, for it appeared that the incident with Madame Trotsky's china was by no means the only one of its kind. He mobilised all his friends and connections and managed to save himself and even to retain some minor post. But of course neither he nor Madame Trotsky was an exception: one set of Communists put itself in the place of another, and behaved exactly as the first had done.

2. MADAME LIET

She ought to have been called 'comrade Liet': she
was a Communist and occupied important posts, but
the word 'comrade' was so out of keeping with her
that even members of the Party succumbed to the
temptation to call her 'madame'—behind her back,
of course.

She was what is called a *belle femme;* she had her hair
done at a hairdresser's, received people at her office
draped in a flowered shawl, and was by no means above
caring which of the men presented reports to her; professional women had no chance with her—she despised
them.

No one knew who was responsible for raising her to
the post of Chief of the Museums Department which, at
the beginning of the revolution, had been held by
Madame Trotsky. Until 1928 museum workers did
not know her even by name, and were much surprised
to read of her appointment in the newspapers; a few
months later she disappeared from our horizon and was
never heard of again. She certainly would have been
more in place as the manageress of a fashionable shop
or a restaurant, where her underlings would have had
a bad time of it—but the reasons for her rise and fall
had nothing to do with her qualifications and no one
knew what they were. When, just before the revolution,
the Tsar's ministers replaced one another so quickly that
people joked about 'the ministers' leap-frog,' there had
at any rate been a lot of talk and some of the rumours
penetrated into the press; the same rapid changes occur
under the Soviet Government, but no one dares discuss

them. Madame Liet's appointment coincided with the worst period in my work: the year before I had been appointed keeper of the Stroganov House Museum, and now it was to be sold, like the houses of the Yusupovs, Paleys and Shuvalovs, which had also been turned into museums after the revolution. First the library was to be sold and then the rest. So far we had succeeded in preserving the Stroganov House, for it really was of quite exceptional historical interest. It was built in the eighteenth century by Rastrelli, the famous architect of the Imperial palaces. The collection of pictures it contained dated back to the time when Catherine II began collecting pictures for the Hermitage. The Stroganovs were a distinguished family of merchants who colonised the Eastern boundaries of the state of Moscovy, were the first to exploit the natural resources of the Urals, and in 1582 equipped Yermak's expedition to Siberia. In the eighteenth century they were among the first to follow Peter the Great to St. Petersburg and played a prominent part in society. Alexander Stroganov, the owner of the Rastrelli house, was the founder of the first public library in Russia. His own library included all the books published in Western Europe from 1765 to 1815, the year of his death. Besides newly printed books, he bought rare editions, manuscripts, maps, engravings. Nowhere else in Russia was there such a collection of literary treasures.

Throughout the hardest years of the revolution they were preserved, classified and catalogued; acquaintance with the museum was included in school programs, and crowds of students and visitors passed through it in endless succession. But in 1928 the Museum Department proposed to 'liquidate' it.

Our only hope was that the newly appointed mysterious Madame Liet would understand the absurdity of selling national treasures and take pity on our museum. One never knew—she might be a sensible woman after all.

She was to arrive from Moscow, and I was expecting her with greater agitation than if a house of my own had been at stake.

At last my colleagues at the Hermitage rang me up to say she had been there and was going on to the Stroganov House.

"You needn't be very hopeful," they warned me.

"How do you mean?"

"You'll see for yourself."

I did see . . .

She looked like a fashion plate: a lovely coat with a big fur collar, a tiny fashionable hat and high felt overshoes—the dream of every woman in the U.S.S.R.

When foreign tourists admire the fact that Soviet women do not trouble about clothes, I always wonder whether they have in mind those 'ladies in authority' who probably appear to them poorly and tastelessly dressed, or Soviet citizens who are too poor to buy any clothes. Such felt boots, for instance, cost at least 200 roubles, the usual monthly salary being 100.

Madame Liet walked majestically through the halls, without asking a single question and barely turning her head when I tried too insistently to draw her attention to something particularly beautiful or striking. She might have looked at our wonderful collection from sheer curiosity, apart from the fact that she was in charge of all the museums—but no, it was in vain I tried to impress her with information, references, argu ments. Communists' minds are impervious to human considerations. I might have been talking to a stone wall, except that she looked at me with growing disfavour. By the time she went away I knew that I had not saved the Stroganov House and had ruined myself. The only thing she understood from my words was that I would do my utmost to defend the museum and that the best means of hastening the 'liquidation' of it was to get me out of the way.

Indeed, a few days later I read in the *Evening Red Gazette* that the keeper of the Stroganov House had been dismissed from her post 'for disorder in the store-room.' It was all up with me.

Such a dismissal made it impossible for me ever to obtain work in any other museum, and so I went to the Director of the Hermitage, who supervised the Stroganov House as well.

"Yes, I've read it," the Director said sympathetically. He was a good, honest, simple-hearted man, a former revolutionary. He knew nothing about art, of course; he called 'candelabras' 'gardelabras,' said 'analogued' instead of 'catalogued,' and never went alone into the Hermitage galleries for fear of losing his way. But he was a kind old man.

"Have you got a store-room at the museum?" he asked.

"No, we haven't."

"You haven't? That's bad. I don't know what to do. If you had a store-room I would appoint a committee of inquiry and perhaps they would find the disorder was not bad enough to dismiss you for it. But if there's no store-room, it's a bad lookout. It means someone has informed against you. She must have taken a dislike to you, and she is a bit of a Turk, that lady."

"What am I to do?"

"Write an explanation. I'll send it on to her; I will give you a good testimonial. There may be changes, you know . . . "

It was the kind of situation described by the saying "prove that you are not a camel*": there was no store-room, but I had to prove that there was no disorder in it.

I was out of work for two months and had no right to apply for a job. My friends did not advise me to go and see Madame Liet: she would not receive me, and besides she might be angry and do me more mischief. There was no one to whom I could complain of her order, for she herself was the highest court of appeal in our Department. All that was left me was to become a housewife, dependent upon my husband—after ten years of museum work. Suddenly the director of the Hermitage rang me up one morning.

"Would you like to receive a reprimand?" he asked in a cheerful voice.

"I should love to," I answered laughing, for a reprimand meant that I was reinstated in my job.

"It is unjust, of course, but an order has been received to reinstate you and pay arrears in your salary—so that shows they know you are innocent—and to make you a reprimand. What am I to reprimand you for?" he added with vexation.

"Anything you like—what does it matter!"

* A hare escaping from U.S.S.R. was stopped by the frontier guards: "Why are you running away?" they asked.—"Camels are being taken to the collective farms." "What has that to do with you? You are a hare."—"Try to prove to the G.P.U. that I am not a camel!"

"Three reprimands mean a dismissal from one's post."

"Why, I've just been dismissed without a single one."

"It's all that spiteful woman. Well, there's nothing for it, we must humour her and reprimand you, to show that she was in the right. Come to work to-morrow."

I returned to my job. Madame Liet was removed soon afterwards. No one knew what caused her downfall. It all rested on personal relations among Communists in high places whom ordinary citizens never see.

The Stroganov House was sold. A number of antiques were thrown into the market all at once, so that there was a slump; many of the things were broken and completely spoiled in transport. Only one-tenth of the sum calculated by the 'Finance Plan' was realised. After that some of the responsible officials quarrelled, some were taken to the G.P.U., and the new ones appointed in their place proposed to sell wisely and profitably some things from the Hermitage and the palace-museums. While an official was in favour he hastened to exercise his power to the full; none of them ever did any real work or understood what it was they were destroying so pitilessly.

FOR LOVE AND FOR MONEY

I

A FRIEND of mine told me this story in 1924.

He met a pretty young girl at my flat. When he made good-natured fun of some new Soviet measures she snapped at him:

"Anyway, it isn't capitalism."

When she had gone, he asked disapprovingly:

"Who is she?"

"Her father is an engineer, her mother a doctor, and she is an art student."

"That means papa and mamma keep her. But I'll tell you about a girl I met the other day. I was going by tram to my office. Or, to be exact, I was only intending to go. It's damned difficult! It was morning, I was late, there was a crowd waiting, everyone as cross as two sticks. I thought to myself: the tram will come up already full, so I had better jump on just before it stops; the whole crowd will rush at it and the militioner won't be able to tell which boarded it while it was in motion. But it was essential to be first. It's a regular art, I can tell you."

"I am sure it is," I said sympathetically. "Personally, I prefer to walk. If I succeed in getting into a tram, I can't get out where I want to in the crush."

"Oh, I'm expert at it. If one knows how to calculate the rate of movement and the forces of one's rivals, one can be sure of getting in. It's a Soviet achievement.

Very well. No sooner had I put my foot on the step than a girl dashed after me and hung on the hand-strap. She would have been pushed off because she was jammed in between a dozen people all struggling to get in, but I put my arm round her, shoved off the other people, and secured room for her to put one foot on the foot-board. She was no longer merely hanging on the strap, and the militioner could not turn her off. I like taking a bold line. Cheered by my success I had a good look at the girl and found she was a delightful creature. Her body was nice and firm and she had pretty little hands. I pressed her hand, because as it happened we were holding on to the same post."

"In short, it was the beginning of a romance," I encouraged him, wondering why he was telling his story in a melancholy voice.

"Pressing the hand is the usual beginning. In Soviet tram romances the advantage is that 'she' is squeezed right against you so that there is no deception about her figure. Then, you must bear in mind, this is spring! All girls look pretty in the spring if only because cotton frocks are cleaner than winter clothes. They go bare-headed too—some have curls at the back, others at the side, and anyway it's better than Soviet hats. Well, it appeared we had to travel together all the way and to get out at the same stop. I followed her—that is, I went to my office, but it was in the same direction—and meanwhile such fantastic and romantic notions developed in my head that I so to speak lost the ground under my feet. I have always been too susceptible.

"She came to a door, opened it, looked back ironi-

cally at me and went in. The door banged in my
face, but I immediately opened it again, rushed in
and found myself beside her. It appeared she had been
waiting just inside the door to see if I would follow
her! And then she pounced upon me. 'What do you
want? In the tram, taking advantage of the crush,
you practically held me in your arms and pressed
my hand, and now you break into the house after me!
Have I given you any excuse for behaving like that?
What do you take me for?' I stood before her like a
donkey. I really had behaved disgracefully, I thought;
the result of Soviet 'social demoralisation,' I suppose,
and general frivolity. I began apologising, and she
burst out laughing. 'How funny you are,' she said.
'I thought you were fearfully insolent, but you are
nothing of the kind. But what did you come here for?'
—'Forgive me,' I said, 'I've behaved rudely and
stupidly, but the fact is I like you awfully. What am
I to do if fate has brought us together in a tram and
not in a house where I might be properly introduced
to you? Please don't be cross with me.'—'I'm not
cross,' she answered. 'Only, I live here, everyone
knows me. What would people think if they saw you?
Goodbye.' And she held out her hand to me. I
asked, 'May I call on you?' 'Certainly not,' she said.
'We are Conservatoire students, three of us living in
one room.' I insisted as though it were a matter of
life and death to me. So silly! Then she said: 'To-
morrow at the Opera House,' and disappeared behind
the door of her flat.

"Well, then I found there were no end of complications. I had a lot to do at my office; I tried to get
tickets for the opera from the Professional Union—

no luck; I went to the box-office and had to pay ten
and a half roubles for a seat. Then, I wondered,
what would I do with her after the theatre? The
restaurants are horrid, fearfully expensive and full of
drunken people. Invite her to my room? It's in the
Soviet code, I know, but I felt doubtful—she was so
young—how would she take it? Would she be offended?
Would she be angry? The following day, however, I
decided to buy a few eatables. I went into Eliseyev's
—no, what is it called now? *At Commercial Prices*. The
prices there certainly are alarming! Cucumbers, for
instance, one rouble each! What is your salary at the
museum?" he asked in a matter of fact tone.

"Sixty roubles a month."*

"I get two hundred and fifty for my two jobs. But
even so, tell me, who can afford these new Socialist prices?
Workmen? They receive, like you, sixty to seventy roubles
a month. You can certainly buy anything. They have
Dutch cheese, and Tilsit, and Gorgonzola, and goodness
knows what else, smoked salmon, fresh salmon, caviare,
all kinds of smoked fish, sausages and ham. The shop
assistants are quick, obsequious, well-groomed. 'Would
you like to try the cheese,' they say and offer you a shaving
on the point of a knife. They pack your shopping in
a basket and hand it to you respectfully, bowing with
their whole being. It's positively revolting!"

"Wait a bit," I interrupted, surprised to find that
he was disgusted by these 'commercial' co-ops opened
immediately after the terrible undisguised famine.
"You've never been a social reformer, have you?"

"But I've never been a hypocrite, either. What's

* In 1932 my salary was 120 roubles per month, but the cost of living
had increased out of all proportion to the rise in wages.

the use of a revolution when in the name of Socialism they first starve the country for three years and then, in the name of the same Socialism, offer us smoked salmon and cheese at prices that are hopelessly beyond the people's means?"

"Anyway, it's much better than famine."

"Oh, I don't dispute that. But to my mind this 'New Economic Policy' is nothing but capitalism, and dishonest, grabbing capitalism at that. But to return to my 'romance,' " he went on sarcastically. "By the evening of the second day I had completely forgotten what she looked like and was dreadfully worried because I didn't even know her name."

"But tell me what business have you at your age and in your position to be running after girls?" I asked disapprovingly.

"You seem to forget that I am not yet forty," he said somewhat piqued. "And besides, there are lots of reasons: boredom, this confounded life which tosses you from place to place . . . and perhaps Soviet easy morality and lack of restraint is a temptation after all. Or it may be that I still want to fall in love," he added with some feeling. "But never mind me.

"Well, at five minutes to eight I walked into the entrance hall. I suddenly recalled quite clearly her lovely eyes, the childish curves of her mouth and her charming smile. And all at once I recognised her in the crowd. She was standing on the steps leading to the stalls. She was very nicely dressed: a dark skirt and a white flimsy blouse with some lace or something. It is astonishing how those girls can still make themselves look smart. Perhaps it's because they show their pretty necks and bare their arms to the elbow. In

short, I fell in love again straight away. I decided
that she was charming, tender, pure, that I was a
boor and that of course it was unthinkable to invite
her to my room after the theatre.

"And so feeling very proud I led her gallantly to
the ninth row of the stalls. I confess it was rather
galling to think that I'd been rooked of two chervonets
while other people bought the same seats for five
roubles each or even less, but still it was nice to have
good places. It appeared it gave her pleasure too.
She conquered me completely when she leaned con-
fidingly towards me and asked, 'Tell me, what is your
name?' I told her and said, laughing, 'And yours?'
I thought it was so *piquant* that we were friends without
knowing each other's name."

"I suppose you recalled Herman's song in the *Queen
of Spades*, 'her name I do not know,' " I teased him.

"Perhaps I did. But do you know what she
answered?"

"What?"

" 'Akulina Ivanovna'!" he said angrily. "There's
Soviet wit for you—to call herself by a ridiculous name
like that! These young people are an extraordinary
mixture of tactlessness and subtlety. She noticed at
once that I didn't like it, and changing her tone
whispered 'Lila. You don't want my full name. I
am only a little girl, not yet of age. I'll be twenty-one
in three months' time. So meanwhile you may call
me Lila.' "

"What did you hear?" I asked, curious to know
what music accompanied their love-making.

"How do you mean?" he asked absent-mindedly.
"Oh, yes, what opera. I believe it was *Love for Three*

Oranges, yes I am sure it was. Only please don't ask
the composer's name," he defended himself jokingly,
though a little sadly. "During these years I've grown
a perfect barbarian and lost the habit of the theatre,
though I don't think the music was up to much. But
she listened attentively. It appeared she wanted to
be a singer, she had a mezzo-soprano voice and they
thought a lot of her at the Conservatoire. At that
point I remember with disgust that the shop assistant
had persuaded me to buy at least half a bottle of
vodka and that I had a bottle of white wine cooling
in a basin of cold water in my room. So vulgar!"

"Oh dear, your ups and downs remind me of a
ship in rough weather," I remarked.

"All Soviet life is like that," he answered sadly.
"With modern young people everything is much
simpler, of course, but you are right about my feelings
—it was like being on a rough sea! For instance, when
during the interval she met a very nice young man,
she gave him a friendly smack on the shoulder and
left me as though I had been her papa or her uncle.
Seeing that I did not like this, she began to flirt with
me more than ever, and assured me that she couldn't
be attracted by a baby like that young man and that
men of about thirty-five were far more interesting.
She told me quite picturesquely but in a way that
made me feel rather suspicious that these boys knew
nothing about love. They were regular hooligans,
she said, invariably brought vodka to evening parties,
instantly got drunk and began fighting and making
rows. She told me that though nowadays romantic
feelings were taboo, it would be very dull to live without
romance or adventure. I felt rather uneasy at the

thought that perhaps I came under the second category.
But on the whole she was charming, though sometimes
I fancied she might begin lecturing me as if she were
thirty-six and I twenty. And yet, you understand, I
could not get rid of a certain sense of responsibility.
And I could not make up my mind about asking her
to my room. The opera was over. We came out into
the street and she said so charmingly, 'Goodness, how
hungry I am!'—'Splendid,' I said, 'come to my place,
I'll give you supper.' 'No,' she argued, 'let us go to a
night dining-room, there is one round the corner.'—I
assured her that it would be much nicer and much
quicker to go to my room. 'No,' she said, 'I won't go,
I certainly won't. And you'll never guess why. Don't
try, or you'll say something silly. It's simply that I
have work to do: copy out some music. It's piece work
and I must give it in to-morrow. It's very dull, but
one has to live. I have no scholarship grant. Goodbye.'—Half in fun, I did not let go her hand. Then
she stopped and said to me very expressively, 'You
understand that if I come, I'll stay. I would like to
come, but I mustn't. Don't tell me that you'll do
"nothing foolish," I wouldn't believe you, good-bye.'

"Well," he went on, obviously still pained by the
memory, "Of course she came. . . . She drank the
vodka with relish, enjoyed the cucumbers as an
after-taste, and it was nearly morning when we thought
of parting. I was ready for anything—reproaches,
tears, a request to marry her—but she said to me in
a thoroughly business-like tone, 'Dear, I've lost an
evening and a night through you. I haven't copied
the music and won't be able to give in my work
to-morrow, so you'll have to give me two chervonets.

I must pay for my room and exist for a couple of days till I get some more money.' I was so taken aback that like a perfect idiot I couldn't say a word.—'Oh, you don't like my asking for money?' she said. 'You think nothing of throwing it away on a theatre or a supper but it shocks you that I should ask for it?' Would you believe it, she spoke in a perfectly ordinary voice, not in the least hysterical, or annoyed, or offended—if anything, slightly sermonising.   She explained that many Conservatoire students make a little income that way, doing it intelligently, of course, and not too often, for getting tired is bad for the voice. 'If it weren't for that,' she said, 'how could we live when we have no help from home? Some of us, indeed, have to send money to our families. What are we to do if there is no other way of earning? To sing in a church choir, for instance, is dangerous— we may be turned out of the Conservatoire for that. And only senior pupils have a chance of singing in cinemas. Isn't it better to make a living as best one can and become a real singer?'

"I wonder what your friend the art student would say to this?" he said in conclusion. "It certainly isn't a 'capitalistic' way of living, is it?"

"No," I said sadly. "Horrid life. We had an easier time of it when we were young."

II

In the winter of 1931-2 I worked as a librarian in Leningrad University. As I walked every morning down the beautiful Neva embankment I could see the

Hermitage on my left. I had been turned out of there after being kept five months in prison for nothing by the G.P.U. On my right was the University where the Labour Exchange sent me. Every day I asked myself in vain: why could I no longer work in the Hermitage which I loved and knew but was allowed to work at the University, though I knew nothing about librarianship? From the Soviet point of view the answer was clear, but I did not find it convincing: at the Hermitage I was known and had a certain amount of influence; at the University no one knew me and I did not count. It was nothing to the Soviets that in the circumstances my work lost in efficiency: their system is simply to stop up the gaps and not to consider the workers.

Now I recall that year with a certain satisfaction, for it widened my experience of Soviet life.

It was a peculiar year at the University. Directions had been issued by the Government to struggle against individualism and to implant the methods of communistic work and creativeness. In such cases no one bothers about the real issue at stake: everyone knows that if orders are given they must be obeyed until they are rescinded. Besides, if one began to ask what, for instance, communistic creativeness meant, one might easily 'deviate' and find oneself discussing the subject with the G.P.U. Experience has shown that the essential thing is to draw up a programme of practical measures for the benefit of one's chiefs, and then to manage as best one can.

Of all the Soviet educational methods I have had occasion to observe, this one was certainly the most absurd. It lasted only a year, during which several of its opponents had been sent to concentration camps. It may have had other results as well, but I speak only of what I saw.

In order to carry out the method in practice, each year's students were divided into 'brigades' of five. Lectures were done away with. Every two or three weeks the professors gave introductory talks and discussed the tasks to be worked out by each group collectively. The group was then examined, also collectively, and if one or two of its members failed, the whole 'brigade' failed and the good students had to coach the unsuccessful ones. The only advantage of this method was that it helped to economise text-books. There was a catastrophic shortage of text-books because the year before there had been a 'general clearance' of professors; many had been deprived of the right to lecture and their text-books were forbidden. But as scarcely any new ones had been published or even written, students were lucky if they could get one text-book between five of them.

I cannot imagine anything more dismal than the University in 1931-2. All the big, beautiful lecture-rooms were empty. Rough partition walls had been put up wherever possible. The unfortunate 'brigades' occupied every available corner, sat in corridors and on the stairs. There naturally was no room for them, as the University building was not adapted for such small groups. The brigades were not allowed in the general library, for that was overcrowded already, but all the special-subject libraries had to admit a certain number of students and to make room for them in the book repositories if necessary. Thus, for instance, the Library of the Statistical Department was inun-

dated with students from the Geographical Section.
The groups were everywhere: one student was reading,
others had to listen. Being read to made them sleepy;
some followed fairly well, others could not understand
a word, wasted time, asked to have the book and read
stumblingly, mispronouncing the words, especially
foreign ones. The rest were angry and abused them;
sometimes they came near fighting, but it was impossible
to part company, for the brigade into which students
were drafted by its 'foreman' had to work as one
whole. The 'foreman' had strict injunctions to combine
the clever students with the backward.

In my opinion the general level of University students
in 1932 was lower than that of the *Rabfak* students
whom we prepared for the University in 1925-6. It
was a new generation which had grown up during
the famine, in overcrowded homes, and been taught
in schools undermined by Soviet educational experiments. Besides, 1932 was a difficult year altogether:
there was once more famine in the Ukraine and the
Northern Caucasus, rations were diminished, and
meals provided at the University dining-room were
scanty and very expensive. The students' grants were
40-60 roubles per month, and a small herring cost
30 copecks, a plate of watery vegetarian soup 15-20
copecks, potato or barley rissoles 20-30 copecks. Meat
was not on the menu oftener than two or three times
a month. Sugar was to be had occasionally but not
more than two teaspoonfuls per head. The students
had also to pay out of their grant for a bed in the
hostel, for the ration of 1 lb. of bread per day and for
their laundry—unless they did the washing themselves
under a cold tap. All were badly dressed, none had

decent footwear, and in cold weather all rushed to
seize places by the stove so as to sit leaning against the
warm bricks. By November all were tired and run
down, and then a fresh trouble came upon them.
Just before the Neva was frozen, barges with firewood
for the University arrived, and all the students, men
and girls, were sent 'voluntarily' to unload them.
Without suitable clothing, gloves or boots, they stood
for hours in the snow and sleet, passing the frozen logs
down the line. Then they ran to the University to
get warm and drink in the dining-room some substitute
for tea without sugar, thawing their cold, stiff fingers
against the sides of the mug.

When foreigners who have been to the U.S.S.R.
say contemptuously that Soviet youth is ignorant I
know that it is true, and bitterly hold my peace. It
is not their fault: they are eager to study. But when
foreigners begin to talk about their whole-hearted
enthusiasm, I lose patience. The students' presence at
'public tasks' is carefully verified and the lists of names
are checked about twenty times. It means a loss of
days and sometimes of weeks of study. I should like
foreigners to see the exhausted boys and girls dozing
in the corners after a day of such 'enthusiasm,' leaning
against the tables, the walls, and one another. The
State needs a new intelligentsia but what does it do to
help it?

I remember that after one of those 'public tasks' I
discovered a young girl asleep on the floor in a corner
of the little gallery that ran alongside the second
storey of the bookshelves. Students were strictly
forbidden to go into that gallery for it was the only
place where I could sort out the books, undisturbed,

and take them off the shelves for a time. But it was very tempting because it was warmer than the hall below and completely isolated. I was angry and went to wake her but I took pity on her when I saw how exhausted she looked. She was a mere child, not more than seventeen or eighteen; her cheeks were rosy with sleep and warmth, but there were dark rings under her eyes. Her fair curls were dishevelled and fell over her face. She rested her head on her grubby little hands covered with scratches. I left her to sleep and went on with my work.

She stretched herself, knocked against the corner of a book-case and woke up with a little cry of pain. "Where am I?" she said, jumping up.

"In the little gallery. And who allowed you to come here, I'd like to know?" I asked sternly.

"I am sorry. I was tired out carrying those logs. I was afraid to go back to the hostel, they'd swear at me for having run away from work. Where are the others?"

"Gone long ago."

"Good, then I'll go too. Thank you. I've had a lovely sleep though I've got pins and needles in my ear."

Although she had been at fault in coming to my gallery she decided that because I had not driven her away she could reckon on my help and support in the future. Hardly a day passed without her coming to ask me some question that puzzled her. Was Lombardy in South or in North America? Was Genoa a country or a town? In what century did Marx live and why had not anyone invented political economy before him? What was there remarkable about the sword of Damocles? And so on. Following her example, others came too, and though I did my best to train them to use the Encyclopædia, they found it was simpler to ask me. In this respect they were less advanced than the Rabfak students of 1925 who used to verify my knowledge by the Encyclopædia.

I am afraid that there has not been much progress made since 1932. For instance, the paper *Za Kommunisticheskoe Prosveshchenie* for August 2nd, 1935, tells about a test set to teachers of geography, a subject to which special attention is to be paid. Here are a few instances:

"What is Japan?"—"A continent."

"Tell me about India."—"India . . . Obviously, it's in Africa."

"Why do you think it's in Africa?"—"It's a hot country. It belongs to Japan. Black people live there."

When the teachers were blamed for not reading up the subject, some of them answered candidly:

"We've got to work in the offices of Village Soviets and Collective Farms. There is absolutely no time to study or to read anything."

The students continually asked me German and English words. In 1932, for the first time after the revolution, one of those languages was made compulsory. French was still prohibited as counter-revolutionary; it was regarded as a sign of sympathy with the old régime when the aristocracy and all cultured people spoke it. Now the position has changed: French is compulsory and German forbidden as a Fascist language.

From the German words that the girl was always asking me I gathered that it was not merely a question of preparing for examination tests but of something personal as well. Thus one day she would ask me, as though casually: "How does one say 'I'll come at eight?' " Another time it would be, "Wait in the street under the clock," or "I want to see you," "I have received your letter," "I cannot come."

It was easy enough to see that she had an affair with a German. And the way she followed me about trying to catch me alone showed equally clearly that she was dying to have a talk with me. She succeeded at last in finding me alone one late afternoon when the students had gone away.

"Can I help you?" she asked very nicely.

"Sort out these journals by the years and months, my arms are simply dropping off after a day's work."

She worked zealously for half an hour and then asked timidly: "Have you guessed that I have an affair with a German?"

"I have," I answered in a tone not encouraging confidences.

"I don't know what to do about him and have no one to advise me."

"Give him up before you've got yourself into a mess."

"I know I ought to give him up, but it seems such a pity. You see, it all happened quite by chance. I was crossing the road and saw a group of people standing. I thought it was an accident, but it appeared a German was asking his way to the Astoria and no one could understand what he was saying. I couldn't explain anything to him because as you know I am none too certain about *rechts* and *links*, but I took him by the sleeve and led him."

"And he?"

"He was very pleased. He said lots of things to me, but all I understood was *schönes Mädchen*. When we came to the square I showed him where the Astoria was and said *Aufwiedersehen*. He invited me to his hotel, but after much thinking I made up a sentence and said '*Ich komme nicht*.' He laughed and asked '*Warum?*' Well, how could I explain, I ask you? I couldn't go to an hotel where there are two G.P.U. detectives to every foreigner. I don't want to be sent to prison and turned out of the University. I would be charged with espionage straight away!" she said with conviction, speaking in a whisper, though there was no one about. "Then he began asking where I lived. It was so funny, like a lesson: he pointed to himself and to the Astoria and said '*Ich wohne in Astoria; wo wohnen Sie?*' and pointed to me and into space. I said to him '*Warum?*' that is, why did he want to know? He said lots and lots in reply, but all I understood was *Schokolade*. It would be interesting to see what German chocolate was like, so I gave him my address on the chance and said seriously '*Sie kommen nicht!*' Would you believe it, he sent me some chocolate by post! Wonderful chocolate—strong, well flavoured, quite different from ours which crumbles like sand. Fortunately the parcel came while the girls were out. I would like to have treated them, but I had to eat it alone for fear they'd talk. If someone reported that I ate chocolate, I would lose my scholarship grant."

"You'd better break with him," I repeated.

"It's very well for you to talk, you've lived your life," she protested. "But we have a thin time of it. Our boys are so coarse, and one dirtier than the other.

I assure you not all of them use soap. And they make a point of being coarse to be like the Party men. The amount of vile language one hears during the day! If you go to a cinema they begin pinching or hugging you in the darkness. It isn't very pleasant, is it? And the German is so considerate. Though one day he frightened me to death! Imagine, just as I came out of the University with the other girls I saw a taxi at the door. One never sees a taxi in our parts—except when foreigners are brought to see the Academy of Science. I looked—and there was my German! I was terrified and rushed back into the entry, saying to the girls I had left my galoshes behind. After a time I peeped out again—he was waiting and had opened the taxi door. I did not know what to do, I was frightened, but it was so funny. I saw the girls had turned the corner, and then I made a dash for the taxi. It was the first time in my life I drove in one!" she said delightedly. "The German kept asking me '*wohin?*' and I merely answered '*noch, noch!*' I don't know what figure I ran him in for, but I drove about to my heart's content. The only trouble is I daren't tell anyone!"

She paused dreamily, recalling her wonderful adventure. I looked at her childishly round cheeks and arms and wondered how far the adventure had gone. It was all very well for the German—he would have his fun and go away, but what would become of the girl?

"You should see what presents he gives me!" she babbled enthusiastically. "He gave me his necktie, three handkerchiefs, a piece of scented soap, a bottle of eau-de-Cologne—all foreign! Look, here's the tie-pin: I like it so much that I wear it on my shift under my blouse. It can't be seen there, but I feel that I've got it on."

She unbuttoned her blouse and showed me the pin. At the time I could not say what it was worth, but now I know it was a sixpenny thing.

"All the other things I've hidden at the bottom of my basket. When I go home for Christmas I'll cut a dash! I'll use his soap then, too, but I daren't do it here—the girls would sniff it out."

She was quite right in this. Owing to the conditions of Soviet life there is an incredible amount of petty spying and greed among University students. The first time that I left my purse inside my coat pocket I lost all its contents. I brought a piece of soap with me because handling books made my hands dirty, but it disappeared as soon as I forgot to lock it inside a bookcase.

"Do you like him, at any rate?" I asked her.

"Of course I do. He is not very young," she said thoughtfully, "but he is not old. He brushes his hair, he shaves every day, he has good clothes. It's a pity I don't know the language and can't follow his gallantries, but in love-making one does not need many words," she added in a tone of experience.

"Mind you don't come to grief!" I remarked disapprovingly.

"What do you mean, come to grief?" she snorted ironically. "It's true, our boys are sure to get one into trouble and there's nothing for it but an abortion —but not he . . ." she gave a low whistle. "Nothing of the kind. It makes me laugh how considerate he is. If the G.P.U. catches me that of course will be

more serious. Well, I trust they won't convict me as
a spy! But what a lot of his chocolate I've eaten!"

In the middle of December the students went away
for the vacation. It was strictly forbidden to call it
the Christmas vacation, but between themselves they
all talked of Christmas and the New Year. It was
the first time that permission had been given to
celebrate the New Year. Until then, 'winter vacation'
was the favourite season for the 'raids of light cavalry'
when Komsomol youth, directed by the G.P.U. and
the Commissariat for Finance, made house to house
searches, requisitioning the remaining brooches, rings,
bracelets and other trinkets which were produced from
their secret hiding-places and worn on holy days as in
the old times.

University staff received no leave for Christmas, and
stern orders were issued saying that no slackness would
be condoned during the vacation. But indeed we were
anxious to make use of the students' absence to finish
sorting out the books and doing other work which had
been hindered by the overcrowding.

The term began in January. The three weeks had
done wonders for the young people, who all looked
rested and better fed, especially those whose families
lived in the provinces. During the first few days the
University re-echoed with their gay shouting and the
library was hardly fit to work in. There was a particular
hubbub round the girl I knew. She sat on a table,
entertaining her audience in a voice that could be
heard all over the place.

"What's the matter with you?" I asked crossly as
I came up to quiet them and send them out of the
library.

"I've got married!" she answered triumphantly.

"Quick work! Fixed it all up in three weeks?"

"Not in three weeks but in three days!" she cried boastfully.

"She married an airman!" her friend explained enviously.

"I suppose you thought it a romantic profession?" said I. The girl burst out laughing.

"Romantic profession? Well, I dare say it is. But, you see, he receives a specialist's rations," she said, amused at my innocence. "We have a flat at Gatchina," she went on with dignity. "They offered us one at the former palace, where some sort of Grand-Dukes used to live. The furniture and the pictures are simply splendid! But it is cold there and there are no kitchens. We chose a flat in a new house with central heating. Come to see us in the spring, my husband will take you back in the car, it will be a nice ride for you," she invited us patronisingly.

"Where did you meet your husband?" I asked, to make up for my unfriendly manner at the beginning.

"The usual thing—at a party," she answered readily. "There was a Christmas tree, but really it was just a drinking party. Though we did dance foxtrot to begin with. I had my eye on him from the first. I wondered where he had come from. It appeared he was staying with a friend. All the girls were after him; they simply gave him no peace. But I am a student of the Leningrad University, so that's one better!"

"Is he young or old?" a senior student, who had so far looked down on other girls and considered herself irresistible, interrupted enviously.

"Airmen are never old," a friend of the bride answered defiantly.

"And even if he isn't so young, what does it matter?" another one chimed in. "Our Maika will grow up some day."

"Clearly," a young man supported her. "Well, tell us how did you rope him in?"

Maika gave him a contemptuous look. "Simply enough. I'm not a fright, or bourgeois refuse, I can dance all right, and know polite conversation. He is not a boor like you! It was all very proper. We danced that evening, and the following day we went to a cinema, and the day after we were out walking and he said all of a sudden, 'Hadn't we better go and register while the Z.A.G.S. office is still open?' I laughed and said, 'Why such hurry?' And he replied, 'To-morrow my leave is up and I have to go back to Gatchina, so I might as well take a nice little wife with me.'—'Well, why not?' said I. So we went and got registered. We went home to tea and said 'Congratulate us on our marriage.' "

"You desperate character!" her friend cried delightedly.

"There's nothing in it," Maika answered with feigned modesty. "If I no longer like him I can always get a divorce. But look, girls, what silk stockings he's given me! And shoes too, and knickers," she boasted, lifting her skirt and showing her leg.

It was queer to watch them. In my days University students were different, I said to myself, in the way old people do.

A GIRL STUDENT

In 1918, one year after the revolution, I had to give up my post in a secondary school where I had taught for nine years. There was more than one reason for it. To begin with, I could not endure the educational policy of the Government which played havoc with public education. It assumed that nothing good had existed under the old régime and that therefore everything ought to be done away with and started afresh. The progressive private schools suffered even more than the conservative State schools; the destruction was wholesale, and the result was such chaos that a decent new type of school has not emerged from it yet.

Secondly, teachers' salaries suddenly dropped lower than those of any other workers, including half-skilled labourers. Judging from the Soviet newspapers, the position is still very much the same. Before the revolution teachers in secondary schools received 200 gold roubles a month, in elementary schools 60 to 80 roubles in the towns, and 40 to 50 roubles in the country. In 1932 teachers in 'workers' schools' received 120 Soviet roubles and in elementary schools in the country about 50 roubles. Before the revolution one rouble bought 20 lbs. of bread, in 1932 it bought only one pound; before the revolution one rouble bought 6 lbs. of sugar, and in 1932—only $\frac{1}{2}$ lb.; before the revolution one rouble bought 5 lbs. butter, and in 1932 only $\frac{1}{4}$ lb.

Judging from newspapers and official price-lists the cost of living has risen since 1932 by another 50 to 60 per cent, while wages have risen only by 20 to 25 per cent.

And so I gave up teaching and took a job in a museum. The salary was very little better, but the work was much easier and more interesting.

In 1923, however, I was tempted to take up teaching once more and, while working at the museum, agreed to take a class in history at the *Rabfak*—the working people's university.

It was a new, and I must say, a good institution. The revolution found young peasants and factory workers at a very low level of culture and education. It was essential to give them a chance to improve themselves, as many of them were already taking part in the political and economic life of the country, and there was not time to wait for a new generation to grow up. As years passed, it became obvious that it would not be easy to provide regular schooling for the young generation throughout the country; the *Rabfak* was modified, but still played an important part in popular education. It had several advantages: the age of admission was from 16 to 30, so that only those who really wanted to study went there; they were easier to teach than schoolchildren, for many of them had already learned a good deal from life; the Government treated the *Rabfak* better than other schools, spent more money on it and selected the best teachers, since it was specially intended for working people. The difficulty was that only some of the students had Government grants; the majority worked eight hours a day in factories and studied for four hours in the evening. Many found this too tiring and during the four years' course about half of the

students dropped out. Every year the suggestion was
raised that *Rabfak* students should be allowed to leave
off work an hour earlier, for hardly any of them had
time to get a meal before the classes began—but
nothing came of it.

I liked teaching at the *Rabfak*. In my second year I
had six groups of thirty pupils. I was engaged every
evening till half-past eleven; sometimes I felt utterly
exhausted, but I could not forsake them—they were
just as overworked as I was. It was delightful to watch
their progress and see how clumsy lads who could
scarcely put two words together and said 'levorution'
and 'rabolatory' instead of 'revolution' and 'laboratory,'
learned to use their brains, to express their thoughts
clearly and understand complex historical situations.
One also had to teach them to behave more or less
decently, and above all not to pick quarrels with one
another and be rough with the girls.

The girls were our misfortune. They were not many,
only one or two in every group; they were usually more
backward than the men and, what was worse, introduced disorder by their very presence, even if they were
plain and not inclined to flirt. The young men were not
used to any restraint; the Soviet Government zealously
fostered in them 'a contempt for bourgeois morality,'
they had not as yet acquired any moral standards of
their own, and every day there was some 'painful
incident,' especially with the first-year students. They
'grabbed' at the girls and made crude jokes more
reminiscent of the farmyard than suggestive of any
conscious depravity. The girls squealed with excitement and were quite ready in their turn to pinch, or
lean against a man in a 'comradely' way. But the men

outnumbered the girls; they were rougher and more true to the principle of 'keeping to the point,' and so there were plenty of tragic complications, especially among those who lived in hostels. The boys there were unmolested, but the girls were jeered at and badgered until they yielded. And when they did yield, there was the trouble of having abortions, and either meekly bearing the men's jokes, or of parrying them off with abuse. In literature it is all very well to speak of the freedom of choice and the pride of motherhood, but in life I have met too many senseless tragedies and seen girls completely ruin their life and health.

These 'non-academic' complications became a real calamity when I had to accept into one of my classes a girl who was a real beauty. Tall and slim but strong, well-made and graceful, she looked so lovely that even our teachers could not take their eyes off her. And as luck would have it she was utterly different from the other girl students, so that one couldn't help noticing her. All the others had short hair and were always dishevelled because it was not easy to get to a hairdresser: one had to save up fifty copecks and wait an hour or two in a queue. She had beautiful fair hair which she plaited neatly in a long thick plait. Other girls wore skirts above the knee, exaggerating the fashion for short skirts, and either tried to make themselves smart by wearing something bright and tawdry or affected such simplicity that their blouses looked like men's nightshirts. She dressed in simple washing frocks, threadbare but clean and well ironed. She looked so neat that she had to undergo a particularly searching cross-examination about her social origin. But everything proved to be in order: she had no father,

and her mother was a dressmaker who died during the
years of famine. One of the members of the Admission
Committee raised the objection that perhaps her father
was a bourgeois, since she was an illegitimate child;
but it was pointed out to him that she might complain
of his making difficulties "on the basis of old-fashioned
conventions," and he subsided. Though indeed when
he saw her he no longer wanted to make any objections.
Beauty affects Communists no less than it does capital-
ists; and in the dull, hard and poor Soviet life tempta-
tions have all the more power.

At first our new student caused a lot of trouble.
Learning that her name was Dunya, the men followed
her about with a silly street song:

> "Dunya lets down her hair
> All the sailors stand and stare.
> Dunya, Dunya, Dunya—ya,
> Pretty Communist, ya—ha!"

One would look into the corridor and say reproachfully "Comrades, you are no longer children, you
know"—but in another corner of the room someone
snorted with laughter and began in a breaking falsetto:

> "Dunya puts on a new frock
> All the students run amok,"

and the rest could not resist joining in the refrain:

> "Dunya, Dunya, Dunya—ya,
> Pretty Communist, ya—ha!"

They prided themselves on being 'qualified proletarians' and looked down upon us as miserable remnants
of the old régime, but when opportunity arose they

behaved exactly like young calves that race about with
their tails in the air. I felt angry, but the head of the
Rabfak, an experienced educationalist and a wise old
man, only smiled good-naturedly.

"It's just as well," he said, "else they'd be so stuck up
we could do nothing with them."

He thought it was all mere childishness and was completely at a loss when a very unpleasant affair was
brought to his notice. One of the older students, who
already held the post of a 'people's judge,' said to him
one day that a certain young man ought to be transferred to another *Rabfak* because he was on intimate
terms with our Communist woman-superintendent and
this created 'an awkward situation.'

This Communist was a coarse middle-aged woman,
anxious to make the most of life while there was still
time. Round-shouldered, with a fat flabby body and
short legs, her hair always dirty, she seemed greasy
through and through. No one liked her, but since she
was a person of some importance, students who were
not too particular did not mind giving her a push or a
slap on the back, as though she were one of themselves
and saying with a grin, 'I see I've made a mistake.'
One, more enterprising than the others and lazy at his
work, went further. This gained him all sorts of privi-
leges, but the others resented it and there was a great
deal of unpleasantness. It never entered anyone's head
to ask her to retire: she had been appointed by the Party
and no one wanted to get into trouble by opposing her.
On the other hand, it was galling to let a comrade
profit by her favours, and perhaps, too, they felt
instinctively disgusted with the sordidness of it all. The
favourite's fate was quickly settled: the Communist 'cell'

had him transferred to another *Rabfak*, taking advantage of the lady's temporary absence. He was angry and, trusting that she would stand up for him, made a row and was turned out altogether. What her feelings were remained a mystery. All we knew was that she did not dare to intercede for him, but was more than usual down on the girls, especially on Dunya. There was no reason for it except that Dunya was young and pretty and she—old and ugly. It is a familiar story, and the Soviet peculiarity of it lay only in the fact that it happened within the walls of an educational institution.

Gradually, however, Dunya settled down. At first she seemed to be up in arms against everyone. Tamarka, her only friend in the class, advised her to change her name. She had done so herself: having been Aksinya all her life she now bore the name of the famous Georgian queen. Why shouldn't Dunya do the same? It wasn't the old régime—you could call yourself anything you liked—Eleonora, Cleopatra, Maya—in honour of May 1st. And an excellent thing it was. "No," said Dunya obstinately. "I'll just be what I am." It was her favourite retort.

The men quieted down to a certain extent. At first they kept badgering her and called her a bourgeois, a spick and span young lady, a 'touch-me-not,' and every offensive name they could think of. She snapped back at them. After a time they became used to her and left her more or less in peace. It must be said too that work and the struggle to get food took up so much of their energy that they had not much to spare. Towards Christmas or, as it is now called, the winter vacation, some were ailing, others so run down with overwork and underfeeding that their only concern was to keep awake during the classes; a few were seriously ill. One had ulceration of the stomach, caused, apparently, by the bad bread which was adulterated with all sorts of things including straw and chaff; another suffered from malaria which he had caught in the summer and could not get rid of, because there was no quinine obtainable; two or three were obviously in consumption. Besides, all had to work extra hard for the half-yearly examinations. An order had been suddenly issued that these were to be in writing instead of oral as usual—and writing was the weak spot of *Rabfak* students. Many of them had a fair command of language, since most of them were used to speaking at meetings, but practically all found writing difficult. It was the case even with the most aristocratic of our pupils—the judge, a former political instructor in the Red Army, a Red director of a tramcar station and a co-operative store manager, though they were all quick and business-like men.

"I am used to my secretary writing for me," the judge said with a sigh.

"Writing is sheer waste of time," the political instructor grumbled, "the chief thing is to be politically sound and to have ideas—and I have plenty."

The humbler students were simply in a panic, especially one, a very nice and modest young man, who worked very intelligently.

"What is your profession?" I asked sympathetically, noticing for the first time that his hands were shaking.

"Corking beer bottles, that's all," he answered resentfully.

At that time Dunya apparently helped many of them by lending them her notes—text-books were for the most part unobtainable, and the students learned simply by listening to the lectures and taking notes. She corrected their mistakes in spelling and taught them to write difficult words.

"Our Dunya is a good sort, and she has brains," the older students commended her. "At first, of course, we thought she was rather a bourgeois, but she's turned out all right. She'll be a useful girl."

Dunya, too, had lost much of her vigour. One evening she and I left the classroom together but as we came out of the front door we hesitated. A fearful snowstorm was raging. Street lamps could not be seen for dense whirls of snow. Causeways and pavements were obliterated, and snowdrifts rose like sand dunes by the water butts and lamp posts. I looked doubtfully at my feet, wondering how I should dive into the snow-drifts in my light galoshes, and saw that Dunya had no galoshes at all but only worn and probably leaky shoes.

"Where do you live?" I asked her.

"At the Obvodny," she answered, obviously hesitating as to what she was to do.

We were at the Kamenno-ostrovsky, at the other end of the town.

"How do you get there?"

"By tram," she answered, looking at the snow-covered tram lines.

There was no tram in sight. Two or three men with spades, who had been sent to clear the line, were busy in the distance, but the results of their work were not perceptible.

"Why so glum, Dunya?" one of the students who was late leaving the school called to her. "Come to the hostel with me, I'll keep you warm."

She turned away without answering.

"You'll be frozen! The crossing-sweeper will discover your corpse to-morrow under the snow."

"Get along with you!" she answered irritably, and wrapping an old scarf round her nose and mouth moved decidedly forward. "Let me see you home, comrade," she said to me, taking me solicitously by the arm.

"You must come to me for the night, Dunya," I said.

"Why should I?" she answered with her usual air of defiant independence.

"Because you'll be frozen to death if you don't. It is more than 20 R. below zero."

She could not argue because snow was blinding us and we could hardly breathe for the wind. We had to turn our backs to it at every step to draw breath.

"Where shall I put her?" I reflected on the way. "In the servant's room she would probably be more comfortable, but she might be offended at my not treating her as an equal." In either case she would have to sleep on the floor because there was no spare bed and I myself slept on the sofa. But that did not matter, no one in U.S.S.R. bothers about material discomfort—it is the spiritual atmosphere that is so painful.

Dunya followed me obediently, but when the servant opened the door she hesitated. My servant at that time was a young girl who loved clothes and was ready to spend her all for the sake of a new rag. She scanned Dunya in such a way that I instantly decided to have the bed made up in my room.

"Give us some tea, please," I said. "And afterwards take the mattress off my sofa and make up a bed on the floor in my room."

"Tea is ready," she muttered ungraciously. She resented the fact that Dunya was also young, but much prettier than herself and that she had to wait upon a girl poorer than she was and obviously 'not a lady.' She looked disgruntled, but did not dare to disobey and made the bed, scrutinising Dunya with much interest meanwhile. Dunya was obviously put out: she felt confused by the unfamiliar surroundings, a piano, a lot of books and above all the presence of this cheeky girl who should be a comrade, but could not be treated in proper proletarian fashion. It was curious to see distinct hostility between the two girls who, one would have thought, were social equals. Was it the result of the Soviet training in class distinctions? I wondered. One was well fed and well dressed because I, a bourgeois, earned her keep by teaching another, a real proletarian who was hungry and ragged—and they despised each other. How ridiculous it all was!

We soon finished tea. I went to wash and when I returned Dunya was already in bed. She had folded her clothes so that the skirt lay on the top and concealed her undergarments. She was covered by the blanket right up to her neck. I would have gladly lent her a nightgown, but I was afraid it would make her all the more shy and miserable. I put out the light. Dunya lay quietly but she was not asleep. I could not sleep either—the presence of a stranger always disturbs one.

"Dunya, are you warm enough?" I asked after a time. "There's a shawl on the armchair near you."

"Yes, I am warm," she answered in an agitated voice. I had never heard her speak in that tone before. "What would have become of me if you hadn't brought me here . . . Oh, nothing, though," she interrupted herself. "I would have gone into some doorway and slept peacefully till the morning on the stairs."

"Don't you ever sleep at the hostel? Some of our girls live there."

"I know," she answered contemptuously. "But I don't fancy spending the night with them. Tamarka alone is enough for me . . . " She broke off suddenly.

Proletarian etiquette forbade her to discuss the subject with me, though we all knew the story. Tamarka had already had two abortions and said openly that she was not sure with whom she was living at the moment. There had been some trouble about her because she arranged drinking parties on several occasions and it was rumoured that she sniffed cocaine. There was nothing surprising in this: young people had it drilled into them that bourgeois morality was no good, 'conventions' were silly and everyone had a right to live as they pleased.

"What I want is to be a teacher," she said dreamily all of a sudden.

I smiled: it was so childish—she came to a teacher's home, found it warm and clean, and wanted her own life to be the same.

"No, not like you," she continued, as though guessing my thoughts. "I'm not a match for you. Our boys say you are very clever. I suppose you don't know that we tried to catch you out. We looked things up in the Encyclopædia on purpose and asked you questions. We wanted to find out if you really knew everything or just pretended. All sorts of people take up teaching nowadays."

"Was this how you got rid of the geography teacher?"

"That's the way!" she said gaily. "He had no business to be teaching. He thought if he was a Communist he could do what he pleased. Let him have as many Government posts as he likes, Party men are wanted there, but we want proper teachers."

This distrust was very typical. It was 'class difference' again: they had no good teachers of their own class and were suspicious of us, the 'bourgeois.' How stupid it all was, I thought.

"I want to go to the country, to teach in a simple village school," she went on.

"Have you lived in the country before?" I asked cautiously, knowing how careful one must be with personal questions, for everyone is afraid of saying too much.

"No, we have always lived in town."

"Then why do you want to go to the country?"

"I hate Petersburg . . . Leningrad," she corrected herself. "I know everything here and I hate it. You have probably never been in our parts, on the Obvodny? It is just the same as before the revolution, worse in fact: dirt, fights, quarrels, hooliganism. When I get off the tram I have to run, to escape hooligans. I am afraid to go up my own stairs, homeless children may be hiding there. Our flat is so crowded that one can scarcely breathe. We used to live in it just the three of us—my mother, auntie and I. We had two rooms and a kitchen. We slept in one room and used the other for fittings and seeing clients. Now a whole family has been put into that room—husband, wife and two children. When mother and auntie died during the famine I had a factory girl from the Red Triangle put into my room. Every bit of her clothing stinks of chemicals. Now at least she is no longer sick every day, but it used to be dreadful—she came home from the factory hungry but could not swallow anything for sickness. The ventilation there is very bad."

"Do you think it will be better in the country?"

"Of course," she answered with conviction. "I'll tell you what I saw at the Education Department. I went there to inquire about a post. The school is in a big village, and a factory is going to be built close by. In two or three years there will be a Socialist town there. Everything has been planned out. Every workman will have his own flat in the general block. Trees will be planted in the main street and there will be two public gardens. Then of course there will be an Education Hall with a club, a theatre and a cinema. There will be a factory kitchen, a common dining hall, light and airy, not like the one in our *Rabfak*," she said, speaking as though all these things were already in existence.

"Do you believe these plans will be carried out?" I asked cautiously. It had never occurred to me before that Soviet propaganda can have such an effect on the young. I thought they knew from experience what all these projects were worth.

"Of course. You know, it isn't easy for the new régime to deal with the legacy of the past. Just think what a lot of old stuff there is in this town—men, things, houses—and it all is like a dead weight on the new. It is no use thinking of rebuilding the old town, but there everything will be started afresh. The plans are drawn up by well-known architects, Fomin and Shchuko, I believe."

"Yes, they designed a lot of buildings before the revolution, too."

"Perhaps. But now their work is quite different. You know, the Education House model shows what it will look like at night: lights in the windows, a glass-roofed porch, a motor standing on the asphalt pavement outside. Very pretty. Do you think they draw up plans like that in capitalist countries?"

"I expect they do. And they build, too."

"You don't believe in us, I see! But you don't know what a lot of building there is going on in the provinces. I do so want to see it all instead of sitting in this dirty old hole, poisoned by the Tsarist régime."

Dunya went on dreaming of how Russia would overtake and leave behind the capitalist world of which she knew absolutely nothing. She wanted to believe, to create a new life never seen before. Well, all that was perfectly natural. The only sad part of it was that an ordinary good motor car seemed to her a wonderful achievement and the building of two or three houses —an important event. There was no sense of proportion in her dreams, for she could not remember how fast building had been going on in pre-war Russia and did not know what 'rotten capitalism' was still capable of doing.

I had no chance of any more heart to heart talks with Dunya. The following morning she got up very early, dressed quickly without disturbing me, made her bed and tiptoed out of the room. No one in the flat was getting up yet, but she had to be at her work at seven.

Two more years passed. Dunya and other students in her class were finishing their course at the *Rabfak*. Before leaving they decided to have an evening party. They asked for the loan of one of the rooms at the hostel. The younger students had already left and there was hardly anyone in the house. They scrubbed the floor, tidied the room and decorated it with green branches and bundles of lilac gathered in other people's gardens. They covered the tables with clean sheets and spread homespun ornamental towels down the centres to make it look more like tablecloths. The weather was warm, the teachers came in summer dresses, all smartened themselves up and were rather excited.

"Shall we ever meet again, I wonder?" people asked.

"They'll send us to the ends of the earth to work off our schooling," Fedya said in his deep bass.

"Don't worry, Fedya, Socialism has no need of Shaliapins!" they teased him.

Fedya had a beautiful voice. But there was nothing to be done about it, for he was being sent to the building of Turksib.

"Just look at our Dunya!"

"Dunya, Dunya, Dunya-ya" the young men started in a chorus.

"That girl will waste her life," they joked. "Look at her—a regular beauty like a capitalistic Mary Pickford, but she hasn't taken notice of any of us boys. What the devil is she keeping her virtue for? These aren't the bad old times."

"Shut up, Vanya! Don't pester Dunya, it is her own affair."

"It's provoking. She is our own sort and yet . . . "

"Dry up, you devil! Shut your maw!" they shouted at him from all sides.

"Sit down to tea," said Dunya, slightly frowning.

She was the only girl left in the class. Tamarka had given it up long ago. She had had several abortions, but on one occasion there was not room for her at the

hospital and she had to go on carrying the child. Her
studies suffered in consequence, and her comrades gave
her no peace with their jokes.

"Whom will you sue for alimony, Tamarka?"

"Better sue the one who never grabbed you," they
guffawed.

"Mind you have a girl, you see there aren't enough
girl students to go round."

No one remembered Tamarka now. They were
drinking tea, shouting, joking, making merry. Dunya
called to me from the other end of the table:

"I am going in the autumn. Do you remember? The
place I told you."

"Why don't you try for the University?" I shouted
back.

"There aren't enough vacancies. Never mind. I'll
begin work all the sooner."

Out of the thirty who were in this class at the beginning only twenty completed the three years' course and
only five were allowed to go on to a University, though
all were eager to study. In U.S.S.R. the only thing one
can hoard is knowledge, and specialisation alone gives
one some kind of advantage, so that higher education is
not a luxury but a most vital need. There is certainly a
shortage of properly qualified specialists, but so there is
of men with a moderate amount of technical knowledge,
and since the Government is always in a hurry with its
plans, most students are not allowed to finish their
education. As soon as they have learned enough to go
on with, they are sent into the depths of the country—
to stop up the gaps somehow, for the time being.

We were making merry together for the last time,
knowing that Soviet life would throw us all so far apart

that we should probably never meet again. And this proved more or less to be the case.

Five years passed. It was early spring of 1932. It was my last spring in Russia. I had before me a risky escape and was leaving behind all with whom my life had been spent. I wanted to do something more during my last months in Russia, but I felt paralysed. The Soviet law condemns to penal servitude all who are suspected of assisting an escape abroad, or who merely fail to report it to the authorities, and so I was careful to avoid everyone. But I had an old friend, a lonely man forgotten by all; he had been in hopeless exile for years. I wanted to see him for the last time. In order to do so I had to sneak away from town, so that no one in my office should notice it. I planned and planned, but could think of nothing: I needed two consecutive days, and the only holidays are November 7, January 21 (the day of Lenin's death) and May 1. Suddenly we were told that March 8 was 'working women's international day' and we women could stay away from the office. March 9 happened to be my off-day, and so everything fitted in beautifully. At that time of the year trains were not overcrowded, there was practically no risk of meeting any acquaintances, and everything might pass completely unnoticed.

And indeed it all worked quite smoothly, and on the night of March 9, I was returning to town with a certain sense of satisfaction.

The cold and dirty carriage was permeated with the acrid smell of a disinfectant, which had been poured on the wooden seats and the floor. The glass in one of the windows was broken and so the passengers were crowded in another compartment where one could not breathe for tobacco smoke and human stench. I could not go to sleep: my sides ached with the hardness of the boards, my heart ached with weariness, my head ached with the noise, the shaking and the two sleepless nights. Everything in the carriage squeaked and rattled, and after every stop at a station the train seemed to go into convulsions: it jerked forward, then jerked back, then jerked again but made no progress, and only after two more desperate jerks moved on.

During the night a young woman came into the carriage at one of the stations. She tried the other compartment, but the stench that came through the half-open door made her draw back. She sat down on the seat opposite me. It was half dark, the bit of candle in the lantern was almost burnt out, and I could not make up my mind who she was. A large 'Turkish' shawl, such as were worn in the middle of the nineteenth century, covered her head and shoulders and was tied in a knot at the back. Peasant boots were showing from under her short skirt. It was a queer combination of town clothes, probably a legacy from her grandmother, and country footwear—a defence against the impassable mud of the roads.

She undid the knot with some difficulty and took off the shawl. I saw that she had on a hand-knitted little beret, a thin but well-fitting overcoat and a dark cotton dress. There could be no doubt: it was Dunya. I recognised all her quick graceful movements. She carefully pulled off her boots, undid the newspaper which she had wrapped round her legs and feet for warmth, and folding it neatly put it into her little basket. Her town stockings were worn out of all shape but darned and reinforced on the soles with pieces of another stocking. She wrapped her feet in the shawl, pulling the rest of it over herself and lay on her back with her head on the basket. It made too high a pillow, she was uncomfortable and turned on her side. Now she was lying with her face towards me.

She looked taller and thinner and had grown more beautiful, but if I saw such a face in a portrait I should ask 'whose face is it, so dead, so devastated?' What had happened to her?

She opened her eyes, looked at me indifferently and asked "Do you recognise me?"

"I do," I answered, feeling excited and interested at the meeting, though she obviously did not care in the least and was not even interested to find out why I should be knocking about in trains in the middle of winter.

"Have I changed?" she asked casually.

"Yes."

"You are the same, except that you look much older."

"I've been in prison."

"Lots of people are in prison now," she answered indifferently. "Are you in exile?"

"No."

"All the villages round us are full of exiles," she explained.

"What do they do? How do they live?"

"They just die off," she answered in the same toneless voice.

"Dunya, what has happened to you?" I asked raising myself on my elbow and gazing at her.

"Nothing," she answered curtly, turning so sharply that the basket under her head gave a bang.

"We won't talk if you don't want to," I said drily.

"What's the good of talking when life is beastly," she said bitterly.

"Not much good, but sometimes if you meet a friend . . . "

"That doesn't happen often," she interrupted ironically.

"Exactly. So you should value it all the more," I added instructively.

Our conversation sounded like wrangling, but I understood that Dunya was quarrelling not with me but with life. I had no particular desire to comfort or dissuade her: life certainly was beastly. But it seemed to me that it ought to have been kinder to her than it was to me.

"You are a regular intellectual," she said crossly. "Why should you care about other people? Do you remember how you saved me from frost that night? Much good it was! . . . But you could not explain to me then that I had my head full of nonsense, that I was fascinated by ridiculous Soviet plans when in truth all was chaos. What did they teach us? Political literacy, political economy, history of class struggle, history of the Party. What did it all come to? That in all the world there was a crisis, exploitation, decay, and we alone had new life and were building up Socialism. I've seen enough of it and to spare. Live in the country, then you'll learn something."

"But you were going to a factory, to a Socialist town."

"A Socialist town, indeed! Five years ago I came to the station and had to wade five miles through impassable mud to the village—and it is exactly the same now. For five years they've been talking about a motor

bus; this year they started one at last and it broke down
within a week. There are no spare parts for mending
it, of course. The boy who drove it was sent to prison
for breaking machinery. It's called wrecking. But he
had never seen such a machine in his life before. The
instructor explained to him at one go all about it and
put him at the wheel. They built the factory and three
years later it dawned on them it was in the wrong place:
raw material cannot be brought there and there aren't
enough workers. They appointed special recruiters
lately whose duty is to provide workers. They promise
the men goodness knows what and bring a party, but
less than half of it remains after the first week's wages
have been paid. The men get all the blame, but how
are they to stay when for the whole lot of them is only
one proper building with so-called flats—that is one
room for each family; the cooking has to be done in the
communal kitchen. All the rest have to live in barracks
with plank shelves for beds. It is so cold in winter that
people with children are afraid of their freezing to death,
so they make dugouts and live underground like moles.
And the school! Do you know what it says on my
school board?—'Church school with four years' course,'
and over it is written 'Karl Liebknecht's Labour school.'
The new paint is bad and half of the letters have come
off. And village people aren't likely to know who Karl
Liebknecht was."

"But surely there's no harm in making use of old
buildings," I protested feebly.

"And have you seen any new school buildings?" she
asked irritably.

"That doesn't mean that there aren't any."

"Nor does it mean that there are many of them. And

the children!   Barefoot, dirty, dishevelled, spiteful."

"Have they grown used to you?"

"Which ones?" she asked gloomily.   "Half the village was wiped out when they began liquidating the *kulaks*.   Whole families were sent into exile, children and all.   They were driven with the butt ends of rifles into cattle trucks and treated worse than cattle—no food, no water, no clothes.   How many of them survived, I wonder?   What's the good of my teaching them to read and write?   The sooner they die the better, they'd be out of their misery, anyway."

"Dunya, you must apply for leave and have a holiday," I said seriously.   Her nerves were obviously on edge, and in such a condition to talk of the joys of Soviet life meant simply to reduce oneself to despair.   But one had to live, and work, and keep oneself in hand.

"I did have a holiday," she said sadly.   "I am ashamed to think of it.   Do you remember how I used to keep our boys off?" she asked with a bitter smile. "And then . . . it all happened like a vulgar novel.   I was sent to the Crimea, to a sanatorium.   For the first time in my life I saw the real sea.   I bathed till I was exhausted. . . .   What roses!   Dark cypresses wreathed in white roses, roses on the walls of the houses, roses hanging over fences. . . .   Sometimes as one came out in the morning after a windy night all the paths would be covered with rose petals as with a carpet.   I came out with my bare feet on purpose, it was no nice and soft to tread on.   We had plenty to eat and nothing to do. . . . We were sent there only for a fortnight, it's true, but we felt as though we could live that easy, carefree life for ever.   Love-making began straight away.   I didn't give in, though.   Probably because several men were

after me at once: it was amusing to tease one, to give
hopes to another and then run away by oneself or swim
far out to sea and escape them all. And I would have
escaped altogether had it not been for a drinking party
that a Communist arranged there. He was the only
person who had a room to himself, and altogether there
was no written law for him. He got for the occasion all
sorts of nice things to eat, savouries, sweets, cherries,
strawberries and plenty of wine. Very different from
our *Rabfak* party! At first there were a lot of us there,
drinking, singing and kissing. Then, I don't know how
it happened, all went away. And he kept teasing me
all the evening 'you are afraid! afraid of drinking too
much! Afraid of kissing!' And so in the end I woke up
in his bed in the morning and found him snoring beside
me."

"It isn't only Communists who snore, Dunya," I
tried to joke, noticing what sad eyes she had.

"That's not the point," she said seriously. "You see,
I fancied that morning that perhaps I loved him after
all and that, anyway, it was the beginning of something
new. It was my last day at the sanatorium. I told him
so and he began to sing 'This is the last day, oh my
friends, I can enjoy myself with you. . . . Let's have a
booze, Dunya,' he said, 'and embrace for the last time.
We, Party men, like to make hay while the sun shines.
You are an A1 girl! And you go to your village and
teach snivelling babies till there's nothing left of you.'
That was all."

Dunya sat up and began pulling on her boots.

"You are younger than me, you know, though you
are old enough to be my mother," she said without
looking at me. "It isn't that life hasn't been rough on

you—it's rough on everyone nowadays, but you have had time to grow up soundly, and you live more intelligently. And we, so-called 'youth' . . . Well, goodbye," she broke off absent-mindedly. "I get off here. I've been summoned to the town to a meeting of women workers, and to-morrow morning I have to be at my school."

"Goodbye, Dunya. We shall not meet again," I said, knowing that I really would never see again those difficult, unlucky young people to whom in spite of all I felt so near.

THE GYPSY

I was born and educated in Moscow, but began my independent life in Petersburg after I was married. Consequently there remained as it were two elements in me, and all my friends fell into two categories. Those in Moscow were school and University friends with whom one remained intimate however much both they and I changed in the course of years; those in Petersburg were business friends of my grown-up life. Whenever I came to Moscow I felt ridiculously young and wanted to see everyone as in the old days.

I had not many men friends left in Moscow. I finished the Moscow University in 1913. After graduating most of the men had to serve their year in the Army; in 1914 they were called up during the first mobilisation and nearly all killed at the front. One of those who had survived the war used to meet me every time I came to Moscow. He was a gay, charming and an exceptionally gifted man. When we were young we found fault with him for his 'lack of principles,' but it was nothing of the kind: he was simply light-hearted and could not endure humdrum existence. As a matter of fact he was more intelligent and hardworking than many of us. Having almost completed his course in the Faculty of Arts he changed over to engineering and graduated four years later, though he had to earn his living while he was at the University. Afterwards he made a better career than any of us, in spite of the revolution.

It was remarkable that whenever one wanted him, he invariably turned up in answer to a wire or a telephone call, without groaning and grumbling about urgent business, special committee meetings and so on.

I wired to him in the spring of 1924 asking him to meet me at the former Nicolaevsky station. It was the very best period of the NEP. It seemed as though Russia were on the way to recovery and life might some day become normal again. The train was not late; I bought my ticket in the Wagon-Lits Bureau without any trouble or waiting in a queue; I travelled in a 'soft' carriage with clean bed-clothes, and a samovar busily boiling in the buffet. When the train came in I saw my friend wave his hat to me from a distance and then push his way through the kissing family groups, porters loaded with luggage, children clinging in alarm to their parents, and busy Soviet specialists carrying their papers. When he had made his way to the carriage I saw that in his left hand he had a large bedraggled bouquet of lilies of the valley which he shyly held upside down.

"What's this?" I asked ironically.

"Take it and throw it under the carriage. I don't know what to do with it," he answered flushing red. In his youth he used to turn red like a peony at the least provocation and we teased him unmercifully about it.

"But the bouquet was meant for me, wasn't it?"

"Well, yes, it was. You see, I had intended to meet you in style and yesterday looked at all the flower-shops but could not see anything good. Then I had so much to do that I forgot all about it, and this morning all the shops were closed. In despair I bought from a flower-seller at the corner all her wares and then discovered it was awful rubbish. But I couldn't throw it down in the street in broad daylight, could I?"

I looked at him and laughed. It was so like him to plan something magnificent and end in a fiasco. Under the conditions of Soviet life it must have become the regular thing.

Owing to his energy and skilful elbow-work we managed to be among the first to leave the station but there were no longer any taxis or *izvozchiks* to be had.

"Which tram do we take?" I asked.

"Tram! Certainly not. You'd be bruised all over and then find fault with Moscow. Wait a minute, I'll run and fetch a taxi."

"Let's go by tram!" I pleaded. "It's more certain."

"What? You don't believe in the revival of Socialist prosperity? You doubt the success of the reconstruction policy? One minute, and you shall have a taxi. Please!" He looked at me appealingly and dashed away leaving me on the station steps.

The crowd of passengers surged past me. They made a dash for the trams which were already crammed full of people inside, on the landings and on the footboards. I grew tired of standing and sat down on my suitcase, holding the absurd nosegay made up of tiny bunches. Whirls of dust, sand and rubbish blew up from the station square. I could not go back into the station for if I did, and he returned and went looking for me, the taxi would be instantly snatched up by somebody else. Forty-five minutes passed, but at last he drove up to the station steps. Several people rushed to engage the taxi and went away swearing and disappointed.

He was full of militant triumph.

"Imagine," he told me his victorious adventures, "I could not find a taxi till I got to the Opera House. I jumped on to a tram and stood on the landing, thinking I'd snatch up the first taxi I saw. Not to waste time I had a rouble ready in case a militioner fined me for jumping off a tram in motion. And I didn't see a single taxi, damnation take them! It took me half an hour to get there, and a quarter of an hour back. I was afraid you would be gone. But you see all is in order."

"No drunken men about, but sober ones can't walk straight," I quoted the Soviet proverb.

"Drunken men! Do you suppose I drink nowadays?"

"Why, what do you do at nights, then?" I joked him, though I knew perfectly well that it was not drinking he cared for but having a gay time in good company.

"I'll tell you," he answered irritably. "You know I have at last a room to myself."

"I know you have changed your address."

"It's a whole story. For the last three years I've been saving up certificates and mandates from my various offices to get a room, but it was no good. I slept in the passage in my brother's flat. Then I happened to meet at a pub one of the big whigs in the *Gorotkomhoz**. A regular scoundrel, my boot was just itching to kick him. I made him drunk as a lord two or three times. But as I stood him drinks I thought to myself: it's sheer waste of money. It won't pay me. He'll sleep it off and never think of me again. But would you believe it, I called on him one morning, and there he was, cool and

* Municipal Section of Communal Management.

fresh as a cucumber, offering me an order to occupy a
room in house number so-and-so. 'My dear fellow,
explain!' I said. 'I can't believe my eyes.' 'It's quite
simple,' he replied. 'I told you I wasn't boasting.
I gave you my word of a proletarian. An old woman
died in that house, the former owner. She had been
allowed to live in the tiny room adjoining the porter's
lobby, and the porter's sister occupied the room which I
now intend for you. It appears she had not paid for
that room for a year. I don't know the ins and outs of
it, but anyway it has been decided to put her into the
old woman's place, and the chairman of the House
Committee sent me word about the vacancy. Naturally
we had a drink on it and decided that the room is to
be handed over to you at the order of the *Gorotkomhoz*
as part of room-space requisitioned for demobilised
soldiers, and you must pay 700 roubles to the chairman.
You know yourself, without money you can't get a room
anywhere. And besides, if you don't pay the chairman,
he won't support your claim in court—and the lodgers
are sure to go to law about it. But don't you have any
fears. If I say so, it's sure as sure. I've had pity on you—
I see you are a good fellow, our own sort. Now you may
get married if you feel like it.' "

My friend poured out the whole story at one go and
burst out laughing.

"What about marrying?" I asked jokingly.

"No. That's not in my line. Watching family happiness in our flat is enough for me."

"Indeed?"

"One of my neighbours is a big fellow with weak
nerves. He is an inventor, and at every unsuccessful
experiment—he is trying to invent the *perpetuum mobile*—

he beats his wife and then sobs in a fit of hysterics. His wife is a medical student and gives him Valerian drops to soothe him. She is consumptive and has a child of three who is comparatively quiet but howls loudly when the father begins beating the mother. In another room lives a Red Army officer, dried up and smelly like a dead bug, but he's been married three times this year."

"I am sure you are laying it on!" I said, laughing.

"No need to do that," he answered seriously. "You couldn't invent anything queerer than Soviet life if you tried. All I tell you is perfectly true. Here is the list of his wives. The first was a brunette of generous proportions—a regular dumpling. She had an affair with the Co-op manager. In her husband's absence she went to the Z.A.G.S. office*, got a divorce and moved all her belongings to her new home, though it is two streets away. She managed to do it all while her husband was at his office—a business-like woman! I don't think he was broken-hearted about it; anyway, in a week's time he married again. The second wife was distinctly pretty and distinctly consumptive. I had heard casually that she had lost her job and this was why she married him. Anyway, he has an officer's rations, and that's better than our salaries. But she tried those newly invented injections for tuberculosis and departed this life after the second injection. I did not even notice it—you know, one woman is like another to me if she doesn't happen to attract me—and then it appeared that a third wife was on the scenes. But this one will take a lot of killing."

"Why do you think that?"

* Registry Office.

"She is small, thin and disagreeable like himself. She moved in with her mamma, a squeaky old thing. Last night she gave birth to a baby to the accompaniment of the gramophone and of merry songs coming from the house cashier's party in the flat below. The cashier was celebrating a joyful event: he had been sentenced to a year's imprisonment for stealing 3,500 roubles collected by the lodgers for mending the central heating. His salary was only 75 roubles a month, and now he's secured 3,500 at the cost of one year of prison. But what a quantity of wet napkins there will be in the kitchen now!" he recalled suddenly.

"What has the kitchen to do with you?" I asked, annoyed at his not being able to get away from his domestic impressions.

"My dear, have you dropped from the moon? What has the kitchen to do with me! I may not succeed in boiling a kettle for my tea every morning, but I still have to wash, you know! The bathroom is occupied by a gloomy, dishevelled student. He's fitted a lid over the bath and sleeps on it. In the morning he puts the bedding inside the bath and uses the lid as a table. He cooks his food on it, has his meals and does his reading and writing on it too. It's an excellent arrangement!"

"Has he water as well?" I asked with some interest.

"No, there's no water. The pipes burst during the frost. But he's fixed up a wireless set there with a loud-speaker. How the devil he can stand it, I can't think!"

I listened absent-mindedly to the familiar story, though in Leningrad in those days we were much less crowded. Moscow was overloaded with Government offices. It was a very different place from what it used to be.

In the Lubianka, in the very centre of the town, the G.P.U. had its headquarters. In front there were old houses that had once been occupied by commercial offices and flats. Now all the signboards had been removed, the gates and the front doors were closed. At the back was "the inner prison of the G.P.U."—the most dreaded place in the U.S.S.R.

The Kremlin was closed to the public. Before the revolution cabs used to drive through it, people went for walks there, sightseers came to look at the cathedrals, the palace, the Granovity Hall. It had belonged to the people and not only to the Tsars. Now there were sentries at the gates and the place looked empty and forbidding.

The little streets round the Arbat had grown old: the small wooden houses seemed to slant on one side and looked curiously like dog kennels; the big houses dated back to pre-war times. It was six years since the revolution, but there was so sign of building.

"What an ass I am!" my friend cried suddenly. "I haven't asked you anything about yourself yet, and we have nearly arrived. You must promise to spend an evening with me. What about to-night?"

"Why, I have only just come."

"To-morrow, then?"

"Ring me up."

We found it difficult to arrange a meeting. In the U.S.S.R. all specialists have to attend committees, consultations, meetings, 'regardless of time'; all housewives have to waste hours in queues. No one comes home in time, or has regular meals, or goes to bed at a decent hour. And everyone is in a hurry—though what is it all for?

At last we settled that I was to call at his office between seven and eight. Offices are supposed to close at five, but only typists and clerks leave at that hour. Specialists are not paid overtime and so they are kept at work till all hours.

The office building presented a familiar picture. Lofty spacious rooms had been divided by rough wooden partitions into tiny lobbies, to accommodate the various sections, subsections, etc., into which all Soviet institutions are split up. Constant re-organisation required fresh room to be found in the same old building. Next to the offices of the Local Committee and the Communist Cell the walls were thickly covered with placards inviting the people to subscribe to the State loan, which was compulsory anyhow, and to put their savings in the State Bank, though no one could possibly have any savings. By the door of the Trades Union Office lists of defaulters were hung up. It was astonishing that there were so few of them— the subscription was heavy and gave one no advantages, for the Union was simply a Government institution.

When I arrived most of the staff had gone, and char-women were tidying the offices—carelessly sweeping the dust and cigarette ends off the floors and pouring water into the cracked old decanters that had not been washed for months and had no stoppers. Talking loudly, they disturbed the specialists, who were still at work, and made them move from one table to another. The sweeping raised clouds of dust which descended into the room again as none of the windows were open. The stale, pungent air was awful. In my friend's office the partition wall was fixed to the window which had been divided into two. It could not be made to open and was thickly covered with dust.

"At last!" he cried, jumping up from his writing-desk which was jammed in between two other odd desks, big and clumsy. He hastily began putting away his papers. "Excuse me, I must put these in the drawers or else our char will sweep them all away."

"Don't you lock your table?" I asked.

"What's the good? The Communists have duplicate keys, and nobody else is likely to look into another person's desk."

He put on a shabby old overcoat and led me out through the intricate dark passages.

"Now, where would you like to go? Moscow is one big pot-house, and there is nothing to do but drink. Shall we go to 'Pegasus's Stable'? or to the 'Stray Dog'? or 'The Galosh'?"

"Highbrows trying to be clever?"

"They too have to eat and drink, my dear, those poor rhymers, scribblers and actors. Well, would you like 'Borzhom,' a Caucasian little pub? or 'Medved'? or 'Arbat Number Nine'?—there are gypsies there."

"Let us try Arbat," I said uncertainly.

"Excellent. There is Stesha there, my weakness. Young and fresh as a wild flower."

"So you still fall in love, do you? How many times a year?"

"I don't keep count," he said, slightly nettled. "What should I do if I didn't fall in love and drink? After being pent up all day in a filthy hole like my office one wants some relaxation. Theatre is no good. Would you have me admire the antics of Meyerhold who thinks that the more hideous he makes a play, the more revolutionary

it is? Listen to old operas and watch the scenery getting
shabby and the singers losing their voices, and the
young ones not being trained properly? No, thank you.
I prefer the gypsies. They are simple and unassuming
people. Their women have no truck with Commissars
as the ballet-dancers do. They won't inform against
one, and that's something. Take Stesha, for instance. I
assure you there are few women nowadays so pure and
honest as she is, though I met her at a beer-house. It
was a couple of years ago, at the very beginning of
NEP. I felt out of sorts and wanted some vodka.
They are not allowed to sell vodka in beer-houses, but
I knew they'd give it me. So I went into one, sat down
in the corner and said to the waiter, "Some beer and
Seltzer water, not the effervescent sort, but the one that
burns your lips, you understand?"—"Certainly, by all
means."—"In that case, bring me something hot to eat
as well. Anything that's freshly cooked, ask the chef.
And some salt herring with onion." He instantly
brought me the herring, a mug of beer and some vodka
in a Seltzer water bottle."

"The latest achievement of the revolution!"

"Well, there's nothing bad in that, if it weren't for
their communistic hypocrisy. And so I had a gulp of
vodka and felt warmer and in better spirits. The door
opened and a gypsy girl slipped in. She looked a
regular bundle of clothes: a kerchief on her head, a
shawl on her shoulders, a skirt reaching to the floor.
She peeped in to see where the waiter was, and made
for the table where some proletarians were drinking in
gloomy silence. 'Let me tell your fortune,' she said to
one of them. 'I'll tell you your fate and show you your
luck, what has been, what will be, where your love is!

Put a coin in my hand, dear, handsome man!' She had
a charming, childish voice, clear and ringing, and they
swore at her in such a filthy way . . . people are coarse.
And you know, she didn't turn a hair—she must have
been used to it. She came up to my table, but the waiter
caught sight of her and shouted 'Clear out! Haven't I
told you you've no business here? Off with you!' I was
furious—'How dare you? I've invited her. Bring
another chair.' I asked her what she would like to eat
and added, just as though she were a grown-up woman,
'You'll do me great pleasure if you have lunch with me.'
Her eyes laughed and she said 'May I have some
chicken?' But the foolish child was afraid of the
waiter and sat at the very edge of the chair. Presently
she looked at me and asked, 'May I take my things off?
It's hot here.' 'You may,' I said. She undid her shawls,
took off her quilted jacket and emerged from her rags
light and graceful like a bird. She had a small head
covered with curls, a white neck and huge eyes, like a
wonderful doll. I asked her how old she was. 'I don't
know,' she said hesitatingly.—'How is that?'—'I don't
know, because I have to say that I am sixteen.'—
'Why?'—'Or they wouldn't let me into a beer-house.'
—'And what do you want in beer-houses?'—'I tell
fortunes.'—'Who sends you?'—'My mother. People
give more to me than to her. My younger sister does it,
too.'—'Have you a father?'—'Father has been killed.
He wouldn't give up his horses. But how can one camp
without horses?'—'Where do you come from?'—'The
Ukraine. We have to live here now.'—'What do you
earn a day?'—'A rouble or two.'—'How long are you
at it?'—'Till dark. Mother does not let us out in the
evening.'—'What do you do in the evening?'—'I

dance.'—'With whom?'—'With my sister: we sing and
dance. Mother knows all sorts of songs. In the daytime
it's dull and cold, and one has to go after drunken
people, they give more.' So you see, this is how I made
friends with Stesha. And do you know what she told
me by my hand?"

"What?"

"That I would die a violent death," he said carelessly. "The amusing thing was, she was so alarmed by
her prediction that she wouldn't take any money from
me: she said fortune-telling doesn't come true if it isn't
paid for."

Talking in this way we reached Arbat. The beer-
house door was open and one could see that the place
was crowded and swathed in grey clouds of tobacco
smoke.

"There's no room," I said, drawing back.

"Nonsense. Bravely forward!" He took me by the
arm and piloted me between the tables put together so
closely that the people formed one continuous mass.

"Misha, hullo!" he called the waiter.

A lively, well set-up lad with a lock of fair hair
jauntily combed over his forehead, came up to us. He
had just roughly plumped down two mugs of beer on
one of the tables, but he stood before my friend respectfully with a bowed head as though waiting for a con-
fidential commission.

"A table for two, close to the platform."

"Certainly," he answered modestly.

There was a disturbance in the corner by the platform: Misha was shifting the tables, asking the people
to move, assuring them it was 'in the course of official
duties,' threatening them with militia and being ex-

tremely amiable. Two minutes later we had a separate
table right by the platform, and Misha stood before us,
bending obsequiously.

"We'll have an omelet with ham, sausages and cabbage, and two bottles of light beer. Give us the omelet
first, and see that the ham is chopped up small and
slightly fried before it is put in."

The waiter disappeared, but my friend was not satis-
fied.

"He is sure to get it wrong. I'd better go and see the
cook. Excuse me, I shan't be a minute."

He seemed to feel quite at home in the place. And
indeed his domestic activities could not find an outlet
elsewhere, as he had no home of his own.

"It's all settled," he said with satisfaction when he
came back. "The choir is here, they'll soon begin to
sing. Stesha is here. The omelet will be first-rate. See
the advantages of the Socialist régime: three roubles to
Misha, one rouble to the cook and all is as it should be.
The instructive inscriptions on the walls are very
appropriate: 'A person who gives tips is no better than
a slave owner; the one who accepts is his slave'; 'Comrade, in accepting tips you lower your human dignity.'
'Customers who are not sober cannot be served.' "

He looked round. It was a mixed public: workmen,
Soviet officials, a few smart-looking military men doing
their best to live up to the old Army ideals of smartness,
many women, many young people.

"Half of the public certainly ought not to be served,"
he decided.

" 'All must struggle with the liquidation of illiteracy,' "
I read one of the placards. "That's neatly worded."

" 'Citizen customers are asked not to use obscene

language,' and underneath is written in pencil '3 roubles'—that is the fine for swearing. Forgive me for bringing you into such an unrefined place, but without me you wouldn't have seen this aspect of Soviet life."

The omelet was brought in.

"That's fine!" my friend said with enthusiasm. "I haven't had any grub since morning, or to be exact since yesterday and am hungry like a wolf."

"That's too bad!" I said indignantly. "This isn't a famine year. There's food enough to go round."

"My dear lady, you know nothing about a bachelor's way of living! To begin with, I woke up yesterday morning with an unpleasant feeling that something was amiss. What was it? It gradually dawned on me—I was completely bankrupt. I searched through all my pockets and found ten coppers. Well, anyway I could go to my office by tram, and borrow from our Communist chief, a comfortable fellow with rations from the Kremlin and always enough to eat. But as soon as I came in my colleague ran up to me: 'My dear man, have you any cash to spare? I am desperately hungry.' He is a family man, but his trouble is that he's been appointed to a job in one town, and his wife in another, and so their budget doesn't balance. So I had to sacrifice the Communist to him. In the lunch-hour interval I dashed off to the chairman of our World Planning Section. It's a fine place, with a lot of furniture from private flats and even a carpet on the floor. He insisted on giving me lunch, but I couldn't very well borrow from him because the first thing he did was to invite me to a party at his flat."

"How is it you have any money now?"

"Like an idiot, I had forgotten that the magazine

Technical Science owed me something for an article. I only remembered it this morning and marched there straight away. I know their cashier, a delightful girl—a blonde with appetising lips. Nothing would have come of it but for her—she settled it all in a trice and gave me three new chervonets."

"Why didn't you go and have a meal?"

"For one thing, I hadn't time, for another, one doesn't feel so hungry when one has money, and thirdly, I was waiting for you."

"And fourthly you were afraid of spending it all before you met me!" I finished his sentence and we both laughed.

"The gypsies are coming," he said, turning to a rickety little door through which the gypsies were coming out on to the platform.

The women walked in one after the other quickly and gracefully and sat down in a semicircle on chairs. The men followed and placed themselves behind them.

The mistress of the choir sat in the middle, resting her plump hands on her knees. She must have been about forty, but like most southern women, looked old for her age. She was wearing a long black silk dress, slightly open at the neck and with long sleeves. Her hair was smoothly brushed back and she had small but good diamond ear-rings. In her right hand she held a white batiste handkerchief edged with lace. Her movements were restrained, dignified and full of authority. Other women were dressed in black or in some dark material with a design of flowers. All had shawls, some of white silk, others of flowered cashmere and two or three had flowers in their hair. They all looked neat and smart in their own way, though their dresses showed signs of wear. One felt that, like all actors and singers, they had pulled themselves together before coming on to the stage and were tense with excitement. None of them were made up, though at that time most Soviet women and girls seemed to think that generous quantities of paint made up for any deficiencies of dress.

"Look, Stesha is on the left, at the very end. Isn't she a beauty?" my friend whispered ecstatically. "See how slim she is! One might hold her waist in one's two hands. And what eyes! She is only sixteen, and so beautiful. Look at her mouth, see how she smiles. She won't look at me, the little wretch. Stesha!" he called in a low voice.

She undoubtedly heard, but obstinately went on looking at the audience at the other side of the room.

"It's because I am not alone. They are very tactful," he comforted himself.

The men gypsies made a strange impression on me. Young, with thick curly hair carefully combed and oiled, clean-shaven, swarthy faces, sensual lips, sad and yet insolent eyes, they all looked rather alike to me. Their Russian shirts, jackets and well-polished boots fitted admirably, but somehow did not seem the right thing for them.

"I don't like men in a gypsy choir," my friend said with a note of discontent in his voice. "They are all right at a fair, selling stolen horses."

"The citizens have eaten their horses," I observed. "And if they went to a factory it would be the end of them."

The audience gradually subsided, though by no means the whole of it.

"I can't sleep at night in my anguish
Bitter thoughts drive sleep away . . . "

the mistress of the choir began in a deep mellow voice.
The guitars accompanied her with a subdued moaning
sound.   The choir waited for the refrain and then
joined in harmoniously but with curious dissonances.
When the refrain ended she sang again alone, and every
time there was more anguish in her voice and more wild
passion in the choir's sudden outcries.   The guitars and
the voices swelled into a wonderful whole of sound. The
women betrayed their emotion in different ways; some
threw back their heads, others moved their shoulders
or waved their hands, but all the gestures were restrained and not meaningless as is so often the case with
opera singers.   The mistress of the choir sat more still
than the others, and only her fingers twitched.   At the
end of the song she bent back, glanced at the man who,
as it were, led the choir with her; he answered her with
a strange twitter of the guitar, two or three of the
women cried out, and the song broke off on queer
discordant notes.

The delighted audience clapped, shouted, cried
"Dasha, more! Dear girl, it was fine!" The gypsies
bowed quietly, without getting up from their chairs,
and straightened their shawls, their hair and their
dresses.   The mistress of the choir wiped her mouth
with her handkerchief, folded her arms and made a
sign to the one who was to begin the next song. It was
a passionate, gay, rollicking song. But everything they
sang was passionate, whether it was gay or sad. Sometimes there was nothing special in the words, but when
they began singing, shouting, screaming each in her

own way and all of them together that "you must kiss once again, once again, many, many times again" the audience went mad with enthusiasm and was ready to shout with them.

"Damnation take them, those children of Herod simply turn one's soul inside out," someone said behind me. "Witches, regular witches!"

"You wait till you see Stesha dance!" my friend persisted.

"Dasha! sing 'The Morning'! 'The Grey Misty Morning'!" a young student shouted obstinately and imploringly, forgetting his girl companion who wanted to have something more cheerful, "with kisses in it."

The public quieted down when the gypsies began to sing and then raised an uproar again.

At last Stesha came forward. She threw off her cheap shiny shawl of bright magenta shot with violet, obviously dyed with aniline dyes. She was young and was not likely to possess any good, old things. Her dress was dark blue with a design of small red roses. The hackneyed "Pompadour" pattern might have been made for her, so fresh did it look on her. Her small firm breasts were clearly outlined by the narrow bodice, and the full skirt did not conceal the graceful lines of her legs. She stepped out simply and modestly, glanced at the audience and at the choir and began to dance.

All the room she had on the platform amounted to something like ten paces by five, so that she could not move to any distance as she danced. But as soon as she began, to the accompaniment of the guitars and the voices, to move her shoulders and arms, setting her whole body in motion from the head downwards, and to glide along without taking her feet off the floor, I understood that she had mastered the art of dancing better than many a ballet girl. And Russian ballet dancers know their trade!

The way she moved her arms, or bent her head or cried out suddenly to the changing accompaniment of the song, now slow and now quick, was utterly unexpected and spontaneous. The women in the semicircle followed her excitedly with their eyes, clapping their hands and nodding their heads as they sang. The men looked on critically and exactingly, cleverly changing the time and twitching the strings of their guitars. At last one of them gave a sudden shout, stamped his foot, and they all began stamping, shouting, screaming. Two more women jumped up and danced, while the others clapped their hands and shouted. The audience banged their mugs against the tables, and the uproar made one think of the hounds of hell let loose. At the same time one of the customers flung a bottle at a neighbour to whom he had taken a dislike, and a hand-to-hand fight began by their table. A dozen waiters surrounded them and with remarkable skill and quickness separated the enemies just as the wild dance came to an end. The audience watched the dance and the fight with equal interest—it all seemed of a piece in the general half-drunken frenzy.

"My word, those waiters are well trained!" an elderly man who wanted to show his knowledge of the world said with enthusiasm. "Jolly clever, and so disciplined! As good as in any bourgeois country!"

"Bring me two more bottles, quick!" a workman demanded.

"Can't be done," the waiter answered sternly. "By

the new order of the Moscow Soviet we are not allowed
to serve more than two bottles per person."

"Nonsense! To begin with, it would mean six bottles
for two persons, and the order says nothing about that,
does it? And besides, as a proletarian, an activist, a
social worker, etc., I'll tell you what: give me my bill!
There, take the money—four bottles of beer, 3 roubles,
and half a rouble for yourself. That's clear, isn't it?
All settled?"

"Yes," the waiter answered reluctantly.

"Now we are fresh customers, see? We begin all over
again—bring us two bottles of beer!"

The workman was delighted at his own resourceful-
ness. His neighbours' sympathies were entirely on his
side: nothing is pleasanter than to defeat a Soviet order.
The waiter went away, obviously wondering if the man
was a Communist and would give him away. He must
have consulted somebody, for a minute later another
waiter came up to the workman, wiped the table with a
cloth as for a new customer and inquired, "What will
you have?"

The workman was in raptures.

"Clever creatures! Jolly clever! The Soviet power
does sharpen people's wits, anyway! Neatly done,
this."

Taking no notice of what he was saying, the non-
committal waiter brought two more bottles of beer.

My friend was indignantly watching someone in the
audience.

"Just see how those wretches try to ape Stesha,"
he said irritably. "That cow of a woman over there
twitching her fat shoulder! You know who the man
with her is? A very important Communist from the

Kremlin. And there is the scraggy cashier from the 'Fat and Bone Trust,' painted like a cheap doll, flirting with a man whom she obviously cannot stand."

"Never mind her. Look at that girl on the right, isn't she charming?"

"Fair, rosy, a little *à la* Venus of Milos. She is all right for a quiet, comfortable life but not for a Soviet romance. Come, I'll introduce you to Stesha. They are very grateful for any recognition. It's a dog's life, you know."

We went out into the corridor. The gypsies were resting in a narrow passage by the cloakrooms. A horrible stench came from there, but there was nowhere else for them to be. The men were excitedly discussing the fight and, with a thorough knowledge of the business, examining the victim who had received 'first-aid' from the waiters in the kitchen. They smothered his bleeding wounds in collodium which made him look perfectly ghastly.

The mistress of the choir saw my friend and, going up to him, took him by the hands.

"Oh, my dear, how horrid it is to sing when drunken men are fighting and there's blood! It upset me so that I am trembling all over, and I've got to sing again."

I began telling her how beautifully they sang and how impressed I was by her musical talent.

"My treasure, but we can sing very differently from that!" she exclaimed, delighted. "Come with your friend and I'll sing such songs for you that you'll forget everything in the world. And it will be a relief to me too. If I hadn't to earn my living, nothing would induce me to sing nowadays. We don't sing for gold now, as we used to, but for a bitter piece of bread. We have nowhere to turn. The people have grown so coarse, such bullies. They all try to drag one into the mud. In the old days singing was a joy to me, a delight. And now it makes me cry. All we sing for, it seems, is that people should drink more Soviet beer."

Stesha, pale with exhaustion and the stuffiness, stood leaning against the wall. A young gypsy stood beside her. There was a hostile expression in his eyes, and the others avoided him.

I heard Stesha say to my friend:

"How do you do! It's long since you came to see us. This is the man I am going to marry."

When the choir made ready to go on to the platform again, we left—the hall was too stuffy and full of drunken people. There were plenty of them in the street, too. We tried to walk in the boulevard but on every seat there were two or three couples making love, some in silence, others with excited giggles and occasional shrieks.

"They've got nowhere else to go," my friend said apologetically. "Probably none of them have a room to themselves, so they all come out into the street. Disgusting."

We turned into the winding little streets near Arbat. They were quiet and empty. We walked along the broken down pavement feeling anything but gay.

·　·　·　·　·

The NEP was over. Stalin was busy reversing Lenin's policy in all directions. Once more there were ration cards, distribution depots, underfeeding or downright famine and political terror. The people in the streets looked greyer, shabbier, thinner. Shops and

restaurants closed, but pot-houses did excellent trade.
The only food they sold was dry salt fish and soaked
peas, but there was plenty of vodka. Soviet life had
other aspects, of course, but the tremendous sale of
vodka was very typical of that period.

Smelly, impure vodka reeking of raw spirit was sold
in places where nothing but tooth-powder and gum
could be bought. There were not enough proper
bottles and it was sold in bottles that had been used for
milk, beer or mineral water, badly washed and
corked up with old broken corks. It was ridiculously
expensive and cost twenty times as much as it did under
Tsarism. It could not be bought in small quantities:
sometimes even pint bottles were not available but only
quarts. When there was a shortage of vodka, people
drank eau-de-Cologne, *vegetal* and other toilet concoc-
tions made with wood-spirit. Working people drank
spirit varnish. People drank because they had not
enough to eat, and a hungry man needs something to
fortify him; and those who had enough food drank to
drown their misery. They mostly drank by themselves
because all gatherings were dangerous. It was a terrible
time.

I heard that my friend had been transferred to
Leningrad, but I did not want to look for him: there
had been several arrests among my husband's colleagues
and I kept away from everyone, for fear of compromising people. He did, however, come to call on
me at the museum.

"What wind brought you here?" I asked joyfully.

"It is my off day. I had nowhere to go and was
wandering about the Nevsky when I saw that the
museum was open and that your name was on the

notice. So I've called. I have long been meaning to find you."

"How are you getting on?"

"Abominably. And you?"

"The same. I am preparing the museum for sale. Didn't you see on the notice that this is the last day?"

"So I had a bit of luck after all, finding you here."

"Where do you live?"

"Making ready for Solovki

> Where it's the Government's intention
> To keep me in strict detention."

"Oh, nonsense."

"You know very well it isn't nonsense. That's what we are coming to. The worse the famine, the more necessary the terror. Is your husband all right?"

"So far."

"God grant he may be."

We walked in silence through the rooms of the doomed museum, though he scarcely noticed them.

"Have you listened to the gypsies any more?" I asked him, recalling Moscow and our last meeting.

"Would you believe it, I met Stesha here the other day. You remember Stesha, don't you?"

"I do, though NEP and even famine seem as far off as one's childhood."

"That's true. Well, this was how it happened," he went on, brightening up. "You see, I got dead sick of drinking by myself. I wanted a bit of excitement. Anything to make one forget about the arrests and the shootings. Suddenly a friend rang me up. 'Come to the corner of such and such a street.' I did and stood

there waiting for him. He drove up in a taxi with his
wife and another lady. She too did not know what to
do with herself for misery but, of course, she began to
flirt, the silly hen. She asked me coquettishly, 'Do you
know where we are going? Don't try to guess, you
never, never will.'—'I don't care where we go,' I
answered, but remembered in time to add 'with you
it would be delightful anywhere.' It's a good thing my
tongue is used to saying those sort of things. 'Oh,
don't,' she chirped. 'You mustn't look at me to-day
(When did I look at you at all, my good woman, I
wondered); we are going to the gypsies, to real gypsies
in the Novaya Derevnya,' she added in a whisper. I
cheered up at that—it would be jolly, after all, to hear
that devilish singing again. So there are still some of
them left, I thought. I had been told that gypsy choirs
were exiled wholesale to the North as a 'pernicious,
demoralising element.' Suddenly I saw my friend stop
the taxi at a gate and give the chauffeur 35 roubles for
a twenty minutes' drive. Whatever for? I wondered.
But it appeared it was all a conspiracy. The lady was
in raptures, of course. 'We'll go through a passage in
the yard,' she prattled, 'so as not to leave a clue. You
know all taximen are employed by the G.P.U. and
report there what fares they had. We are going to turn
into another street, then round a corner, and then it's
quite near. Isn't it lovely?' I can't stand this Nat
Pinkerton business. I let her go first and asked my
friend where did he get the taxi? It would have been
much simpler to go by tram. 'I assure you, it's perfectly all right,' he said. 'I got the taxi at the corner by
the Hotel d'Europe. You know they are kept there for
foreigners. To the ordinary citizens they have to say

they are engaged. I promised my man three chervonets over and above his fare. One may as well do things in style! And there is no danger of his following us, because he can't leave his taxi, and it is too far to drive round. I have weighed it all. We mustn't get the gypsies into trouble, you know. There are so few of them left, and they are all watched.' I swore at myself for coming—it would be beastly to let the gypsies down. But I knew, of course, that Novaya Derevnya was their old haunt and that gypsies did not betray one another."

He gave a crooked smile.

"What's the matter?" I asked.

"I remembered that we drove past the *Technical Bureau* in the Shpalerka. It will be a good thing if I end my days there and not at Solovki."

"Don't be morbid," I said angrily.

"It's all very well to say that, but I know there are about a score of our best specialists there already. They are taken out to work by day and are locked up in solitary cells for the night."

"Come, tell me about the gypsies. I know all about the *Bureau* myself."

"What is there to tell? Oh, yes, Stesha. Imagine, she was the first person I saw when we came in! She had filled out and grown taller and more beautiful—devilishly beautiful! What health, what wild, natural vitality! A true woman. She has a baby . . . Well, what else? We unpacked the food we had with us, had some drink, listened to their singing. Stesha sang, her husband sang, they called in a neighbour, the old mother joined in and even the baby assisted. A Russian baby would have screamed himself blue in the face, but this one sat on his grandmother's lap, waving his little arms, his eyes shining, thoroughly enjoying the noise and the singing. I asked Stesha why she didn't put him to bed. 'It's all right, he is a gypsy,' she said; 'he will sleep in the morning. And anyway he wouldn't go to sleep now.' I asked where her sister was, and she just waved her hand: 'Where we shall all be soon. I don't know how we are to go on: we may not tell fortunes, we may not sing. All we live by is that people come here to listen to our singing and give us something. We sometimes get asked to go out, but that's risky. The only people who can afford to ask us nowadays are Communists and G.P.U. men, and they are the very ones to give us away.' At that moment her husband called her to sing and I suddenly felt that this was the last time I was seeing her. How do you explain that, you clever woman?"

"It's nerves," I answered, knowing that it was not an answer.

•   •   •   •   •

Eighteen months passed. During that time my friend had been shot, my husband sent to penal servitude, and I had been in prison. As soon as I was released I went to see him at Kem. While I was there I saw a party of women prisoners marching through the frozen mud of the road. There were many gypsies among them. Most of them were old, thin, dishevelled and scarcely able to drag themselves along. When the escort swore at them they raised a fearful outcry. There was one young girl among them and a young woman carrying with difficulty a child of about two, wrapped up in a shawl. I did not know whether it was Stesha; I no longer remembered by then what she looked like.

Last year I read in Soviet newspapers that on the eve of the new year 1935 tables could be engaged in restaurants and a gypsy choir would be singing. I wondered how many of the gypsies were still left and how long they would be allowed to go free. And I asked myself if Stesha had survived, and to how many more men she would foretell a violent death.

A PEASANT WOMAN

THE word 'madame' immediately calls before my mind the image of a typical Frenchwoman. I at once picture to myself a tall, once handsome woman with red-dyed hair, free gestures and emphatic speech, confidently and thoughtlessly treading the downward path of age. Or I think of a plump little woman who makes up for the stiffness of her tightly corseted body by the lively movements of her head and fat little hands. But the 'madame' I met in my wanderings abroad was a calm, stern, sensible Siberian woman.

It is not worth while to tell by what chance a woman born and bred in the depths of Siberia married a Frenchman and changed from Fedosya Vassilyevna into Madame Petit. Many foreigners, especially Frenchmen and Germans, used to come to Russia before the revolution. Some of them saved money and went home again, others settled there for good. The revolution ruined them all and threw them out of the country in a state of utter destitution. Those who had not made up their minds to abandon everything at once and flee for their lives found themselves in a desperate plight and, as the Soviet expression is, 'died post haste,' leaving their families one legacy—foreign citizenship. Thanks to this legacy, Fedosya Vassilyevna managed to reach France with her three children and was transformed into Madame Petit.

"It's all one to me, what they call me," she said smiling. "If it's to be 'madame,' there's nothing for it. Anyway, the madames here get enough to eat, I see, and our citizens are starving."

I met her when she was already settled in Paris. We were both invited to tea by a nice, hospitable Russian family.

The table was covered with a pinkish cloth and laden with plates of cakes, pastries and biscuits. There was thinly cut bread in a basket and a piece of cheese under a glass cover.

After fifteen years in the U.S.S.R. I had not yet grown accustomed to the sight of an attractively laid tea-table. I could see that Fedosya Vassilyevna felt the same. At first she would not have anything to eat, then out of politeness took something from the dish nearest to her and put it down on her plate, biting off a little piece.

"I am not hungry," she said. "I've had dinner to-day, not long ago, I mean," she added, recalling that we were in a country where one is supposed to have dinner every day.

I liked looking at her and listening to her plain, quiet speech. We were different: she was a peasant, I—an intellectual, but we had one thing in common that drew us very close together: our experience of Soviet Russia. Destitution, cold, hunger, fear, helplessness—one can only understand all this if one has been through it.

I felt that neither she nor I had yet entered thoroughly into our new 'bourgeois' life.

She was wearing a neat black dress with an old-fashioned trimming. It evidently was not her own.

Someone had given it to her and she had put it on without thinking whether it suited her or whether she liked it. I too had worn for months things that someone had sent me instead of having clothes made for myself. So long as a dress was in good condition and had no holes in it, it seemed to be all that one required. She had a smart and fashionable handbag, obviously a present. I too had a bag given to me. She was holding hers tight, afraid of losing it; I, equally unused to handbags, kept leaving mine in the most unlikely places. Other people did not notice these little things about us, but I knew that we had both been branded by our Soviet experience for the rest of our lives.

"Where do you come from?" I asked her.

"You don't know our parts. I am from Siberia, a long way off," she said sadly, certain that she could not meet anyone from her part of the country in a strange land.

"From Krasnoyarsk?"

"Very nearly," she answered, cheering up. "To the north of it, but on the Yenissey. Do you mean to say you know our parts?"

"Yes, I've lived there. I come from Tomsk."

"I know it. Just fancy now, meeting a neighbour in a foreign place! One never can tell. Are you from Tomsk itself?"

"Yes, right from the town."

"It's a fine town, a rich one."

"Your parts aren't bad either."

"I won't boast, but they certainly weren't bad. Plenty of room. And of course before the revolution we were very well off. But we thought nothing of it then. If a peasant lived on bread and potatoes we reckoned he was as poor as poor could be, though he had a good store of cabbage and cucumbers and was sure to have a cow. People don't live like that nowadays. They haven't enough bread, let alone bread and potatoes. And they don't even think of cows."

"Had you a cow?"

"A cow! Why, we used to have three, though we weren't considered rich *kulaks*. When the revolution came, the Red Army soldiers killed one of our cows, another we had to sell for taxes, and the third died, though we took ever such care of it. There wasn't enough fodder, and besides every beast has its proper span of life."

"I suppose you couldn't manage to buy another one in its place?"

"Not likely! We were driven out of our cottage and had everything taken from us. We had to live in my mother's old hut. My husband died there, and mother soon followed him. It was from underfeeding. They gave every bit of food to the children."

"Did you go on to a collective farm?"

"They wouldn't take me. A woman with three small children isn't much of a catch. And I didn't want to go either. It isn't as though there were any order or sense there. It's nothing but misery. I'll tell you what it was like, if you care to know. To begin with, they put in a lot of strangers as overseers. They knew nothing about our parts, and wouldn't listen to anyone. 'You live in the old-fashioned way,' they said, 'and we want to build up a new life.' Well, first of all, they took all the deer they could get hold of. They were going to have a special farm to breed more of them, if you please. They drove everybody's deer into one big shed. The deer trampled down the ground and stood there in the mud, all crowded together. And deer are free animals, you know; they need plenty of room, fresh air and cleanliness. In a month or two they all died, everyone of them. Breeding deer, indeed! Why, they can't manage horses."

"Can't feed them, I suppose?"

"It's partly that and partly negligence. Every horse, good or bad, needs attention. On a collective farm a horse doesn't belong to anyone. A man finishes his work, puts the horse in the stable and that's all. There's no one to give it food or drink at the proper time or to cover it with a cloth in cold weather. Spring came and nearly all the horses had died—there were none for ploughing. The overseers were dismissed for mismanagement. The new ones ordered the peasants to plough with cows. We'll see to it later, they said, and meanwhile the work must be done according to plan. The peasants had to do as they were told, or they'd be sent to prison straight away. So they harnessed the cows. It was a sight! The men were ploughing and the women waiting in the furrow to get a drop of milk from the cow. At that rate, of course, a cow can't last long. Soon neither men nor beasts could stand on their feet. One day I saw a peasant come out ploughing with an ox; his ox fell, the man tried to lift it up, and fell too. People came up to them and saw they were both dead. If men have a bad time, I suppose it has to be, they may have deserved it, but why should dumb beasts suffer? One can't bear to see it."

She was silent and so was I. I knew Siberia very

well and liked it better than Russia in Europe. Siberia
has never had landed gentry or destitute peasants.
Siberian peasants managed their farms well and were
prosperous and there really was 'plenty of room' in
those parts. The ruin of that rich country grieved me
even more than the plight of the Russian peasants
who had been rich only in the North and in the
Cossack region.

"At the collective farms they never gather all their
harvest in before the winter," she went on. "In the
old days no one ever dreamed of leaving any of it till
the snow came, but now they always do," she said
sorrowfully. "They get through the bulk of the work
after a fashion and then send the feebler workers—
kitchen maids and anyone they can spare—to gather
in the rest. There may be three or four feet of snow
on the ground, a hard frost, and they send them to
cut down the remaining sunflowers. The women have
no leggings, no one has proper clothes. All get frost-
bitten, of course. No end of them are taken to the
hospital; some have their legs cut off and others die
of themselves. They send women to saw timber in the
forest, too. A woman can't refuse because she is not
strong enough or because she has a child that can't
be left alone. She has no right to. She must take the
child to the crèche. It's none of her business what
will become of him there—she's got to do as she is
told. Women work in timber yards, too. And at
penal camps they do all manner of work. As I was
travelling in the train I saw women making bridges,
repairing the line, building dams. The loads they have
to lift—it's frightening to see! Women never did such
work before. They are certainly men's equals now!"

"And how did you get on?"

"Oh, I just kept body and soul together. I used to
be up with the daylight—hunger would not let me
sleep longer, much as I would have liked to. The
children got up early too for the same reason. I used
to close the shutters to darken the room, but it made
no difference—one can't sleep if one is hungry. My
eldest boy, he was twelve then, at once set off foraging:
fishing, or looking for mushrooms, or, in the spring,
looking for some sort of roots. Some roots are sweet,
you know. In the autumn he sometimes stole from
kitchen gardens or from the railway station when stores
were brought there. He told me he had picked things
up in the road, for he knew I didn't allow stealing.
But there is no stopping a child when he is hungry.
When he took the young ones with him I always
knew he was going thieving. And indeed I didn't
forbid him stealing collective farms' goods. Everyone
did that. For instance, when corn was sent off by rail
they brought sacks and sacks of it to the station and
left it there under rain and snow till the time came for
loading up. They set some decrepit old man to watch
it, of course, but he couldn't keep awake for ever.
The children waited till he dozed off and made a
hole in the sack to get the corn. Sometimes he out-
witted them and only pretended to go to sleep. If
he caught them he gave them a whipping or pulled
their ears. All sorts of things happened. The children
did not tell me everything, and indeed I hadn't time
to listen to them. As soon as it was light I had to
run and see if there were any queues waiting. If there
was a queue it meant that provisions of some sort had
been brought—radishes, or cucumbers, or onions; we

took anything that was going so long as it was food."

"Didn't you get any bread?"

"I was supposed to have a pound of bread a day for myself and one for every child—that is four pounds a day altogether. But what's the good of rations when there is no bread to be had? We had proper riots about it. Women went in a crowd to the co-op, banged on the door and shouted for the manager. He came out one day. 'Have you gone silly?' he said. And they all shouted:

" 'It's you who've gone silly with eating too much!'

" 'Just look at the fat brute!'

" 'Give us bread!'

" 'Death is better than such a life!'

"Others simply went for him with their fists. He stood on the steps kicking them off, but he didn't dare to hit out for fear they'd do for him. When the women grew tired of shouting he began soothing them and explaining ever so nicely that he wasn't responsible himself, but he would telegraph somewhere and ask for bread to be sent at once. Well, they went home and the next day again there was nothing to buy. It was simply terrible, the state people were reduced to. At the market-place one suddenly heard a cry, 'Comrades, brothers, help, I'm dying!'—and it was some respectable man or woman lying on the ground and shouting. They had come to the end of their tether. Well, people would give fifteen or twenty copecks—but there's no buying anything with that. Or again one would hear shouts—a man was being beaten. He had taken a cup of flour from a market-woman as though to see what it was like and run off, trying to eat the flour on the way. And market-women are well organised, you know—they immediately tripped him up and began beating him. If the man was clever he tried to fall near their wares: while they were beating him he protected his head with his hands and made haste to seize with his mouth what he could —milk cheese, raw potatoes, anything. We had a neighbour who had spent all his life in penal servitude —he was a regular bandit. He would no sooner be let out than he did something again and was locked up once more. When the revolution came the bolsheviks released him at once: he had suffered under Tsarism, they said. Of course while there was anything to steal, he lived by stealing, and afterwards he went about swollen with hunger, begging in Christ's name. He used to come to me and say 'Do you know, neighbour, I tell you as before God, I would give all the years that are still left me for one single day of our prison fare in the old days! What a life that was! They gave us two and a half pounds of bread a day, and white rolls on Sundays. Much good freedom is to me now when there's nothing to eat!' But he didn't live long, anyway. When they begin to swell, they soon die."

"What did you have to eat in those days?"

"Whatever I could find. I did my best to get a little flour. I didn't bake bread. You give a child a piece of bread, and it's gone in no time. I used to make flour-porridge: it's hot, it tastes good and goes further. The children liked potatoes, too, but there weren't any to be had. Sometimes I used to get potato peelings and bake cakes of them—there was a factory near us where they made treacle. I had a friend there, else I wouldn't have been given any peelings. But I must say we were often reduced to boiling grass for food. There is a special grass that has seed pods on it and we collected those seeds and cooked them. True, many people died of it, but we used it to eke out our rations."

"And perhaps to hasten death?"

"Perhaps," she answered calmly.

"Were people in Government service better off?"

"I don't know what to say. The heads may have been better off, but small officials were worse off than I. Their rations weren't enough to live on, and they had no time to go in search of food. They couldn't keep house at all. They came home from the office hungry and there was nothing they could buy in the evening—everything was sold out in the morning. You can't think what we did eat!" she said smiling suddenly. "A woman ran in to tell me that they were selling tea at the co-op, made of some sort of roots. I rushed off and was in time to buy some. A tremendous crowd came after me, all for this tea, but there wasn't any more of it left, though they only sold a small packet or two to each customer. Those who did succeed in buying any, ate it on the spot, munching the roots or the berries, whatever they were. When a substitute for coffee was brought to the co-ops it too was sold out at once. We mixed it with potato peelings and baked cakes of it."

I listened to her and thought: I too made flour-porridge, I too baked cakes of potato peelings. At one time I was better off than she, but I knew that the chief feature of Soviet life is the agonising, ever-present thought about food. There was a curious equality between her and me, and indeed it was so with all of us.

Our hostess was offering us biscuits and jam.

"Won't you have something? Let me give you some more tea." Madame Petit took a biscuit and put it on her plate.

"Do your children like it here? Do they play?" I asked, following the train of my thoughts.

"They have enough to eat, so of course they play," she answered, understanding what was in my mind.

"Do they go to school?"

"The eldest does."

"How do they manage about the language?"

"They are getting used to it."

"Did they get any schooling at home?"

"It was misery, not schooling," she said angrily. She had spoken calmly, almost indifferently till then, as all peasant women do, accepting their troubles as something inevitable.

"Forty degrees of frost outside, a snowstorm, they come to the school and the room hasn't been heated. Schooling, indeed! They did nothing at school. The teachers understood—they too were perishing with cold and hunger. What could they do? Besides, they were short of books, of copy-books, of pencils. And in schools attached to Children's Homes it was nothing but vice. The homeless children in there are professional thieves and they teach others their trade and much else besides. The filth of it ruins them for life."

She was agitated and ceased speaking, probably feeling that she had said too much. I did not venture to ask what had roused her, knowing how bitter memories can be.

I also knew from my own experience how difficult

it was to make a child go to school. I had no end
of arguments and even quarrels with my son about
it. I received a complaint from his teachers that he
refused to take his cap off in the class-room. I asked
him why. "And if it's cold?" he answered defiantly.
—"But you are allowed to keep your coat on," I
answered.—"I can't put my coat over my head, can
I? Why did they make us shave our heads in the
middle of winter? Because one of the children was
verminous? Much it matters! And why didn't they
shave the girls? It's the girls who breed lice. There,
you've nothing to say!" he added triumphantly seeing
that I had no answer ready. And indeed I had nothing
to say. In Leningrad there was not enough fuel to
heat the schools. The children went about with
chilblains, their hands blue, swollen and itching. There
were a good many thieves among them too. They
stole cap, gloves, galoshes, pens, pencils, anything
that was left about.

Yes, it was bitter to recall life in the U.S.S.R.
Whatever we spoke of, it touched one on the raw.

"What about women?" our hostess asked. "They
say many women occupy important positions now."

"Oh, yes!" she answered ironically. "A woman is
sure to be elected on to a committee of management.
She is delighted and doesn't see that she is an exception
while thousands are toiling like slaves. But her life
isn't anything to envy, either. She loses the habit
of a woman's work: she hasn't time to mend a tear,
she forgets how to cook, for she gets her food from a
communal kitchen. And what sort of food is that?
Watery soup or porridge that makes you sick, but
you've got to eat it because there's nothing else. It

doesn't improve one's health either. No, I can tell you, if a woman has an important post, her children are homeless and her husband too. She doesn't need him any more."

"Come, come!" I said jokingly, though I knew she was largely right.

"I assure you. Forgive me for putting it so crudely, but we are all women here: if a bull is to be of any use to cows he must be well fed. Besides, a woman knows nowadays that a husband will not support her, and as for the rest she can have all she wants without marriage if her conscience lets her. They are not so keen on that now, but if it hadn't been for the famine, I don't know what we should have come to! There is no morality left, life has simply been turned upside down. For a decent woman it's simply unendurable."

Fedosya Vassilyevna spoke with great heat and animation. Bookish words found their way into her speech. The revolution in domestic life had evidently touched her to the quick.

"There is no advantage in being a wife," she said, evidently presenting somebody's case. "She is sure to be tripped up, and the other woman, the new wife, will have the same rights, though the first one may have worn herself out with work for the family. I'll tell you a case—if you aren't tired of listening," she interrupted her story, though we could see she wanted to tell it.

"Do go on, please."

"The man was a Communist. He had lived with his wife for thirty years and they had grown-up children. You know, in the old days people used to marry early. He was about fifty and she was less, though

she looked older: children age one, and she had had
seventeen. Some died in infancy, others grew up,
some were still at home. After the revolution her
husband began to rise. He was a capable man and
a Communist too. They made him director of a Soviet
farm. The farm was close to the town, and he sent
his wife back to the village to look after their house
and the children. At first he wrote to her—such nice
polite letters, too, and sent her money. And then he
stopped writing. She wondered if he was ill, but all
of a sudden a letter came saying that she must not
come to see him or expect any more letters from him
because he had begun a new life. Well, we all know
what a new life means. She packed up at once and
went to the town. She came straight to his flat and
tried the door, but he did not let her in. 'Wait a
minute,' he said. 'Don't be silly,' she said, 'you know
who I am,' but still he did not open the door. At
last he let her in. She could see he had been hastily
putting himself to rights, and there was a powder box
on the chest of drawers and some skirts hanging on
the wall. Her legs gave way under her. She had
expected it, and yet she couldn't believe it. 'I've got
married,' he told her. 'I can see,' she said. 'You have
ribbons and powder all over the place. What's come
over you? You are not a boy.' And she saw he had
shaved and had his hair cut and made himself look
a regular dandy. 'You don't give me complete satisfaction,' he said. 'My new wife is young and educated,
she has been to a secondary school.' She cursed and
went away. He gave her 700 roubles and promised
to send more for the children. They had lived together
happily till then. All she said to him was, 'We'll see

what she'll be like when she has borne you seven children, to say nothing of seventeen.' Well, some time passed and he came to her village. He arrived looking very humble, and as soon as he came into the cottage he fell at her feet asking her forgiveness. She understood then that his new marriage had not been a success. After all, he was an old man, no pleasure to a young creature.

"And here's another case. A wife came to visit her husband. He was a Communist and had been given a post somewhere at a distance. She came and found that meanwhile he had married a teacher. The teacher, of course, was an educated woman and the wife was a simple peasant. She set up a wail, but there was nothing for it: he had divorced her in her absence and married the teacher legally. Tears were of no use. So she went back to her village, collected all her children—and they had a great many—took them to her husband and left them with him. The new wife received them all right and put them into decent clothes. Both he and she were earning very well, they were Communists. After a while the mother came again to have a look at the children; she missed them dreadfully. Her husband was sitting with his new wife, making love to her. His landlady said to him, 'Aren't you ashamed of yourself! You've got a wife and children and that's how you carry on! The example you set them!' And he said, 'A very good example. You have old-fashioned prejudices and ours is conscious life.' And his first wife said to the landlady as though to apologise, 'I miss them very much, but what am I to do? I can't take them back because I can't keep them. The allowance he gives me won't buy anything nowadays, and he isn't likely to give me his Communist rations. It grieves me to think what my poor children will learn here, but there's nothing I can do.'

"And sometimes a husband brings a new wife to his house and they live together: the old wife does the cooking and the new one goes to the office. Just like the Tatars or the Kirghis. Only with them the old wife is treated with respect and with us she has to lie low because of course she's been formally divorced and can be turned out into the street any moment.

"And that's called a new life! Some women delegates came to us and explained that now we weren't slaves any more but free women and told us how we should treat our husbands, but we aren't such fools as all that! We never were slaves in our own homes so long as the law was for us. As though divorce were any good to a decent woman! It's not easy to be left alone with the children in one's old age. It's worse than being a widow, and they call it freedom. Well, those delegates didn't hit it off with us. We made a proper row and turned them out in disgrace. We didn't spare words," she added with satisfaction, recalling a victorious encounter.

"Don't you feel rather lonely here?" I asked, thinking how hard it must be for this staunch Siberian to find herself in utterly alien surroundings.

"Why should I, when I have work," she answered simply. "And I hope to bring up my children properly."

Again I felt that our thoughts were the same: *to bring up our children properly*.

Both she and I might have many sad thoughts to struggle against; a time might come when we would both feel home-sick. But it gave us courage to know that our children had now a chance of living a normal life instead of being warped by cold, hunger, cruelty and senseless experiments, in surroundings which made it impossible to bring them up as ordinary decent men. One of us might have to scrub floors and the other to write books; we knew that we were both doing honest work for the sake of our children's future. We both felt confident that we had done right in bringing them to foreign countries. If only the countries that received us so hospitably would understand what misery drove us to deprive our children of their native land!

A SOVIET WRITER

I was already abroad when Marietta Shaginian, one of the most orthodox Soviet writers, published her *Diaries* in the U.S.S.R. Throughout the revolution she has never been suspected of any 'deviations.' Stalin himself has approved of her, and so I hope that I may write about her without any risk of getting her into trouble. Besides, she can say with perfect truthfulness that she and I are so different from each other that we quarrelled more than we lived in peace. But she will understand what her *Diaries* mean to me. I could never indulge in the luxury of a diary, not even in a slightly doctored form like hers, to pass the censor. I have lost everything, every relic of the past. Her *Diaries* mention so many people, books, thoughts, details that I seem to live over our quarrels, meetings and reconciliations once more.

We were fellow-students some twenty-five years ago at the Moscow University. We are the same age and our children, her girl and my boy, were born in the same year. When we first met, she was considered a rising star in poetry. Her charming book of poems *Orientalia* was a great success. She herself, young and very pretty, with thick glossy black hair, large black eyes, olive coloured skin and a sharply curved red mouth, was a striking figure. Well-known writers fell in love with her, she appeared at the most fashionable literary clubs, and people said she ought to marry Andrey Biely who was as young and as fashionable as she.

It was a fascinating time.

Moscow and Petersburg tried to outshine each other with concerts and operas; an exhibition of pictures was an event; the production of a new play excited the whole town; both young and old lost their heads about poets and writers. Russians whose names are now so well known abroad—Scriabin, Rachmaninov, Shaliapin, Anna Pavlova, Bakst, Benois, Rörich, Tchehov— had all won their fame during the brilliant blossoming period of Russian culture before the revolution. Bolsheviks in their desire to get rid of the past dismiss it all under the name of Tsarism and call this blossoming time unprincipled, useless, highbrow, and so on; but they cannot deny its reality. Nor can they deny that we, the generation that had grown up before the revolution, are, so far, the last representatives of Russian culture. During eighteen years they haven't produced a single first rate artist or writer from among their own 'lads,' to say nothing of the girls.

Perhaps we ought not to take much credit for our 'culture.' Before the revolution, especially before the war, young people found life easy. There was so much demand for intellectual work that we easily found jobs which not only secured us our keep—the dream of present-day young people—but paid for theatres, concerts, books, two or three new dresses a year, trips to the Crimea, the Caucasus and abroad.

I did not learn till many years later that Marietta's father, a doctor with an excellent practice, had died when she was still at school. While at the University she had to work for her living, as indeed most of us had.

But we did not mind that: it was far more fun spending money that one had earned, and there was no occasion for anyone with a head on his shoulders to suffer from destitution. In Marietta's case there was no doubt of it: poetesses were the fashion, literary work was well paid, and she could look forward with confidence to success and perhaps to fame. The revolution parted us, and for years I heard nothing about her though I loved her tenderly and disinterestedly.

It was a terrible time: everyone seemed to have hidden away, sunk through the ground, as it were; everyone was left alone with his own sorrow and hunger. Petersburg where I had moved just before the revolution was growing empty and dying out. Trams were not working, shops were shut, front doors permanently closed. The houses were neglected, the windows were never cleaned, the broken window-panes were replaced by pieces of cardboard, paint was coming off the walls, the stucco and woodwork were crumbling, the roofs showed rusty iron.

It was at that time, early in 1921, that I met Marietta. We were glad to see each other. But it was a strange joy—there was so much sorrow in it at the thought of what we had become.

We were standing on the pavement which had not been cleaned once during the winter and was buried a foot deep in snow, trodden down into grooves and hollows. The snow in the street rose much higher, because there was very little traffic in those days—only carts with goods for the co-operative stores and a few Government cars. Huge snowdrifts alternated with deep hollows. The horses, exhausted by perpetual underfeeding, found this very trying, especially on the

steep ascent to the town bridges. Frozen horses' car-
casses often lay about there; no one took them away—
the best parts were cut off by the people and the rest
was left to the dogs.

Marietta who had once dressed smartly and ele-
gantly was wearing a shapeless overcoat of peasant
cloth with a worn kangaroo collar that I remembered
from our Moscow days. She had nothing but thin
worn shoes on her feet and on her head a miserable little
hat knitted by her own unskilled fingers.

"Come to my place," she said, examining me with
pity and affection, and shaking her head.

My get-up was little better than hers. Its chief
advantage were top-boots made of sealskins which my
husband brought me from an expedition to the North.
Warm footwear was essential in those days, and I did
not take off my boots either at home or at the office.

"Tell me about yourself," said Marietta looking at
me closely with her short-sighted eyes, kind and
humorous, and almost touching me with her nose and
lips.

But it was no use telling her anything because during
those years she had grown almost completely deaf.
Deafness was hereditary in her family and the conditions of Soviet life had obviously made it much worse.

Taking me by the hand she brought me to a large
house at the corner of the Nevsky and Moika. Before
the revolution it belonged to the Eliseyevs, rich merchants, and now it was turned into 'The House of
Arts,' i.e., a hostel for writers, painters, actors, etc. It
was intended to be a centre of artistic life: it had
a hall for meetings and concerts, a grand piano, a
library. But meanwhile the multifarious population of

the house, young and old, with brilliant names and
hopes of future fame, was chiefly occupied in obtaining
some sort of food. It was the third year after the revolution, the civil war was over, the bolsheviks were un-
disputed masters of the country; the hopeless, desperate
famine which began precisely at that time was due not
to a failure of crops or military operations but to the
policy of the Soviet Government.

"No dinner to-day"—or rather, no food at all—
Marietta put down in her diary more than once. She
had been to Moscow to try to obtain a writer's ration
card.

"I have been sent several times to Ostozhenka, to the
Commissariat of Public Education, to give par-
ticulars about myself, but after I got my feet wet
through about ten times and had a bad throat, they
told me I could not have the ration card."

A few months later she wrote: "I have no bread and
no food of any kind except herrings. I know I have been
again omitted from the June list of candidates for
rations."

A month after that she was in a regular panic: "a
terrible famine is threatening Russia. They say that
millions of starving people are moving like an avalanche
towards Moscow, destroying everything on the way.
There is famine on the Volga and in the North; crops
have failed in parts of the Ukraine, too. Things are
bad on the Kuban, in Northern Caucasus and on the
Don. It is rumoured that the plague had been brought
to the Volga from Persia."

What she said about the 'avalanche' was a mistake:
the starving millions were too exhausted to move and
most of them died in their own villages.

It is hard to imagine how we, who lived safely in
Petersburg and Moscow, managed to feed at that time.

Alexandra Lvovna Tolstoy describes in her book the
lunches at the Rumyantsevsky Museum: "Professors,
scholars, museum assistants, taking off their gloves,
warmed their hands against steaming mugs which they
carried carefully, anxious not to spill a drop of the
precious liquid. We called it tea, but it was made of
dry carrots and strawberry leaves. Everyone un-
wrapped his packet with lunch: a piece of ration bread,
two potatoes, a dry salt fish.

" 'Carrots are extremely nourishing,' said one of the
professors, unwrapping a piece of newspaper with two
dark looking boiled potatoes; 'they can perfectly well
take the place of bread.'

" 'Yes, but you can't always get carrots. You know
my wife makes wonderful cakes: she adds potato
peelings to rye flour and puts in an apple when she
can.'

"I tried not to notice the hungry eyes, the trembling
greedy hands."*

Another calamity was the cold.

Marietta writes in her diary: "I have a huge room
upholstered in greenish plush, with a lovely bed big
enough for three, and central heating."

I remember that was the room to which she brought
me on the day we met. It really was huge. There was
a greenish plush carpet on the floor, but all that remained of the central heating were some cold radiators
which were no longer in working order. The tempera-
ture was below freezing. There was a small iron stove
in the corner, but had it been heated day and night it

* *I Worked for the Soviet*, by Alexandra Tolstoy.

could not have warmed the room, and firewood was such a rarity that the stove could only be used like a bonfire to warm oneself by the side of it, especially one's hands. Marietta wrote in her diary on January 19, 1921: "I meant to work but desperate cold drove me to bed." She told me that sometimes she did not undress for weeks together and only took off her overcoat to throw it on the top of the blanket under which she crept.

On February 3, 1921, a literary evening was arranged for her benefit. It ended rather sadly: the room had not been heated; she was determined not to appear in her wretched overcoat and put on her best dress, tying an orange bow in her hair—and caught a desperate cold. She wrote: "The audience was small. They met me and took leave of me coldly. It was very cold, my voice and my hands trembled."

Shivering figures wrapped up in all the clothes they could muster sat huddled up in the cold half-dark hall. There still were many poets and artists among them, men of fine intellect and rare talent, but they were all hopelessly cold, hungry, exhausted. Marietta's poems about the languid air of the East smelling of jasmine and myrrh, about fragrant melons, the desert longing for cold clear water and maidens throwing rose petals into a bowl, sounded unreal and hollow. Very likely they were just as good as her poems of five years before, but we were no longer capable of appreciating them.

She was taken ill immediately after that evening and wrote in her diary: "I woke up in the night shivering and in high fever. My only food was the slops they call soup, rusks and hot water, so I could not fight my illness." Fortunately that year the typhus epidemic had subsided. But this is what she wrote about a well-known literary critic, V. Tchukovsky: "Last year he and his mother were ill with typhus. They lay in an empty flat and had no one to look after them. His mother died and her corpse was gnawn by rats. He was unconscious at that time and the rats gnawed his hand (he still carries it in a sling). That's a bit of *couleur locale* of Petersburg in 1920 for you."

In 1921 all were distressed by the news that Alexander Blok was dying—perhaps the best Russian poet after Pushkin and certainly the greatest of modern poets. He was the first to accept the revolution and to give it expression in his art.

He was still young and possessed an indescribable charm. I saw him only once, about a year before his death. We lived within a stone-throw of his flat, and his mother and aunt, two small, frail old ladies who simply worshipped him, sometimes ran in to me to ask whether I could procure a little flour, or pearl barley, or half a pound of butter—"it's for Sasha, you know." They trembled with exhaustion and the constant fear that 'Sasha,' the greatest of Russian poets, their own adored Sasha might die of hunger like other people. As I piloted them along the dark corridor into our former drawing-room which now served as bedroom, study and dining-room, I felt that their weak little arms were nothing but skin and bone.

"We've only called for a moment," they muttered. "Have you managed to get anything?"

One day as I came down into the street, once so lively but now completely deserted, I saw one of the sisters. She was walking unsteadily, shuddering from time to time, looking down and shaking her head. I went right up to her and carefully took her by the arm.

"Ah!" she cried out and clutched at my shoulders. "It's you! You must save me! I said to myself that before I come to our door I must meet someone who will help me. I had nothing but ill-luck all day. A horrible day. Refusals everywhere—no money, no food. I am desperate, I can hardly stand on my feet."

She had not the strength to walk up the stairs to my flat. I made her sit down on the seat by the gate and brought her a few handfuls of pearl barley—an honestly measured half of all the food I possessed.

I happened once to have a little butter, and as they had not been to see me for some time, I decided to go to them myself in the hope that Blok would be out. I knew that the poor women did it all in secret so as not to worry him. As it was, the poet had to accept work in the State publishing office and did his best to eke out a livelihood, like everyone else.

In answer to my quiet ring the door was flung open with a quick, strong movement, and I saw Blok standing in the semi-darkness of the small entry. He was tall, thin and very pale. I do not know whether he was handsome—beauty is a matter of taste—but there was something rare and gracious about his shapely figure, his mellow clear voice and his whole manner.

In the summer of 1921 he was dying. It was not literally of hunger, but of underfeeding and of the general conditions of Soviet life which he, as a poet, must have found harder to bear than other people. When it was too late for anything to help him, and life was slowly ebbing away from him as he lay there, utterly exhausted, some member of the Government sent him a supply of foodstuffs which had been plentiful in the

Kremlin all the time but were not intended for the citizens.

I remember, people stopped one another in the street asking for news of Blok . . . Maietta was in an agony of helpless despair. She pounced on me crying, "Surely, God can work a miracle for Blok?"

She was religious in those days and there was a great deal of sincerity, passion and sorrow in her faith.

Blok died—and with him died, perhaps, the last free Russian poet. No one of us, I would have thought, could ever forget this, especially not Marietta who literally beat her head against the wall at the time and was almost insane with grief. But seven years passed and on February 9, 1928, she wrote in her diary: "I have received Blok's *Diary* and it upset my work. I began to recall my past, the environment which I have left. What saves me is lack of memory. I have terribly little strength left, I want to keep it and instinctively I travel light (without memory). And when I begin to recall the past, the weight of many years falls upon my shoulders."

Not to remember is one of the main principles of Soviet life. Otherwise how could one have the strength to obey, to follow the ever-changing curve of the Government policy?

Blok died in 1921; during the period of 'military Communism' between 1917 and 1921 died dozens of scientists, scholars, artists, writers and millions of obscure citizens. When rebellions became a menace to the power of the Soviets, Lenin declared that that policy had been a mistake and orders were given to forget it.

"But it's all different now!" well-meaning foreigners say. "All that is past."

"And what about the famine of 1931-32 when Ukraine and North Caucasus were dying out?"

"But that may have been exaggerated," they reply.

In Soviet Russia it is an unwritten law that every time the Government changes its policy, the past must be forgotten.

Soon after Blok's death came another terrible loss— the shooting of Gumilyov, the poet who was, perhaps, the next best to him. Marietta has not ventured to mention him in her diary, but as I do not 'travel light, without memory,' I can fill up the omission.

The news of Gumilyov's execution was a shock even to those who had never read his poetry or indeed any poetry at all. Almost all of us remembered from our school days that André Chenier was beheaded during the French Revolution. Pushkin translated his last poem; Chenier's execution became for us a symbol of the most senseless crime of which a tyranny could be guilty. Now a Russian poet had been shot without a trial, without any explanation of the reasons. It is dreadful to recall it even now.

I went to the House of Arts where he had lived. He left a wife and child. On the same day another writer from the same House had been shot—Uhtomsky. There was a general sense of uneasiness in the House. People were afraid to talk, but silence was a strain. On the landing by Marietta's door I saw two young writers. Both were agitated, and seeing me, whom they knew but slightly, they made a movement to run away but thought better of it.

"Have you come to see Marietta Sergeyevne?" one of them asked hesitatingly.

"Yes. Is she at home?"

"She is. But she's locked herself in and we don't know what's the matter. Do you know what has happened here?" he asked cautiously.

"Yes, I know. You go, I'll try to get in to her."

They went away with obvious relief. I bent down to the key-hole but could not see anything because the key was in the lock. I put my ear to the door but could hear nothing. I took a pencil and succeeded in pushing out the key. Marietta was too deaf to hear it fall. Now I could see that she was sitting at the table, crying.

I waited by the door, listening and peeping through the keyhole from time to time. She would not hear an ordinary knock, and I did not want to make a noise and attract other people's attention to her. I waited till she got up and began walking up and down the room. When she came near the door, I knocked. She opened the door, threw her arms round me without speaking and led me to the other end of the room where she had hung up her 'time-table,' which included study of Marxism, of current politics, the history of the Party and so on. She loved making time-tables and programmes though she never carried them out, for she was constitutionally incapable of anything systematic and was fantastic and emotional through and through. But at every new period of her life she always drew up a fresh 'time-table.' Neatly divided into squares filled in with her beautiful small hand-writing, the time-table had a pencil mark drawn right through it, and underneath stood the words "Write poetry. Gumilyov."

"It was he wrote this: write poetry. Poetry—this is all that is left of him now. But I cannot write poetry any more," she said sadly in a low voice.

And then in a different, not at all a lyrical tone, she asked of no one in particular a question which I shall never forget:

"Has anyone the right to kill a poet?"

Two months later I happened to call at the office of 'Universal Literature' to be paid for the translation of Balzac, which, alas, soon came to an end because some-one made the discovery that Balzac's art was 'a product of a bourgeois environment.'

When I came up to the cashier's desk, a young and pretty woman was standing in front of it. The receipt book lay before her, but she could not bring herself to sign it.

"I've been told that I was to receive a large sum of money, that my husband had it owing to him for his work."

"This is all that is due to him," the cashier said drily. I could not resist peeping into the receipt book. The young woman had her finger on the name of Gumilyov. The sum of money had been large two or three months before, but by the time all the formalities had been completed and the payment could be made Gumilyov had been shot and the value of the money due to him had dwindled down to less than the price of one pound of butter. The widow stood there not knowing what to do: signing the receipt meant giving up all further claim to what was her last resource, and perhaps there was some mistake about it which she did not under-stand.

"Don't keep me waiting," the cashier said impatiently.

She signed and in her distress forgot to take her 'thousands.'

"Take your money!" the cashier shouted angrily. Soviet officials like to be treated with gratitude and respect.

The widow turned round in alarm, hastily thrust the money into her bag and went away.

By comparison with the terrible misfortune which had overtaken her, the incident with the money was, of course, a trifle. And it is only fair to say that since then the Soviet Government has perfected its methods: two or three years later, instead of paying the wives of its victims any outstanding debts, it confiscated everything they possessed, including their last rags and the children's toys.

Yes, in those years the writers passed through a cruel training. I believe it was in the following winter that another tragedy took place which Marietta forgot to mention in her diary.

I went to see her one morning about something. As I came in at the gate an objectionable individual standing in the yard called to me:

"Whom do you want to see?"

I told him. In the U.S.S.R. it is better not to argue on such occasions. Another specimen of the same type was in the street behind me. They let me pass, from which I gathered that Marietta was safe.

I found her standing in the middle of the room in agitation, fully dressed and ready to go out.

"Come along, quick!" She flew towards me. "We must warn Victor, there's an ambush in his room. He may return any moment."

"Where are we to go?"

"To the gates."

"There are two detectives there. They'll take us straight to the Tcheka."

"You are a coward! It's a matter of life and death to him," and Marietta abused me with all her Eastern eloquence until I explained to her that if Victor had not slept at home he must have been warned.

"Then let us go to the Nevsky."

I agreed. I knew she would not stay at home and I could not let her go into the streets by herself, for she would be sure to run into one of the detectives and say to him something she should not.

We went into the Nevsky. I held her arm and pushed her with my elbow, as we had arranged, every time that we passed a detective. She was too short-sighted to recognise them and, besides, unlike me, she had had no experience in that line before the revolution to help her. Soviet spies in no way differed in type from those of the old régime.

There were several of them on either side of the Morskaya, at the corner of the Nevsky, and farther on as far as Moika. Marietta stared at them and when we had passed them asked "that man? And that one too? How dreadful!"

It certainly was disgusting. A few days before Victor had been quite rightly regarded as one of the leading Soviet writers; then some stupid information was given against him, and here he was being hunted like a wild animal. The main street was lined with detectives and as soon as he appeared they would all rush after him; someone would shout 'thief' and the passers by would join in the chase not knowing whom they were after. Such is the psychology of the crowd.

"Let us go to the Gosizdat,"* Marietta insisted.

There were no reasonable grounds for going there but it was risky to reason with Marietta in the street, for the detectives were no doubt on duty just between the Gosizdat and the House of Arts. Besides, I was acting merely as a conscientious guide and it was not my business to argue.

We went in and climbed to the second story where the editors' offices were—there was not a soul anywhere. The house seemed deserted. We went on to the third story and turned into a corridor. There, on a bench in a window recess, sat Victor covering his face with a newspaper.

I did not doubt that he was a brave man and that at the front he may have been cool and daring, but I felt frightened for him then. He was within a stone-throw of the street in which they were hunting for him, two streets away from his home where his wife had been caught in the ambush.

"I must clear out," he said when we had told him all we had noticed. "Pity I put on my galoshes," he added in a matter of fact tone. "If I have to run I must throw them away, and I know I'll never get another pair."

I cannot think how a man so essentially in sympathy with the revolution as he was could have been suspected by the Tcheka. It was absurd. But Gumilyov's summary execution made it obvious that the first thing was to escape; one might try to parley with the authorities afterwards. Victor escaped abroad, his wife was arrested and kept in prison for months. I do not know how he managed to come to terms with the Government, but he was finally allowed to return and even to

* The State Publishing Company.

publish his work. But although he is more gifted than many of the Soviet writers he has not succeeded in winning a prominent place in literature.

Those years of famine and terror killed off many writers, and made others change. To say that they 'sold themselves' to the bolsheviks would be crude and unfair. To say that they became 'regenerated' and sincerely accepted bolshevism would be simply untrue. No one in Soviet Russia doubts that the bolshevik power is a terrible tyranny, and that its strength lies in its ruthlessness and cruelty. No one is enthusiastic about it, but . . . one has to live. People have been taught to adapt themselves to the Communist régime, not by Government slogans, which are sheer bombast, but by Soviet life.

Reading Marietta's *Diaries* I see once more how people changed and why.

Up to 1921 she wrote novels and sometimes poems, studied Goethe and Balzac, was keen on the theory of music and of other arts.

In 1923 she began to write about brandy, cotton, textile industry, fruit-drying, coal, marganese ore, geology, agriculture, chemistry, hydrotechnics and so on in spite of being hopelessly ignorant with regard to all these matters. Like the Communists whom the Party commandeers one day to manage a match factory, the next to be directors of the Neurological Institute, then to run the 'Red Triangle' rubber works, and afterwards to superintend the Hermitage, she rushed from one thing to another, without studying any one subject properly. A true poet and a gifted writer, she has become a mediocre journalist, writing dull novels to order. The Government gives so-called 'social orders'

to Soviet literature; the writers at any rate receive a
fee for their labours, but the readers have no inducement to wade through those productions.

Such a transformation has not been easy for her.
Summing up the year 1924, she wrote in her diary on
the New Year's eve: "It has been a year of misery and
almost entirely uncreative." But in 1925 she persevered
in writing about industrial subjects.

At that period I saw little of her: I invariably found
her tired and cross, though now her whole family lived
with her, her rooms were warm and they had plenty of
food. After reading her *Diaries* I understood what was
tormenting her and why she could not give artistic form
to her impressions of the factories of Halturin's Name,
The Red Banner, the Red Lighthouse, the Soviet Star,
and others which she had investigated. Many pages of
her *Diaries* contain the raw material of her investiga-
tions and are printed not for the benefit of the public
who will certainly not bother to read them, but in
order to illustrate the 'social' aspect of her literary work.
Here are some of those entries:

"A workman whose job is to pick out the wet wool
is no better than a convict. Water drips all the time on
to his feet. He receives 45 roubles a month for this."

"The drying place is horrible—it's a niche full of hot
steam, the dyers who have to run in there are instantly
bathed in sweat. The ventilation is bad, the air is
damp and stuffy and poisoned with chemicals."

"In the polishing section there is no ventilation and
air is full of acrid black dust."

"The saddler was very gloomy. He swore and complained."

Here are the entries about the workers' budgets:

"A single woman receives 43 roubles 72 copecks per month; has enough to eat. Goes to the bath-house once a fortnight, to the theatre once a month, to the cinema five times a month. For dinner she has soup and macaroni, for lunch—bread and tea."

"People with families live poorly, wages are insufficient. No papers, no cinema, no cigarettes, no amusements."

"A dyer, a family man. Very poor. They live on tea, bread, meatless soup and porridge."

"A charwoman—25 roubles 55 copecks per month; a widow with three children. Extremely poor.

"A weaver, single woman. 31 roubles 86 copecks. Fairly well off.

"An assistant, a girl of 18. Smokes, has nice things to eat. Goes to the club and to see friends."

"Husband and wife. Fairly cultured. Spend all they earn on food and only buy clothes when inevitable."

"A workman, family man. Chief food—potatoes with oil and tea (not real tea). Wages insufficient. The wife is quarrelsome and looks an old woman though only 36. Complained bitterly of poverty."

"A working woman called Vassilyeva. Has a mother and a little daughter of 8. They share the room with 10 other people; one blanket has to do for four people. The house is damp, dirty, horrible. Had belonged to the Komsomol but couldn't afford it—no proper clothes and no time."

Many pages of Marietta's *Diaries* are taken up with entries of this kind and among them is a remarkable saying of an old workman: "We were slaves of the gentry, then slaves of capital, and now we are slaves of labour."

After a year of such work and of fruitless efforts to create of this material a novel reflecting 'industrial enthusiasm,' Marietta wrote down on the eve of 1926: "My decision is taken: give up Leningrad which has drained all our strength."

When I now recall what I know about the working people's life in the U.S.S.R. I find that little has changed since the time when Marietta made her notes. On July 7, 1935, *Pravda* published the following paragraph about the factory *Tochizmeritel* (exact measuring instruments) of the name of Molotov: "Great quantities of mercury are used at the factory and in some parts the air is saturated with its vapours. The ventilation does not work, the floors are not covered with linoleum, the workrooms where mercury is used are not isolated. As a result, in the first half of 1935 more than 600 workers fell ill (there are about 3,000 in the factory); 32 of them, men and women, had to be pensioned off. Cases of premature labour have increased. Mercury may be found in chinks of tables and floors, on the stairs and in the corridors." Many similar paragraphs might be quoted. The following communication in the paper *Trud*, in June 1935, throws light on the working women's life: "At the Ramensky Factory (with 4,000 women workers), near Moscow, the doctors have drawn attention to disquieting figures: in the first six months of 1934 there were two miscarriages to every five normal cases of labour; in the first six months of 1935 there were five miscarriages to every five normal cases." The evidence quoted by the paper shows that life has grown much harder and that women find it impossible to live on their regular wages during the 'maternity leave of absence,' and so they work up to the very last hour so as to be paid for overtime and for piece work. "There are cases of babies being born before the mother has had time to leave the loom."

Such communications are printed in the papers 'by way of self-criticism' when one lot of Communists in power is trying to undermine another, but no book on the subject would be allowed. So naturally all that remained to Marietta was to abandon the material she had collected and to go away for a change.

She settled in the Caucasus. We met each other seldom, only when she came to Petersburg on business. She assured me that Erivan was a cultural centre like Goethe's Weimar, with educated people, exciting discussions, lovely music. She said that quantities of coloured marble had been discovered in the Caucasus and that all the new buildings would be more beautiful than those of ancient Rome. But when I asked one day if I could come to her on a visit she cried, "My dear, you are mad! The idea of your going to Erivan! Why, I haven't yet a room to myself and my family lives in a hut with an earthen floor."

It was very typical of her. There were two distinct selves in her: one half of her being was so keenly sensitive that sometimes painful impressions made her positively ill, and the other could remain deaf and blind to all she did not want to see or hear. Giving rein to her temperamental creative imagination, she could be easily carried away into the wildest realms of fantasy. It was all the easier for her because of her deafness and shortsightedness. I remember one day she and I were going to my summer lodgings and missed the train. The filthy Detskoselsky (formerly Tsarskoselsky) station was re-echoing with swearing, quarrels, complaints,

drunken rows. A long-distance train for Vitebsk was
leaving and people were fighting for seats. I took
Marietta aside and found places for us at a little table,
asking for some incredibly expensive and incredibly
smelly lemonade. One is not allowed to sit at the
tables without asking for refreshments, because the
artel of buffet-keepers pay an enormous rent and have
to raise the money somehow. Ten paces away from
us some town urchins were engaged in a fierce fight
over a stolen ten-copeck piece. The waiter swore at
them in disgusting language but did not venture to
separate them and merely kicked them from time to
time towards the exit. Marietta, happily absorbed in
her note book, asked me absent-mindedly "What is
it?"

"They're fighting," I shouted into her ear.

"Laughing?" she repeated. "That's good. Laughter
is a great thing."

She heard only what was said to her specially and
often specially intended for her. If she did not like it
she drew slightly away and ceased to hear. Her big,
beautiful black eyes did not see farther than her
writing-desk even if she wore spectacles. When she
took them off she generally lowered her eyelids and her
bright humorous glance rested only on what she wanted
to see. As she had also renounced memory her condition was simply ideal for a Soviet writer. Not to see,
not to hear, not to remember, are the three essentials:
it is then easy to believe what is required and to adopt
without any hesitations or deviations each new turn in
the 'general line of the Party.' I think that this is also
the condition of foreign writers and journalists who
come to Soviet Russia. They do not hear, for they do

not understand the language, they see little because everything that may produce an unpleasant impression is carefully withheld from them, and they know nothing of Russia's past, which is as good as having no memory.

The only trouble is that those who read their books are not aware of their limitations!

But what one can forgive to foreigners one cannot forgive to one's own people. When Marietta definitely became one of the 'officially recognised' writers her readers often pitched into me, knowing that I was a friend of hers. Her popularity with the general public was decreasing as fast as it increased in the ruling circles.

"Have you heard what your Marietta has done?" an important engineer, once a great admirer of hers, pounced upon me. That was in 1928, after the 'Mines case' with which the attack on specialists began.

"What is it?" I asked uneasily, knowing that with her fantastic temperament she could do a lot of mischief now that writers had been ordered to go in for 'social work.' I also knew that I could never persuade anyone that she had not 'sold herself' to the Government.

"She is not content, if you please, with writing idiotic articles and passing for a specialist on cotton, iron, marganese ore, wine-making and goodness knows what!" the engineer was fuming. "She's taken up a more profitable line—rousing 'the social sense'! or to put it simply, informing against us, the real specialists."

"What nonsense!" I interrupted him with a heavy heart.

"Do you want facts? By all means. Do you know what Dzorages is?"

"I have no idea."

"It's an electrical power station in the Caucasus. But that's not the point. The point is that such stations are all the fashion nowadays, and so Marietta decided to go there and settle right by the building site—she was going, if you please, to write an 'industrial' novel. Heaven only knows how the building went on—as elsewhere, no doubt. Absurd, fantastic plans, desperate hurry, delays about the money and the materials, shortage of labour, Communist superintendents, intrigues—and we, engineers, as scapegoats. Idiots that we are to go in for constructive work instead of becoming modest and quiet factory hands! And in that place, just imagine the confusion—Caucasian officials, Communist officials, U.S.S.R. officials—a carriage-load of them! And Marietta in the thick of it—a revolutionary writer, a representative of the social element, and so on and so on. . . . An old woman, fat as a pillow, growing a moustache . . . "

"That will do!" I stopped him. "To begin with, she is forty, and secondly you must talk calmly or else I'll get cross with you before I know what it's all about."

"Calmly!" he shrugged his shoulders. "We'll only be calm when we've been shot, you know. A nice sort of calm. So just imagine: there's a mountain river there, the bridge wasn't finished and the spring floods washed away what there was of it. Nothing could be worse because, as Mayakovsky, that poet of genius, has said, Communists and G.P.U. men are always eager to apply the principle of 'making elephants out of midges and selling ivory.' And our clever Marietta stepped in and asked with a learned air 'Is it reasonable to build wooden bridges across mountain rivers, for the piers would

naturally make the river angry?" How do you like that?
Make the river angry!"

"But look here, it's simply absurd, like all her technical arguments," I laughed.

"Wait a minute, this isn't the whole story. After that
Marietta rushed to Tiflis—I beg your pardon, I should
have said, she heroically climbed into a goods truck and
on arriving at Tiflis raised a storm about the 'un-
healthy atmosphere' at Dzorages and showed the
Peasant and Workmen's Inspection a thundering
article she had written or, in plain language, a piggish
tell-tale story."

"What was the end of it?" I asked gloomily. It was
dreadful to think both of the men whom she got into
trouble and of her, who was sure bitterly to repent of
her fit of folly.

"Fortunately, she overshot the mark. The investi-
gating committee sent by the Inspection had to admit
that her 'communication' was only twenty-five per
cent true. You can well imagine how much truth there
was in it if even the Inspection found it was not more
than twenty-five per cent! No one has been shot, but
lots of people have been dismissed or imprisoned,
and as usual the most honest and decent ones."

Four years later I read in her diary:

"April 14, 1928. My article has appeared to-day. I
am getting more and more desperate. I know that I
ought not to have taken upon myself to be the accuser
because I am weak, kind, and soft-hearted. I know that
I have played the part of a match thrown into a room
full of gas. If truth were the only force at work I would
have felt better, for the alarm I caused might have led
to their listening to me, weighing carefully everything

I said and verifying all the details before publishing the article. But now my words have been immediately caught up, the whole machinery has been set in motion, and trifles have suddenly assumed enormous proportions. And yet there was no ill-will on my part, but on the contrary a desire to do everything as I ought."

"April 15, 1928. P. has called. He is indignant at my article. He assures me that there is a persecution of specialists going on, and that one can't go on working in such conditions. . . . I feel like an animal at bay— can it be that I have done wrong?"

She ought to have asked herself that question sooner, but Soviet policy is least of all calculated to foster a sense of pity: if a few people are shot or exiled by mistake, what does it matter? There are plenty of others left.

When in 1931 I was let out of prison I heard that Marietta had left the Caucasus once more and moved to Moscow. It was strange to read in her diary for February 10, 1931:

"I went out in the morning in search of fuel. We are freezing. All the week we've been heating the stove with rubbish and coal refuse which my sister, daughter and servant picked up in the sanatorium back yard."

Ten years before she had been freezing too—conditions of life in the U.S.S.R. do not improve quickly! Or, rather, they do improve as soon as free play is given to private initiative, but with every new advance on the 'socialistic front' get catastrophically worse again. How often we have seen this rise and fall! No one believes any longer that prosperity, however relative, will last; and people suffer from privations more than before because their strength and power of endurance are giving way.

In 1931 I thought of going to see Marietta. But I recalled that when she heard of my five months in prison she sent me a message to say she was very glad and hoped that prison had forced me to think over the whole of my life and made me into a true Soviet citizen.

It is true that in prison I did think over the whole of my life, but the result was the very reverse of what she hoped for; and so I decided not to meet her any more.

ALIMONY

"In Moscow last year there was one new marriage per 80 inhabitants, but one divorce per 200 inhabitants. In the first five months of 1935 the number of divorces equalled 38.3 per cent of the new marriages registered. In May this percentage reached 44.3 per cent. It is high time to declare frivolity in family affairs a crime, and unfaithfulness an offence against the morality of the Socialist régime." (*Izvestia*, July 4, 1935.)

This is the unexpected verdict of the Soviet Government which for seventeen years has been doing its best to destroy the family. Why it did it, is a mystery. It was obvious to every sane person that there was nothing socialistic or revolutionary in a policy which gave free play to the most unpleasant human instincts and to people of the most objectionable type. But, anyway, for seventeen years it all went under the banner of freedom. Freedom of love, freedom of the individual, freedom of choice—and as a result "all adults in Moscow have been married on the average 1.3 times. Nearly 2.3 of the divorced couples have children, but only about 10 per cent make arrangements for their support. The Soviet courts spend much of their time in hunting for runaway fathers who have meanwhile founded new families in distant towns." (*Izvestia*, July 4, 1935.)

It is curious that this particular aspect of Soviet

policy—'freedom of love,' divorce and abortions—should have roused such enthusiasm among foreigners, especially women. It does not seem to have occurred to any of them to ask whether easy divorce is to the man's or to the woman's advantage. It obviously does not benefit Soviet women who grow old before their time, can have no personal income or property, have no right to claim support from the husband while they are still capable of work and can at best claim for their children no more than a half of their husband's official salary, which often has to be shared between his children by two or three wives.

I can well imagine how counter-revolutionary the assertion that homeless children are the result of Government policy would seem if some private person made it ! But here is the alarming official admission that only 10 per cent of the children of divorced couples are provided for. What of the remaining 90 per cent?

I recall two typical instances of divorce. The first is my own.

This was how it happened. After one of the new decrees about housing—which appeared, by the way, at least twice a year and each time made housing conditions worse—my husband and I found ourselves in a desperate plight. The new decree curtailed the amount of space allowed per person and raised the rents out of all proportion. We had a flat of three rooms, leading one out of the other; the third was quite tiny. It had been a bathroom but we moved the bath into a specially screened-off corner of the kitchen. A year before, this flat had cost 40 roubles a month, in the autumn it was 80 roubles, and in the spring it rose to

150 roubles, while we earned only 300 roubles per month between us. Obviously we had to move. To do so we had (1) to find citizens living in a smaller flat and wanting to move to a bigger one, and (2) to obtain permission for the exchange from the respective house-committees. We found the first fairly easily, but our house-committee refused point-blank to allow the exchange. There was a good reason for it: we paid a rent of 150 roubles while the new lodgers would have to pay only 60. This was because the rent was calculated in proportion to the highest salary earned by any single member of a family. My husband earned 240 roubles a month, and we had to pay a rent of 150 roubles, though I earned only 60 and we had a child to keep and a servant. The people with whom we wanted to exchange were a family of four wage-earners, but as each of them earned only 150 roubles per month, their rent was calculated on the basis of that figure and amounted to only 60 roubles, although their joint income was 600 roubles. Thus we had to pay half of our total income as rent, while they would have to pay for the same flat only one-tenth of their joint income. But Soviet decrees do not take such trifles into account: it's law, and there it is. The citizens must make the best of it. The house-committee did not allow the exchange because they needed money for the upkeep of the house and naturally did not want to lose lodgers who paid a high rent. But we could not afford to stay and had to find some way out.

After much thought I came to the conclusion that the only solution was divorce. If we were divorced, and my husband went away for a time, the rent would have to be calculated on the basis of my salary and fall to about 40 roubles. The house-committee would not like that and would give permission for the exchange. I was determined to counteract absurd Soviet decrees by equally absurd Soviet remedies. As to the divorce, we did not mind in the least. Many of my colleagues were divorced for similar typically Soviet reasons: because a husband and wife were allowed only one room between them, while divorced people could have one each; because a husband and wife were not allowed to serve in the same office, and so on. For the same reasons many people who were really married did not register their marriage. These tricks did not help against serious trouble: if the husband lost his job or was arrested, his wife, whether not yet registered or already divorced, generally shared his fate. But in small matters trickery was indispensable: all were doing their best 'to get round' the law—this is an essential feature of Soviet life.

And so we had to have a divorce. I went to find out how it was done.

The registry office (Z.A.G.S.) in which people were married, divorced, and obtained birth and death certificates looked like any other Soviet institution—it was dirty, the floor was spat on and covered with cigarette ends, and there was a queue waiting. In one of the rooms a typical Soviet girl, tired, unwashed and carelessly made up, sat at a table covered with red cotton material. Couples waiting to be married or divorced sat on odd chairs placed against the walls. They all looked so bored with the tedious loss of time in the queue that even a Soviet specialist on marriage could not be certain with what object they had come, and looked questioningly at each in turn.

"Make us man and wife, comrade," a man said with affected jocosity, obviously an intellectual. Both he and his intended wife looked uncomfortable.

"I claim divorce!" a factory hand who had had a drop too much announced jauntily. "We have nothing to lose except chains . . . the chains of matrimony," he joked to the entertainment of the weary audience.

"Where is your wife?" the young lady interrupted him sternly. She had no time to spare for jokes.

"That's nothing to do with me. I've done with her. She shan't have any more of my wages."

"Any children?"

"Sorry, I've failed in that line. Maybe somebody else will take my place. But she is old and scraggy."

"No unnecessary words, citizen," the young lady stopped him drily, looking menacingly at the giggling audience. "Fill up the form. Next."

People came up one by one or in couples. Divorce could be had at the wish of one of the parties. No evidence was taken or verified and there were no witnesses. It is no wonder that by 1935, when people used to orderliness in family relations had died out, every grown-up citizen in the U.S.S.R. had been married 1.3 times and that 90 per cent of the children were more or less homeless.

"What do you want, citizen?" the young lady asked me disapprovingly when I came up to her table. Soviet officials of her type do not like intellectuals—there is always a danger of their finding something amiss; it's safer with one's own sort, the proletarians.

"I want to divorce my husband," I said seriously.

"Any children?"

"One son."

"Your papers."

I gave her my labour cards.

"Citizen, you are not married. I cannot give you a divorce. Next!"

"Allow me to point out, citizen," I said, standing my ground, "it says here that I was married on July 22, 1915."

"You may regard church marriage as invalid."

"Thank you, but I want a certificate of divorce."

"What do you want it for?" she asked crossly, with a suspicious glance at me.

"So that I can claim alimony for my son," I answered firmly. She hesitated.

"But all the same, I can't give you a divorce, citizen," she protested feebly, without explaining her reasons.

"What am I to do, then?" I insisted.

"Register your marriage and then get a divorce."

"But don't you think that such a formal way out is rather like deception?" I said sanctimoniously.

The young lady was quite abashed.

"Come to-morrow with your husband, and if he confirms that you are married I will divorce you," she said hastily, anxious to get rid of such an awkward customer.

"Thank you," I answered imperturbably and with-drew, followed by black looks from people in the queue who had lost another five minutes through me.

The following day we were divorced, and I sent to the house-committee a request for the revaluation of the flat. The rent fell from 150 roubles to 38 roubles and a few copecks. To vent his annoyance the chair-man of the committee said to me jeeringly:

"You'll have a hard time of it. You can't claim alimony, for you are in work."

"I will get 60 roubles a month for my son's keep," I answered modestly.

"You'd better look out for a smaller flat. We'll have to put more people into your present one."

This was just what I wanted. A month later I received permission to exchange my flat. With the other house-committee there was less difficulty: they did not want to let me in at first because my salary was low, but I promised them that I would get married.

"Whom will you marry?" the chairman of the house-committee asked: he was interested in my future husband's salary.

"A specialist with a salary of 240," I answered confidently. Thus we obtained another flat and of course were married again. It did not mean anything to us, and we would not have attached importance to formalities of that sort under the old régime either. But Soviet law-givers ought to have taken less than seventeen years to understand that their method of registering marriages and divorces is a meaningless and sometimes a wicked farce.

The second time I came across this aspect of Soviet life was at the People's Tribunal. It was in the summer of 1930 at Oranienbaum, a little town near Leningrad. In Peter the Great's time Oranienbaum was an estate of Menshikov's, then it became Crown property, and in the nineteenth century was the residence of the dukes of Mecklenburg-Strelitz. It has a beautiful park left from those days, and two palaces. One of them was kept up after a fashion as a museum, the other had been completely robbed and was fast going to rack and ruin

under the patronage of the Forestry Institute to which
it had been given. The town buildings, summer residences and streets were in such a state of dilapidation
and decay that they might be within 4,000 and not
40 miles of Leningrad. Many houses had fallen down
and been pulled to pieces for fuel; instead of fences there
were bits of barbed wire stretching from one tree to
another. At the corner of the main street the Soviets
had intended to make a public garden, though right
opposite there was a huge park planted in the eighteenth century. A post with the inscription: "No Litter
to be Deposited Here" was put in the middle of the
waste piece of ground. A heap of incredible filth and
rubbish, rusty iron, broken bricks, etc., rapidly accumu-
lated round the post. It was undoubtedly one of the
dirtiest spots in the town. Almost opposite were the
militia-station and the Volost Committee; beside it, at
the corner, was the Municipal Co-op and next to it the
Tribunal. The house it occupied had been requisitioned from a rich tradesman. The doors were open
day and night. The stairs and the rooms were un-
believably dirty. Even in the U.S.S.R. one did not
often see anything like it. The parquet floor, black
with dirt, was broken down and nails stuck out from
under it; the paint on the doors and windows had worn
off and the woodwork was covered with ink, pencil
marks and scratches by way of decoration. There is
nothing people will not do from boredom!

On the walls there were portraits of Lenin, Stalin
and Dzerzhinsky put in old unsuitable frames, gilded or
covered with velvet, that had obviously belonged to a
boudoir or a drawing-room. Between the portraits
there were papers fixed with drawing-pins saying, 'Do

not Spit,' 'Do not Smoke,' but the floor was covered with traces of spitting and smoking. A bumble bee, flown in from the park, and a swarm of flies were beating against the window panes that had not been washed or cleaned from time immemorial. Dirty, poor, shabbily dressed people wandered about between rough deal benches.

The sitting was to have begun at ten o'clock; my case, the fifth on the list, was supposed to be heard at twelve, but it was past twelve already, and there was nothing doing. They said the chairman had not yet arrived. Meanwhile the litigants poured out their sorrows and troubles to whomever they could find. One man's complaint was that the Co-op had cheated him of a rouble due to him for chopping firewood; another had had a front tooth knocked out in a drunken fight, which he described with some spirit. I had not had time to find out about the others, because I was accosted by a squint-eyed, crooked woman with a piercing voice. Her unwashed face was sunburnt and weatherbeaten, her hands and feet were deformed by hard work, but far from being crushed and despondent she was bristling with spite.

"Citizen, my dear, there's a good woman, write out for me a statement against my husband."

"What is your case?"

"My case? The usual thing, alimony," she answered briskly, ready with the story of all her wrongs and injuries.

"Fancy a hideous woman like that having a child!" I could not help thinking.

"Write it out for me, my dear," she went on, sitting down beside me. "There's a citizen in the next room writing out statements for fifty copecks, but she won't do it for me. She says she has written out one for my husband against me and so, if you please, she cannot write one for me against him. She is that honest, would you believe it! But what am I to do if I can't read or write?"

I tried to explain to her that if her case had already been submitted to the court there was no need for her to make a fresh statement. She was angry and decided that I refused because fifty copecks was not enough for me. Fortunately at that moment the judges came in: the chairman—a lively young man of twenty-five, a fat old working-woman who was evidently doing her utmost to keep awake in the sultry heat, and a man looking like an old-fashioned clerk who watched anxiously every movement of the chairman.

All stood up as usual. The judges sat down, and so did we.

"Citizen Kuzmichova!" said the chairman so loudly that one might think he had a huge hall full of people before him.

"I am here," the crooked woman answered petulantly.

"Citizen Kuzmichov!" the judge roared again as though wishing to show his power by shouting.

"Here," a thin little man answered in a frightened squeak. It was hard to tell what age he and his wife were—they might be thirty or forty; he seemed the younger of the two, but just as misshapen in his way. He held his head on one side, hunched up his shoulders and ostentatiously thrust forward his right hand, two fingers of which were missing.

It appeared they had once been married, then he

divorced her, promising to pay three roubles a month for their daughter's keep. Now he had another family and did not give a penny to his first wife. Altogether he owed her 114 roubles.

Three roubles a month was an absurdly small sum— one could not do anything with it. Evidently the promise had been made in 1924 or 1925 when three roubles bought something like 36 lbs. of flour or cereals; in 1930 they could only buy 3 or 4 lbs. of bread. But in the general scarcity, the wife, on a particularly hard day, must have reckoned up that the debt amounted to 114 roubles and decided to claim it at all costs.

"Citizen-judge," she wailed, "I don't want anything from him, the dog, the scoundrel . . . "

"Citizen, don't use expressions," the judge remarked indifferently.

"I don't want anything from him," she went on without stopping, "but I do want 114 roubles, because my girl has to go to school in the autumn and I must get her some shoes and a dress of some sort. Let him give the money—her father, curse him!" she screamed.

"Citizen Kuzmichov, why don't you pay the alimony?" the judge pounced on him. "Do you hear, the child has to go to school?"

"I did pay. I am out of work now; I am invalided," he wailed piteously.

"Nothing of the sort!" his former wife burst out. "He was born without those two fingers, why, he's always been called Ivan Fingerless, no one calls him Kuzmichov."

"Don't butt in, citizen. Tell me, comrade, why are you out of work?" the judge asked sympathetically.

The quarrelsome woman was obviously 'gnawing at his liver' as the Soviet expression has it.

"I'm a sick man," the man drawled despondently, exaggerating his weakness. "You see my hand," he thrust his deformed hand forward. "And my chest, too . . . "

"Have you a certificate? Have you been to a doctor?" the judge asked briskly, while the fat jury-woman dozed, overpowered by the stuffiness of the room. "Haven't you? Why not? You must go to a doctor, he'll put you right. This isn't the old régime. Why did you give up your job?"

"He never gave up no job," the woman burst in again. "He is a carpenter, he makes stools and he doesn't want a job. It wouldn't pay him to serve the Soviets, he says, when he's got a good trade. It's not like me who's got to run round scrubbing floors and washing clothes by the day."

"Don't answer when you are not asked, citizen. A court of law isn't a market-place; you be quiet," the judge said reproachfully, trying to silence her.

"That old liar will bamboozle you, and I'm to keep quiet!" the woman went on, determined to get in as many words as she possibly could.

"Shut up!" the judge shouted, and she subsided for a time.

The judge began sympathetically questioning her husband about his earnings and asking how much of the debt he could repay.

"Surely you can pay three roubles a month?" he remonstrated with him.

"I can do that and I promise to, but I can't promise about the debt."

"How much can you pay back, on your honour?"

"I can manage ten roubles but nothing more, on my honour as a proletarian."

"Ten isn't enough. Pay up half, and then pay the three roubles regularly every month," the judge bargained with him as though it were his own personal concern.

But the woman could endure no longer and set up a wail:

"A half! I've got to clothe the child and buy her shoes! She has to go to school. I've worn myself to the bone, charring, and he says 'pay half'!"

"Citizen, screaming is not allowed. Tell me, do you agree or not?"

"Agree! Agree to what? How am I to provide for the child? And that ugly brute there has bought a pig!"

"A pig cannot pay alimony," joked the judge, deafened by the woman's piercing voice.

"A pig doesn't pay. But she's got a litter."

"A litter? How many?" asked the judge with interest. His whole attitude to the case completely changed. In 1930 a pound of bacon cost 10 roubles, and to possess a pig which had just had a family was as good as being a capitalist.

"Eight little ones!" the wife declared triumphantly.

"Six," the husband answered sadly, feeling that he had lost his case.

"Eight. He's sold two, everybody knows that," the woman insisted.

"Eh, my man, so that's what it is!" the judge said threateningly. "Trying to deceive the Soviets! I won't let that pass. Confess, how much did you get for the two little pigs?"

The silent juryman riveted his eyes on the sickly

carpenter who turned out to be a rich man. The fat
jurywoman, wakened by the judge's menacing shouts,
vainly tried to grasp what had happened. The audience,
consisting of petitioners and respondents waiting their
turn, began whispering and exchanging looks.

"She's tripped him up fine!"

"He's that sorry for himself, but he's got a pig!"

"Where does he live?" busily asked the most prosperous looking man in the room. He was evidently
wondering if he couldn't buy a sucking pig cheap from
the carpenter when the law would come down on him.

"Speak! What did you sell the little pigs for?"

"Forty roubles each. I couldn't afford to feed them,"
the carpenter whispered piteously.

"Nonsense, you sold them for sixty each, everybody
knows that," the woman insisted staunchly.

"I see I've got to talk to you differently," said the
judge. "Two little pigs at 60 roubles each, and you
have six more at home, and a pig . . . " he reckoned in
his mind. "In short, the matter is clear," he concluded.
"The court withdraws for consultation."

He briskly walked into the next room accompanied
by his silent colleagues and the secretary.

In about twenty-five minutes they reappeared. The
time had obviously been taken up not by discussing the
decision, which was clear to all, but by formulating it
and writing it down.

"Stand up!" said the judge.

We all stood up.

He began reading in a loud, unnatural voice solemnly
worded sentences saying that the People's Tribunal of
such and such a district, on such and such a date,
having heard the case of citizens So-and-so . . . The

longer he read the more he lost the meaning of what he was reading. He stumbled at different 'words, consulted the secretary, cleared his throat, puffed out his chest, and suddenly raised his voice in the middle of a sentence. The audience struggled hard to follow, but could not make head or tail of it. Having read the paper to the end he drew a breath, turned to the respondent and shouted at him in his ordinary voice:

"In short, you must pay your debt in full. Understand? If you don't pay it, I'll sell your pig. Understand?"

This was certainly satisfactory.

Then the case about the tooth knocked out during a fight came on (the judge's comment was "Don't fight another time, your teeth aren't a saleable article!"); then the one about the rouble which the Co-operative failed to pay (the comment was "You should have had a proper agreement and not drag people into a court of law for nothing"). Then there was another case about alimony.

A scraggy, freckled girl with white eyelashes and reddish hair, shy and unhappy, muttered something incomprehensible, holding in her trembling hand a piece of paper with an official stamp on it. The judge conscientiously tried to listen and grasp what it was all about, but suddenly lost patience and stretched out his hand for the paper.

"Give me the paper, citizen. What document is this?"

She walked up to him overcome with confusion and ready to burst into tears.

"A copy . . . from the registry office . . . at Habarovsk," he read, omitting unnecessary words, "dissolution of marriage . . . at the request of citizen Nicolaev,

Ivan Petrovitch, between him and his wife, citizen Anna Semyonovna Nicolaev . . . " I see. Have you a child?" he asked the girl.

"A baby daughter," she answered almost inaudibly. "Five months old."

"At work?"

"Do you mean me?" she asked in alarm.

"Clearly. Your little daughter's only work at present is to soil napkins," he joked to the delight of the audience and the greater confusion of the girl.

"I am a cashier at the 'Peasant's House,' " she said loudly, with hysterical notes in her voice. "My salary is 65 roubles a month, I pay 20 a month to a nurse, I have no one to leave baby with. I cannot feed her myself, I have nothing to live on and am in debt all round."

"Don't get excited, citizen," the judge, used to such stories, interrupted her. "We'll give you the full amount of alimony, but . . . " he threw up his hands, "we'll send the verdict to Habarovsk where your husband had a post, and if meanwhile he has moved to another town . . . you can see for yourself how it is. It's not easy to find a man in the Far East, and perhaps he was there for a time only. In short, we'll look for him. The matter is clear."

"Thank you," she whispered, understanding very well that her case was hopeless. A man who had lived with her for a year while he was in charge of the 'Peasant's House' at Oranienbaum and divorced her the moment he was transferred to a post in another town, would certainly not trouble about her and the child again. Soviet official bodies, slow, unwieldy and formalistic, were not likely to trace him—especially at a distance of nearly a fortnight's railway journey.

I was completely engrossed by my observations—they were new to me, for my time was entirely taken up with museum work. I actually forgot about my own 'case' and was somewhat surprised when the judge read out:

"The case of removing citizen Tchernavin from the premises occupied by her." Citizen, why don't you vacate the premises but allow the case to go into court? You ought to know better, one would have thought, and yet you can't do what is expected of you!" The judge pounced on me before he had finished reading the petition of the Forestry Institute about my removal. Soviet officials, especially Communists, have a habit of attacking one straight away, 'trying it on' in the hope that one will give in from sheer fright.

"Because I hired the premises from the Forestry Institute for a summer residence from June 1 to September 1, and according to Section 2 of the contract I was to pay the rent in three instalments, on June 1, July 1 and . . ."

"Citizen!" the judge interrupted me wearily, afraid that I would adopt another Soviet method and try to stupify him by quoting paragraphs and references, "this isn't Paris, you know! Keep to the point."

It was funny his mentioning Paris. I suppose my appearance at this out-of-the-way tribunal made him think of something very remote. Litigants were wrangling about one or three roubles and here was I paying 200 roubles for a summer cottage!

"I took the cottage for three months, have paid the money in full, and am now on my holidays. Besides, I am doing work for the Education Department at

Oranienbaum and I do not intend to give up my cottage to an employee like myself simply because his mother-in-law has come to stay with him."

"Comrade," the judge turned politely to the representative of the Forestry Institute, "why do you insist on the citizen's removal?"

"She doesn't pay rent," he lied at random.

"The receipts are attached to my statement," I replied.

The judge looked at the documents, reckoned in his mind and did the calculation in pencil.

"All has been paid, comrade," he said, as though regretting that all was in order. "Do you belong to the Party?" he asked the Institute representative cautiously.

"Yes, I'm a member," the man answered complacently.

"Call on me later and we'll have a talk," the judge added sympathetically, "but you can't turn out the citizen on that ground."

No, it could not be done on that ground, but would be done with pleasure on any other. But I was not worrying about that. I knew I could appeal to a higher court and let the case drag on till my holidays were over.

MY SERVANT MASHA

Why, are there any servants in U.S.S.R.? Yes, but they are called 'domestic workers.' In order to obtain food one has to keep a servant—unless the family is lucky enough to have an old aunt, a grandmother or some other relative who is not fit to go out to work and can look after housekeeping. Otherwise one risks being left without anything to eat.

This is how a Soviet house-wife's day is mapped out. At seven o'clock in the morning she must run out to fetch the bread and take her turn in two or three queues outside the co-ops which open at nine. The co-ops might be selling something that can be bought on the ration cards: salt, cereals, soap—and it is essential to be there before the goods are sold out. Then she must scour the neighbourhood to see if anything is being sold without ration cards: half-rotten potatoes, cabbage, tinned fish, etc. If it happens to be a day on which sugar or butter can be had on children's ration cards, or margarine on the 1st category ration cards, she must leave everything and stand in a queue for hours. In case of complete failure she must run to the free market and in the general crush and hustle snatch something as cheaply as she can—a piece of stale meat or fish or a doubtful sausage. And in any case she must stand in a queue for paraffin, for all cooking is done on primus stoves and there never is enough oil. Soon after three o'clock she must run home, light the primus stove and do her best to cook something more or less eatable with the bad and scanty provisions. About five all office workers, factory hands, students and schoolchildren come home to the overcrowded flats where many families live together. The young ones clamour for food, the elderly groan with weariness, but also try to peep inside the saucepans. Sometimes the family has to sit down to dinner without waiting for everyone to come back, because people are often kept at their work after hours. The remains of the food have to be warmed up for the late comers.

By the time that offices close, co-ops are still open, but they have nothing left to sell and the free markets are closed. In public dining-rooms the food is either horribly bad or very expensive. It is no wonder then that servants are indispensable and are kept both by office workers and by factory hands.

It is not difficult to find a servant: all the peasant girls who in the summer manage to eke out a livelihood on collective farms, kitchen gardens or derelict individual small holdings, in the autumn try to get into towns where they hope to go into a factory. Their reasoning is simple enough: the State robs the peasants, both on the collective and on the individual farms, but feeds factory workers. Obviously it is more alluring to receive two and a half pounds or even one pound of bread a day on a ration card than to produce the bread and be left in winter on starvation rations or without any rations at all with nothing but cabbage, mangel-tops, dried fungi and chaff-soup. Besides, in the country a girl has no chance of buying any clothes or shoes.

But it is impossible to get a job at a factory without belonging to a trade union, and in order to join one a girl must begin either as a seasonal worker, which is very hard, or as a domestic servant. After six months she can join the *Narpit* union and then try for admission to a factory. Everyone knows this method of working one's way up, and in my own case, for instance, I had as servants not only a succession of peasant girls, but a doctor's widow and the divorced wife of a civil servant who earned three times as much as I did but paid her no alimony because she could work. U.S.S.R. citizens have to be up to all sorts of tricks.

But no one wants to remain a servant, and as soon as a girl has joined the Union she at once begins to look out for some other job. Factory life is not easy. The work-rooms are stuffy and overcrowded, and the conditions often are so insanitary that the workers suffer from poisoning; but at any rate the working day is limited to so many hours. Besides, there is always a chance of earning an extra rouble; there is the company of one's own sort of people; one can struggle for a better position and hope to get on the Factory Committee and become something like a manager. A domestic servant has no future. Her working day is long, in spite of all the efforts of the Union to limit it to eight hours and ensure a two hours' rest in the middle of the day. This is utterly impracticable, for if a servant does not do her best to obtain food for her employers, regardless of time and weather, she herself will have nothing to eat. Her salary of 40-50 roubles a month is high as compared with the factory worker's wage of 100-120 roubles which do not include board and lodging; but on the other hand factory workers can get manufactured goods more cheaply, while a servant's 40 roubles will not buy anything. A pair of shoes costs about 100 roubles, a dress the same, an overcoat, of which she has been dreaming in the country, is 200 roubles. Discontented with her position she is rude to her mistress who is tired out by office work and annoyed at having the house-work done badly and carelessly. When the servant leaves, the mistress feels blessed relief for a day or two, but is soon worked off her feet. She cannot manage both her office work and her housekeeping, and begins to look for a fresh one. In a family with small children there can be no question of doing without a servant, for they cannot be left alone all day.

My family was small, there was not much house-work to do, and we could afford to pay good wages, so that servants stayed with me for a year or two. But now and again I too was faced with the alternative of either giving up my job at the Hermitage or urgently finding a 'deserter from the agricultural front.'

The last time I was left without a servant was at a particularly awkward moment. My husband had just been sent to work at Murmansk with a reminder that "it was better to go voluntarily to Murmansk than compulsorily to Kem." A few days after his departure our son was taken ill with septic appendicitis. I was desperately busy at the Hermitage because we had received orders to prepare as soon as possible for the sale of the Stroganovsky Dom Museum.

The boy had to be taken to a hospital. The operation passed off successfully, but injections of a newly invented serum gave him blood poisoning and his condition was very serious. The woman doctor was in despair and had not the heart to send me away from the hospital, although mothers were not allowed to stay. But I could not get any food there and so somebody had to feed me and cook special things for the boy, for the hospital provided the same semi-starvation diet for all the patients. At a moment's notice my friends found a servant for me—a girl of nineteen. I had not time to make any inquiries about her; all I knew was her name—Masha.

She came to the hospital once a day, brought our food, took my orders and went back to look after our flat.

The unusual circumstances in which she was placed made a strong impression on her, and she was touchingly anxious to do her best. The sick boy, whom she never saw but whose life, she knew, was in danger, appealed to her imagination. After three weeks I had to take him home because in the children's surgical ward an epidemic of scarlet fever, diphtheria and septic angina broke out simultaneously. My Masha looked like one inspired. She regarded everything that I asked her to do as an heroic feat necessary to save the boy's life. She showed wonderful resource in buying a fowl, discovering fresh butter in the market, getting grapes or coffee. Soviet life does, of course, require resource, since the simplest things may be almost unobtainable. They can only be bought at a very high price at the back door of certain 'closed' co-ops or bartered from privileged persons such as foreign specialists.

At home I saw that Masha was a nice girl, clean, pretty and well spoken. There was something romantic

in her character, and the sense of responsibility and
the atmosphere of perpetual care and anxiety in which
we lived seemed to have transfigured her. Perhaps
she had never before felt such intense, poignant pity
and tenderness. And when my boy recovered, she
liked to recall that anxious time which somehow seemed
to her beautiful.

But gradually she learned to take advantage of the
intimacy that my son's illness created between her and
me. Often coming home from my work I had to go
without bread: "Sonny and I had tea and got through
the loaf between us," she would say. The watery
soup was utterly uneatable: "Sonny and I inadvertently
ate up all the potatoes." The rooms had not been
swept or dusted: "Sonny and I ran out to buy galoshes
for him and me."

I tried to explain to her that everyone ought to have
his own duties: my work was at the Hermitage, and
her job was to look after my rooms. She agreed but
it made no difference, for she wanted above all things
to have a good time. In less than six months she
blossomed out into a smart young lady with no end
of admirers. One invited her to the cinema, another
—for a walk, a third had serious intentions, and she
often hid from him. In genuine alarm she used to
get under my bed. Not seeing her anywhere I answered
the door and honestly told her disappointed suitor
that she was not at home. As soon as he had gone she
crept out, shaking with laughter,

What was I to do with her? I had no time to spare,
and no talent for training people in the way they should
go. We might perhaps have lived together amicably
till she found a husband, had it not been for the

terrible year 1930 in which there was a fresh outburst of Soviet terror.

I remember, on the very day when I heard that specialists were being arrested at Murmansk Masha burst into my room with a loud wail, fell at my feet and howled, forgetting all her civilised town ways.

"What's the matter, Masha? Talk sensibly."

"My poor·brother! What will become of him!" she wailed.

She glanced at me surreptitiously, evidently making up her mind whether I could be trusted, decided that I could and told me her story.

The most awful part of it was that her father was not a peasant at all, as it said in her passport, but a gendarme.

She uttered the word with so much fear that one might think she expected me to turn her out of the house straight away.

It appeared that her father had served at a remote railway station and died before the revolution, when Masha was only four and her brother two. After the revolution their mother burned her husband's passport and papers and returned to her native village where she lived in dire poverty. She sent Masha into service when the girl was seven; when her brother Sanka was the same age he became a waiter in a Soviet pub. He was a clever boy; he could read and write, picked up some 'political science' and succeeded in getting into a military school from which he hoped to go on to the officers' training centre. But now one of his comrades discovered that his father had been a gendarme. That meant that he would be expelled from school as a class enemy and forbidden to continue

his education elsewhere. He was on the point of
suicide. And their mother had just been convicted of
illegally selling vodka—an occupation she had engaged
in since her cow had been taken from her.

"You never told me you had a mother, Masha,"
I said reproachfully.

"Much I care about her! A millstone round our
necks, that's what she is. She'll disgrace us now.
Mother go hang, it's my brother I am sorry for. I
used to look after him, I nursed him when he was a
baby."

"If you had helped your mother, she wouldn't have
taken to selling vodka."

"She is not a child, she knew what she was doing,"
she answered crossly. "No one gives me money for
nothing, so why should I give it her?"

"What a shame, Masha! Why, you have all you
want, even a silk frock."

"Well, what if I have? I've got to live. Till I came
to you I'd never had any money to spare. What am
I to do about my brother, tell me! If he cuts his
throat I'll throw myself into the Neva."

I must say that she had never mentioned her brother
before, but she was in genuine distress about him now.
She could not think of anything and did nothing but
sob. She may have considered of course that through
her brother they might get at her, expel her from the
trade union, exile her from Petrograd and spoil her
life so that she too would not know which way to turn.

We had to think of something. The Soviet régime
specialises in traps and strangleholds for its citizens,
and they have to try to find loopholes—if they are
not caught straight away.

"Give me your brother's letter, Masha. You go and make tea—it's the boy's bedtime, and I will think it over."

The letter was tragic and incoherent. The informer had evidently sent in the report about her brother's parentage, but the boy had not yet been expelled from school. In reason, school authorities ought to understand that the father's being a gendarme could not have had any influence on a two-year-old baby, but they were bound to give consideration to a written report. There was only one way out for the boy: to flee to another town and lose himself among the working masses. But he could only go to a town where somebody would take him in as a lodger and thus give him a right to 'living accommodation.' In other words, I had to invite him to Leningrad and put him up at my flat. I knew that it was a risky thing to do: I did not know the boy, Masha was growing less and less dependable, and I should be mixing myself up in other people's troubles when I had plenty of my own.

I could hear from the kitchen the hissing of the primus stove, Masha's sobs and the voice of my boy who was comforting her. Her brother's desperate letter lay on my lap, and on the table lay my husband's carefully worded note from which I could gather that he had been cross-examined by the G.P.U. all day and part of the night, though he was still at liberty.

"Masha!" I called.

She came in, bathed in tears, wiping her eyes with her apron and a wet, tightly screwed up handkerchief. My son clung to her dejectedly.

"Write to your brother and tell him to leave everything and come here at once. So long as there's been no order to expel him, his future isn't ruined. He will find something to do here, and meanwhile he can live with us."

Masha looked at me as though I had done a magical trick: the problem was solved! She was delighted, my boy was delighted. She hugged and kissed him, they both skipped about with joy and at last ran to the bathroom to get him ready for bed. I could hear her telling him with much feeling about her village, her childhood, her brother. They were both laughing and making plans. Then she began to sing a street song evidently recalling her intention to throw herself into the Neva:

> "Calmly and simply
> We jumped from the bridge,
> A barge with timber
> Looked like a ridge."

Perhaps I had done right, I thought—but I was not certain.

A few days later her brother came. He was a nice lad: intelligent, smart, with good manners. He expressed no gratitude, but was obviously happy and full of hope. He managed to secure his papers before any damaging remarks had been entered in them, easily found a job at a factory and began preparing for the *Rabfak*. His prospects improved as mine grew darker and darker.

News came from Murmansk of my husband's room having been searched by the G.P.U. so thoroughly that they actually sifted the sugar and the flour, as though some State secrets could be found there. My turn would probably come next. I had of course no compromising 'documents' of any kind, but I had a boxful of old letters that were dear to me and a number of photographs. The G.P.U. might misconstrue and make trouble over the most innocent things, so I decided to burn everything. It was not so easy as I thought. I tried to do it myself, but it was a slow business and the heaps of ash with half-burnt bits of paper showing from it looked distinctly suspicious. I had to call in Masha. I explained to her what kind of papers they were, read to her one or two amusing pages from the letters and asked her to burn the lot. I took charge of burning the photographs so as not to lead her into the temptation of hiding away the picture of some smartly dressed lady or handsome young man. She was quite willing to help me, but when the job was over she behaved as though she had done me a great service, involving a certain amount of risk on her part. Her brother too was growing more and more independent; he came home late and used my telephone without asking leave. Apparently he too was having difficulties, but now the brother and sister talked by themselves in whispers and no longer confided in me.

In the summer Masha acquired a new and very determined suitor who ousted all the others. At first he wore civilian clothes but afterwards came quite openly in G.P.U. uniform and sat in the kitchen till the small hours of the morning. It was distinctly awkward. I tried talking to Masha but she snapped back:

"G.P.U. agents are men like anyone else. This one is no worse than others: he takes me to the pictures and brings chocolate every day."

"Masha, do you remember what happened to your brother in the winter? Have you forgotten how you cried and abused the Soviets?" I asked, trying to remind her how frightened she had been then.

"That's past and gone. No one is likely to find that out. And if it does leak out, the man may be of use to us."

It was evidently time I parted with Masha. She soon left me of her own accord, however—just in the middle of my holidays. She said she was going to get married and got several wedding presents out of me. She left me her brother as a legacy: having once registered him at my flat I had no right to dislodge him. Altogether, I had got myself into a mess.

I was cross with myself for my idealistic foolishness, but I had no energy to struggle against small things. Not a day passed without some of my friends being arrested. In September forty-eight specialists were shot, in October my husband was arrested. The prospect of prison for me was drawing closer and closer.

If I picked up the telephone receiver I heard the typical click which meant that a G.P.U. observer was listening. If I went into the dark entry I saw a G.P.U. spy waiting in the yard or trying to look in at the lighted window. Once I saw him in animated conversation with Sanka who was evidently explaining to him the arrangement of my rooms. I was not even surprised. It was all of a piece. But it hurt me to think that Masha may have had a hand in it too.

The night of my arrest came. Sanka was not at home, but when the G.P.U. officers came in, he glided in after them. They did not stop him—he was evidently one of them. When, towards the end of the search, I had to take the G.P.U. men into the room where he slept to show them a few more of my belongings, he jumped up and stood by the wall, turning away from me. He was pale and there was a strained look on his face. Now that his treachery had materialised he must have felt rather uncomfortable.

I was taken away. In prison at one of my first interviews with the examining officer I was asked:

"What did you burn last year in March? Who had lunch with you on such and such a day? Whom did you meet at the station on such and such a day by the morning train?"

None of these facts were of the slightest importance, but the G.P.U. collects information so as to impress its victims by knowing everything as though by magic. I answered with business-like precision, pretending not to understand the examining officer's game, but added at the end:

"You can easily find out more details from my former servant Masha."

He said nothing—he saw that I guessed his secret.

When after five months I was released I found that Sanka had been convicted and sent to a penal camp.

"What for?" I asked in surprise.

"After you were arrested," my son told me, "Sanka was simply dreadful: he came home drunk every day, swore at everyone, and once smashed the kitchen window as though he meant to jump out."

"Did he sleep in your room?" I asked in alarm.

"No, he slept in the kitchen. He didn't come in to me. And I slept on the sofa in your room. I could think of you better there," he added apologetically.

"Did he stay here long?"

"Not long. He spent the Komsomol money on drink. And he sold library books for drink too. The library assistant came to see him about it, and in the night G.P.U. men took him away."

"How did you know he'd been sent to a penal camp?"

"The porter told me. And everyone in the yard said 'there, he set a trap for your mother and was caught in it himself.' "

"Did Masha come?"

"No. Sanka's things are still in the passage, no one takes them."

I did not see Masha again. I only heard that she married not the G.P.U. agent, who abandoned her, but the dull suitor whom she disliked.

"She had to hurry," one of the gossips in the yard explained to me.

"She had to take whomever she could get," another one chimed in. "A G.P.U. man isn't likely to pay alimony."

"What next! Alimony, indeed! Why, she went to the hospital and had an abortion."

I did not want to pursue the subject further.

I feel both sorry and vexed when I remember Masha. She was a nice girl—and to think of the dirty work the G.P.U. made her do!

AN ORDINARY WOMAN

She was a perfectly ordinary nice woman—one of those who are pretty in their early youth but soon begin to fade, who never think for themselves and are entirely at the mercy of external events. They generally remain harmlessly commonplace all their lives, but may become intolerable in their silliness. Such women are to be met everywhere, among all nations, but it is only in the U.S.S.R. that one meets them in prison. The G.P.U. is not in the least particular and its agents are so careless and ignorant that they think nothing of arresting the most unlikely people.

When I was put in the same cell with this woman she had been there for three months already, while I was still a mere novice.

"My dear, how glad I am!" she greeted me. "I don't mean, of course, I am glad because you've been arrested, but I am glad for my own sake. You simply can't think how delighted I am! Just fancy, I've been here nearly three months and I haven't even been questioned. I don't know what I am accused of. I am simply at my wits' end. I can't think what I am to do. No one to ask, no one to advise me."

She began talking the moment I was thrust into the cell and went on without stopping although it was late in the night. There was an oppressive thick darkness in the cell, without a glimmer from the sky or from a street lamp. All round us there was a hushed, uneasy silence. It was the hour when prisoners are called up to be cross-examined, when new prisoners are brought in and the G.P.U. car, 'the Black Crow,' hoots hideously outside the prison gates bringing new victims.

From time to time she asked me:

"Are you asleep?"

"No."

"Do I disturb you?"

"No, I like your talking."

I was not asleep because I had not yet learnt to sleep in prison. The clatter of footsteps on the iron staircases made my heart thump. The click of the electric switch in the corridor made me draw myself up nervously. I waited for the approaching footsteps, for the flash of light, the sound of the peephole opening, and then for the darkness, though I knew that nothing further was likely to happen, as it was simply the usual checking which took place every fifteen or twenty minutes. My neighbour could not sleep because she felt starved after three months' silence and solitude. One must experience solitary confinement to understand how irresistible the desire to talk can be.

"Well, you see," she went on indefatigably, "the moment you came in I thought you were the very one I've been waiting for and that you would help me. Just imagine, three months and not a word with anyone! One of the wardresses—you know, the one in the blue blouse—sometimes says 'Good night' to me. As she passes down the corridor she shouts to everyone 'bed time!' but she opens my peephole and says 'good night.' I am so glad she does. I think she must be a nice woman. I should so like to give her something.

Not now, of course, but when I am let out. I suppose that's not allowed, is it?"

"No, of course not."

"And why does she say it? Is she really kind or does she merely pretend?"

"You wait till she lets you down, then you'll know."

"Oh, she wouldn't."

She did not believe me that night, but she soon got into trouble with that wardress for looking out of the window. She was very nearly transferred to another cell for punishment.

"There, you see, I know simply nothing, nothing at all. And you know as soon as I was arrested they brought me to the examining officer. I was nearly off my head, you know—I gave my mother's name wrong, I forgot the number of the house I live in. Did they ask you those questions too?"

"Yes."

"Whatever for?"

"Oh, it's just their way."

"But it's strange, for surely they know all that already? And I was so afraid of giving a wrong answer." She paused. "And then the examining officer asked me if I knew why I was arrested. But how could I possibly know? It made me quite angry. I said he had no business to make fun of me, it was no laughing matter, I had two small children at home. And he suddenly bawled at me: 'Fun, indeed! Why, shooting isn't bad enough for what you have done!' I was so frightened that I burst into tears. I sobbed and sobbed and could not make out what else he was shouting. So silly of me! I expect he was very cross with me. Tell me, it doesn't do to annoy them, does it?"

"Well, no, but their shouting doesn't mean very much. You shouldn't take any notice of it."

"Could they have mixed me up with someone else, I wonder? Why should they shoot me when I haven't done anything? Just think, I am only thirty. When the revolution began I was still at school. We were all delighted, though it was rather frightening. And I never wanted to be a counter-revolutionary: I put up with everything, I tried not to abuse the bolsheviks and never allowed any silly talk about them in front of the children. So why did they put me in prison? My only hope is that they mixed me up with somebody else."

"Yes, such things do happen."

"Good heavens, what am I to do!" she cried in despair. "Do they often call you up to be questioned?"

"Almost every day."

"There, you see, you can explain things to them, but me they don't call up at all. It's dreadful. They'll never let me out at that rate."

"Very likely that's just what they will do."

"No, it cannot be. They never let anyone out of here. I asked a wardress and she merely shook her head."

" 'They will let me out—they will not let me out'— it's like trying one's fortune on daisy petals," I thought but I said nothing to her: I did not want to depress the poor woman who was unhappy enough already.

She did not speak but I could hear that she was still awake. At last I asked:

"Well, and what happened then?"

"Then he said to me, 'Name your friends.' And I said to him 'How can I?—I know half the people in Petersburg. My husband was a doctor and we always kept open house. And now that he has left me and I live with my children on an allowance from him no one wants to see me.' That was a little ruse on my part, you know—I didn't want to mention any names. I don't want to get people into trouble. That was right, wasn't it?"

"Quite right."

"There, you see—and I didn't know if it was right. Then he said 'I'll teach you to talk to me. You will go to your cell now and think over your position. You will call to mind all your doings and the friends who helped you. You won't be let out of here easily. And don't you hope that it's merely an error—these aren't the times of military communism, let me tell you, when people were arrested for nothing and let out by mistake.' I was taken back to my cell. I thought he would call me up the very next day and I would explain him everything. I would offer to tell him my whole life, every day, every hour of it if he likes."

"But the trouble is, you see, that we have nothing to offer them—they ask of us all they want."

"What are we to do then?"

"Wait."

"But I've been waiting for three months. I am afraid he's forgotten all about me."

"Oh, he will think of you some day."

We spent two months together, she and I. She told me her whole life, "down to the last thread," as she put it. She was very serious and business-like about it. Her idea was that if she recalled everything and told it all to me, while I asked her searching and perfidious questions like an examining officer, we might grasp at last why this catastrophe had overtaken her.

We had nothing to do; I was ready to listen to anything so as to think less of my own trouble, and to her it was a little distraction, anyway.

When she began her story she fancied that there had been 'no end of events' in her life. Every birthday and nameday was an event and so was every holiday. The trip to the Crimea marked an epoch. Her father's salary was small, everything had to be carefully planned out, and when any extra expense could be afforded there was general rejoicing in the family. But when we got as far as the revolution the years sped by like months, and it was difficult to tell one from another in the dull, colourless series of days. She married, but somehow all in a hurry. Her husband, a doctor, moved into her parents' flat, he shared her bedroom, and her father gave up his study for the consulting room. Then children came—each of them meant so much trouble that she and her mother almost dropped with weariness in their struggle to find food, and to mend and darn and turn old clothes into new.

"You know, it is only now, in prison, that I have grasped how many years I have lived after the revolution! At home I hadn't a moment to think—one always had to stand in queues for bread or potatoes or something. And milk! I used to go out of town to get it, for of course the children had to have decent milk. Then I had to take them out—they must have fresh air you know, and in the evening I had to do their washing so that the clothes could dry during the night and be ready for them to wear in the morning. And if there was any warm water left I contrived to have a bath."

One evening, when she was feeling very sleepy because she had been standing in a queue for butter from five o'clock in the morning till after mid-day, her husband said to her gloomily that the following morning he was going to settle with his new wife. When she came to this point in her story she broke down and wept.

"That is how I cried all that night," she said. "And I could think of nothing to say to him, nothing at all. I dropped asleep only towards morning, and he dressed quietly and went out. He never came back. He sent for his things and left money for the children, a month in advance. He always sent their allowance punctually. I knew of course that he was bored with me—I never had time to play, or sing, or read, or to take care of my looks. But I couldn't have done anything different, could I?"

"Of course you couldn't," I answered warmly.

"I couldn't!" she repeated passionately. "The children were the chief thing in my life, and I hadn't enough energy left for him. But why have I been parted from them? What is my crime?"

There certainly was no crime. Indeed, there was nothing in the least suspicious about her circumstances: her husband had never been arrested, she never went abroad, her parents were poor and humble. There was nothing to get hold of, so to speak, and yet weeks passed, and she was still in prison. She now spent most of her time lying down, for something had gone wrong with her during the last month. She did not complain of any illness but she was growing so thin that her bones were showing through the skin.

The prison doctor gave her permission to lie down during the hours when prisoners were not allowed to do so, and she scarcely got up from her bed. The story of her life was finished with additions, corrections and commentaries. I had exhausted all my supply of explanations and words of comfort and, as a last resort, taught her two lines of one of Kuzmin's poems:

"Not for you it is to write the story of your life,
For you cannot tell what the end may be."

She repeated them to herself in an endless number of ways day and night, for she scarcely slept at all now. The lively, talkative little woman, quite competent in her way, for she could tidy up the cell very nicely and portion out her provisions from home to last a whole week, was rapidly becoming a sick, unhappy creature whose mind had changed as much as her body. I don't know how many weeks passed in this way. I cannot even recall exactly when the decisive, dramatic day came at last; but I remember all that happened on that day as clearly as though it were but yesterday.

It was the day for receiving parcels from home. The parcels were brought in after 4 o'clock, but she was restless and excited from early morning. The G.P.U. could always refuse to let the prisoners have the parcels, of course. It was not the provisions and the clean under-clothes she was eager to have, but the list of the articles sent, at the end of which stood the signature 'son Nicolay' or 'daughter Nina,' They both wrote a child-ish hand—the boy was ten and the girl eight. One could see how anxious they had been to do it all properly: no corrections or erasions were allowed on the list, and the writing had to be very clear. Not a single word of greeting was permitted—nothing but the bare enumera-tion of the things sent. The children's signatures and their handwriting were the only sign that they were alive and well and that on that day one of them had been to the prison to bring the parcel. But she read the list as though it were a tale of their lives.

"(1) White Bread. My mother saved it up for me. She has long been giving all her ration to the children.

"(2) Sugar—1 lb. I wish they wouldn't send it! I know perfectly well there isn't enough sugar to go round. When I was at home Nina often cried because the tea wasn't sweet, and she wouldn't eat her porridge.

"(3) Butter—½ lb. My husband must have sent that. They couldn't have got any themselves."

Eagerly, hastily, she read and re-read the list. It was left in the cell for a few minutes so that one could check the contents, and then had to be given back. She never checked anything but merely gazed at her children's handwriting and at the naïve signature, and when the warder came for the list, she pressed the paper for the last time to her heart, kissed the words 'son Nicolay' or 'daughter Nina' and reluctantly gave it up.

Then she had to lie down because after so much agitation she had no strength left to unpack the things. The parcel and the list were both a meeting and a parting, her only link with her family. This time she took out of the bag her clean dressing gown which she had sent to be washed at home. She had nothing to take its place and missed it very much all the week. She put it on and lay down, but suddenly jumped up in alarm, holding something in her tightly clutched fingers.

"What's the matter?" I asked.

"It's a louse," she answered in a frightened, trembling voice.

"Well, that's nothing very dreadful. There are lots of them in the parcels office and one must have got

on to your bag," I said reassuringly, though I knew how
difficult it was in prison to keep down the loathsome
parasites which act as typhus carriers.

"What am I to do with it?" she whispered in terror,
not listening to me.

"Here's a piece of paper, put it in and crush it. It
hasn't bitten you, has it?"

"No, I took it off the moment I felt it crawling."

"Well then, there's no danger. It's only if they bite
that they infect you with typhus."

She sat still with one hand outstretched, helplessly
holding the piece of paper in the other. I made her
unclasp her fingers, and picking up the louse that had
stuck to the moist skin, wrapped it up in paper and
threw it down the lavatory.

"There, don't worry, the terrible beast is gone," I
said jokingly as I pulled the plug. She was watching
me with as much superstitious terror as though I were
handling a scorpion or a poisonous snake.

"For you cannot tell what the end may be," she
quoted unexpectedly. "Yes, I can tell. To see a louse
is a bad omen. I haven't long to live."

Nothing I said could divert her from the idea. She
listened to me thinking her own thoughts.

As it happened, she was called up to the examining
officer that very evening. As she left the cell, she said
to me "You see—that's the end."

She did not come back for hours. Though indeed
time always seems long when one is anxiously waiting
for a fellow prisoner to return from an interview with
the G.P.U. examining officer.

She came back looking half dead. I wanted to
question her but I saw that her teeth were clenched

convulsively and that she was not in a condition to speak.

"Lie down," I said to her. "No, undress first, you'll be more comfortable."

She was shivering as though she had come out of icy water. She could not undo any of her hooks or buttons. I helped her to undress and, when she lay down, covered her up with her overcoat and my own. I lay down too because we were supposed to sleep and the light was out. We lay with our heads so close together that our pillows touched.

"Give me your hand," she brought out with difficulty.

I gave her my hand; she placed it on her eyes. Her forehead was cold and her eyelids were burning. We lay for a long time like this, without speaking in the thick prison darkness. It was past midnight. The warders on duty were no longer clattering with their boots on the stairs, taking the prisoners to be examined. All was quiet, except that every fifteen or twenty minutes the light was switched on and the wardress peeped in to see if we were still alive.

"It all happened because of Irina Pavlovna," she said at last in a clear, unnaturally calm voice.

"What Irina Pavlovna?"

"I didn't tumble to it at first either. As soon as I came in he suddenly sprang it on me, 'What is Irina Pavlovna's surname?' And I thought to myself, whom ever does he mean? It sounds like a Grand Duchess. Was there one of that name?"

"I don't know."

"I don't know either but I was frightened. I thought, surely he isn't going to accuse me of a monarchist plot? 'Think it over,' he said and gave me such an ominous look. 'I ask you for the last time.' And suddenly it dawned on me—'Irina Pavlovna Malygin,' I said. 'Then why have you been concealing that name for the last five months?' he asked. 'How could I have been concealing it if I haven't been questioned for the last five months?" I replied 'That may be,' he said, 'but who is this Irina Pavlovna?' 'A dressmaker,' I said. 'When did you make friends with her?' he asked maliciously. I told him I didn't make friends with her but simply ordered a dress from her. And you know, I was answering him and all the time I was utterly puzzled, I didn't know what to think. I simply couldn't believe that these five months of prison—five months that have ruined my health, drained all my strength . . . "

"Don't get excited, go on with the story."

" 'And when was it you made arrangements with her about those *dresses?*" he asked with a jeer, and I suddenly felt that he could do anything to me. He could arrest me for nothing at all and he can kill me too—can't he?"

"Yes, but I don't think it's likely."

"Don't try to comfort me. I see it all now. And I haven't long to live, anyway. But the stupidity of it! A dressmaker had my address and because of her I shall never see Nina and Kolya again. And I do so want to see them before I die."

"Don't be silly. Tell me what happened."

"Nothing. He shouted at me, asked me for names, threatened that I would be kept another five months in prison—and I got quite muddled and couldn't think of anything. My head ached so. It will end badly anyhow, I thought. So I didn't try to recall anything or to think. I simply sat there like one dead. He grew

angry and sent me away. I had been so anxious to be
questioned: I pictured to myself how I would explain
everything to them and be acquitted. And then this
nonsense about the dressmaker, the dress that I wore
out long ago . . . Why did they arrest the dressmaker?''

"Just as they did you, because of somebody else's
address."

She was so tired she could hardly speak. Her thoughts,
like mine, must have hung over her like a nightmare.
Neither of us could sleep. When at seven o'clock the
wardresses began shouting for the prisoners to get up
she said:

"I am not going to get up to-day."

"Why?"

"I don't want to get up at all if one's life can be
ruined so gratuitously. I had never thought badly of
the G.P.U. I thought, of course, they might make
mistakes, mix things up. But they knew all about me,
absolutely all, when they arrested me, when they kept
me here, when they saw that I was slowly dying . . . "

"Don't begin to cry, get up and let us sweep the
floor."

"And what then?"

What then? It was not for us to tell. Our life in
prison and our death were in the hands of a blind force
—but I did not say that to her.

The prison day dragged on. I don't remember a
more depressing morning. The senselessness of it all
paralysed us both.

After dinner the door of our cell was opened and the
wardress said to the unhappy woman:

"Get ready and pack your things."

She was horrified.

"They are taking me away . . . ! You are all that is left me. Ask the wardress on duty, call the Commandant, perhaps they'll allow me to stay with you! I cannot bear to be by myself again!"

"But perhaps you are going home," I said doubtfully.

"I don't believe it," she answered in a broken voice.

"Anything may happen," I said to reassure her.

"All I know is there's nothing they may not do, nothing."

She was led away and I never saw her again.

A SCHOOL FRIEND

THAT was at the end of July 1931. I had been five months in the Shpalerka prison. It was a hot summer. My cell was stuffy and steaming with the heat, day and night, though the sun came into it for a few minutes only.

I could see from my window the iron balconies of the fifth storey where the G.P.U. officers had their flats. They took out mattresses on to the balconies and with their wives and children lay there for hours in bathing costumes. Some of them rubbed themselves with oil and contemplated with satisfaction the sunburnt even bronze of their skin. Sunburn was the fashion.

They were enjoying the summer, but it was different for us. Though indeed at that time I was incapable of feeling anything except fatigue. If I had not been roused at seven o'clock I would not have got up; if the warder whose duty it was to take the prisoners out for a walk had not opened the cell door requesting me to go for ten minutes down to the stinking prison-yard, I would not have left my plank bed. When I returned to the cell I hastened to take off my dress and lie down again with nothing but my shift on.

The wardresses tried to remonstrate with me.

"Why aren't you dressed?"

"It's too hot."

"And what if the chief warder comes in?"

"You'd warn me and I would slip my dress on."

"It's not allowed."

"It's not forbidden. There's nothing about it in the regulations."

They would go away closing the peep-hole with a snort of contempt or without any show of feeling. They knew it was not easy to come to terms with those who had been in prison for some time and were sick and weary of the daily routine.

The only active occupation I engaged in was killing flies. In the course of two or three hours as many as forty or sixty would get into the cell, which was only as big as two good-sized graves. They were simply unendurable: they crawled over one's face and body, over the bed, the pillow, the walls. But it was not easy to make up one's mind to fight them: in the first place, it required moving about and, secondly, I had no weapon but my own hand. I had to hold my palm right over a fly and gradually bring it nearer. If the fly was cleaning its wings, there was no need to hurry, but if it began crawling I had to strike at random. On the whole I had 75 per cent of success, but it was not a pleasant job.

I had some altercations with the wardresses about that too.

"Why are you knocking?" the wardress would ask.

"I am not knocking, I am killing flies."

"Knocking is not allowed."

"Look in and see what I am doing."

Not knowing what to do she would go away, but hearing that I was going on, would come back again.

"Stop killing flies!"

"Why, is it forbidden?"

"No, it isn't, but you mustn't make a noise. I'll call the chief warder."

"Do. You see, here I've killed fifty-eight this morning, let him look at them," I answered unconcernedly, pointing to the small iron table on which the flies I had killed lay in rows. "I shall make it up to a hundred by the evening, and will ask you to give them to my examining officer."

At this she shut the peep-hole in alarm and disappeared for fear of complications which might tell on her and not on me.

One afternoon when I was lying down exhausted by the heat and by my battle with the flies, the key rattled in the door. It was most unusual, for at that hour one was never called up to be examined, nor were any new prisoners brought in. I slipped on my dressing-gown, annoyed at the thought of an intruder. In solitary confinement one actually developes a sense of property.

The door opened and closed again. The key was still rattling in the lock when I raised myself lazily to see who it was. At the same moment the woman who had just been pushed into my cell staggered back hugging her little suitcase with a gesture of dismay. Her fright gave me a shock before I had had time to grasp who she was.

"It's you?" she brought out like a stifled sigh.

"Yes," I answered absent-mindedly as I desperately groped my way through a crowd of memories, trying to discover who she was.

"Murka . . ." I suddenly remembered her name. We were at school together. She was one of the girls not in our 'set,' and for some reason we despised her and used to snub her. She chummed with other girls whom we 'could not stand.'

"You gave me a fright," she said with a smile, as she recovered herself.

"Why?"

"I've always been afraid of you."

"That was about thirty years ago, wasn't it?"

She gave a wry smile.

"I tell everyone that I am only thirty."

"Well, you might be," I said, scrutinising her unceremoniously from old habit.

She had a strange face. It did not seem young, but there were no lines on it. Her skin was fine and smooth and looked as though it had been stretched. Her eyebrows were narrow black lines. I recalled that as a child she had fair eyebrows and brown dishevelled hair. Now her hair was auburn and beautifully waved. Her figure was slim and youthful.

Now I began to remember: there had been a row at school because of her. She used to bring Madame Verbitsky's and Nagrodsky's novels to read surreptitiously during lessons, and the German mistress caught her at it. When she was smaller her mother used to come for her, also always dishevelled but with a coquettish veil on her battered hat. We called her Madame Sloven. It all came very clearly before my mind now, as childish memories do.

"Have you been here long?" I asked, hesitating between my old, instinctive habit of snubbing her and a desire to feel pleased at meeting a relic of my far-away childhood.

"I've been in the common cell," she answered, as

though avoiding my question. But that might have been just her manner. She always was a bit vague.

"How is it I haven't seen you walking in the yard?"

"So you climb on the window and look?" she said, pleased at being able to joke me.

"I climb on the window and look."

"How often have you been left without a walk for doing it?"

"Once, for three days."

"So you dodge them?"

"I do."

She cheered up, but apparently recalling my question which she had not answered, decided to clear up the matter.

"No, I haven't seen you either, I must have been in another wing of the prison."

"That's strange," I thought. "I don't believe there are any common cells in other wings—and she says she's been transferred from a common cell." But I decided not to press the point for she had always been muddle-headed.

"What did they arrest you for?" I asked sympathetically.

"For going abroad," she answered readily. "I went there to learn beauty culture. One must have a profession nowadays, you know. I used to be a typist, but that doesn't pay. If you don't let them make love to you, the Party men won't let you earn anything for overtime—if they don't turn you out of your job altogether. And if you do have any truck with them, there is simply no end to it. The law is supposed to punish them for 'taking advantage of their official position' and for 'social degeneration,' but if you try to get rid of such gallants they'll accuse you at once of bourgeois psychology. And besides, one needs stockings, scent, powder, shoes. A decent pair of shoes costs 200-250 roubles and a typist's salary is 60-80 roubles a month."

"But you've learnt beauty culture now?"

"Yes I have. Fine, isn't it?"

She turned to me with a so-called 'charming' smile, showing me her face.

"Would you like me to smooth out all your wrinkles?"

"Thanks, they'll go of themselves in prison."

"But you won't be in prison all your life, they'll let you out some day."

"To Solovki?"

"Why? Don't quarrel with the examining officer. I expect you do your best to plague him, as you did the science mistress. I can well imagine it! But being hoity-toity is no use, you know."

I listened in surprise to the lively and insolent way in which she said things that are regarded as a very bad sign in prison—a sign of having been prompted by the examining officer.

"What about yourself? Is it for not being hoity-toity that you are here?" I asked sharply.

"Oh, with me it's different," she said lightly. "I've been caught red-handed: dealing in foreign goods. But how can one give beauty treatments without foreign goods? You wouldn't have a single commissar's wife for a client. Have you seen them dyeing hair with Soviet dyes? You mean the hair to be golden and it turns out purplish, you want platinum blonde and it looks greenish. And scent! Do you know what Soviet scent is like?" she asked dramatically.

"No, I haven't tried it."

"Too awful for words! But if you have Origan,
Quelques Fleurs or even Sourire de Paris—you can
worm yourself in anywhere. I paid for my trip abroad
by smuggling in two large bottles of scent."

"Was it then you were caught?"

"No, later, when I had to buy some here from
private hands. '*They*' use their agents as salesmen."

We were silent. I was tired of her chatter. Her
story was not new to me—it was just the way silly
women were caught. She sat examining her nails and
putting some finishing touches to her manicure.

"Won't you tell me something about yourself?" she
asked presently.

"There'll be plenty of time for that. It's so hot.
The flies are too much for me," I answered lazily,
though according to prison etiquette I was in debt
to her: she had apparently told me a good deal about
herself and I had told her nothing as yet.

She stretched her hand for a book lying on the seat.

"Take the other, on the shelf there. This one is a
bore."

"*A Collection of Speeches by Lenin*—do you call that a
bore? Perhaps you think it rubbish, too? You intellectual
women are above that sort of thing, aren't you?" she
asked ironically.

"Out of prison Lenin's speeches may not be a
bore, but here they are worse than boring. . . ." I
suddenly felt so angry that words failed me. "They
are sheer hypocrisy! To hang portraits of Karl Marx
and Rosa Luxemburg in the vile dirty cellar where
they receive parcels for prisoners. . . . Here, in
solitary confinement cells, we may have four books

in ten days and one of them must be about Marxism and Leninism. A nice place for studying the subject!"

"So you are against Marx and Lenin?" she asked, glancing at me with sudden interest.

"I am against those who make prison and penal servitude a consequence of their teaching."

"How did you put it? It sounds very clever!"

"Idiot!" I cut her short in the way I used to at school, though I knew it was I who was an idiot. I was thoroughly done up, my nerves were on edge, and I was saying things which should not be said aloud even to oneself.

She gave an offended snort. I threw off my dressing-gown and began douching myself with water from the tap, splashing on to the asphalt floor and making a wet mess all round. The water was warm and horrid and came in a thin trickle, but anyway it helped me to recover my balance.

"Let us have tea," I invited her, when I had finished splashing.

"I have no tea," she answered in an injured voice. "I have nothing at all, I receive no parcels from home."

"You poor thing! Take that empty mug. I saved up some tea from this morning; there's enough for two. Come to the table."

She moved on to the iron stool. I swept the flies off the table, spread a towel over it, brought out the bread and the sugar. I was sorry to have offended her.

"Wait a minute, I'll treat you to something nice—salted cucumbers! Freshly salted, awfully good."

She gave a bewildered smile, not knowing what to make of the change in my tone.

"You see, I salt the cucumbers myself. We may now receive fresh cucumbers in our parcels, but they turn bitter and flabby the very next day. I hid away a soup bowl left by my last neighbour and now I salt cucumbers in it. All you have to do is to pour in some water and put as much salt as you can spare. Taste it. Only, there's nothing to cut it up with. You have to bite."

I was doing my best to entertain her but she was silent. I grew more and more friendly and began telling her something pleasant that had nothing to do with the prison. She was smiling absent-mindedly. I could not think what was the matter with her. Could she have been so hurt by my calling her an idiot? But no doubt her nerves too were affected by prison.

"It is my name-day to-day," she brought out with an effort at last.

"So it is! July 22nd.* And it's my wedding day! Well, we're both down on our luck. Let me give you some 'fancy cake'—they've taught me here how to make it, look," and I showed her how to soak in tea some dried apricots, put them on slices of white bread and sprinkle them with sugar.

We were allowed to receive in our weekly parcels one small white loaf and 1 lb. of dried fruit. It was a great luxury because it was very difficult to obtain and fearfully expensive.

"Do you like it? Do have some more. I still have three prunes left. We may as well have a treat!"

But Murka suddenly dropped her head on the table, her shoulders twitched, and there was a bubbling in her throat—all the miserable symptoms of a fit of hysterics.

* The day of St. Mary Magdalen.

"Stop it! Don't be silly!" I said sternly and stood with my back to the door so as to close the peep-hole with my head: I could not endure to have wardresses interfering with our emotional upsets.

Murka threw back her head and was on the point of screaming but I stopped her in time.

"Be quiet! If you must, speak in a whisper. Sh-sh! Don't scream."

"I can't, I can't" she muttered, pressing her handkerchief to her lips.

"What is it you can't? Talk sensibly, only don't shout. Don't make a scene.'

"You, you don't know, you don't understand," she stammered, looking frightened.

"There's a lot of things I don't know, but that isn't a reason for you to get hysterical. You can tell me now or presently, but first have a gulp of tea and pull yourself together."

This was not the first attack of hysterics I had seen in prison.

"It's you, it's you who are an idiot! You don't understand that I am a spy. I've sold myself to the G.P.U. And you, you offer me your last, entertain me like a visitor, and may any moment blurt out something you should keep to yourself. And to-morrow they'll call me up and question about you, and I'll gorge myself at the G.P.U. buffet. What am I to do? Good God, what am I to do? I can't stand it, I can't stand it!" She was utterly beside herself.

"First of all, don't scream, it won't help anyone. Talk sensibly. You work for the G.P.U.?" I grasped the situation at last.

"Yes."

"Since when?"

"I don't remember."

"That's not true, but it doesn't matter. How did they get hold of you?"

"I wanted to go abroad. I wanted to escape, never to return to this misery, squalor, filth, horror . . ."

"Don't begin to scream. Did you apply for permission to go abroad?"

"Apply indeed! As though they let many out! Most of us have to make up to 'them,' go into cafés, drink. Please don't look so reproachful. There's nothing terrifying in that: G.P.U. officers are often far more civilised than the Communists, our delightful superiors. That's how they get hold of one, the damned brutes, the blackguards . . ." she added in a changed voice.

"Wait a bit! So you did go abroad?"

"I did."

"Why did you come back?"

"Because of my little girl. My mother is old, untidy, silly, cannot do a thing. They were not allowed out of the country. I thought I would go back, see how things were and somehow contrive to take them away, but, instead, I got myself entangled."

"How do you mean, entangled?"

"They caught me selling scent. They threatened me. They made me give information about my clients. Everyone talks too much. It isn't my fault that women talk, that they give themselves away. Why should I bother about them?"

"But how did you get here?"

"How can I tell! As though I knew 'their' minds! They want to show their power, I suppose, to tighten the noose! It's tight enough already! They can rejoice at their handiwork. Here I've stumbled upon you, what am I to do now? Why are you cross-examining me? What right have you?"

"Don't shout," I interrupted her. "I am not cross-examining you but merely asking questions so that you shouldn't have hysterics. That would be the last straw. Be quiet, do you hear the wardress behind the door?"

I began pacing up and down the cell, lingering by the door as I turned so as to prevent the wardress peeping in. Murka sat with her head thrown back, stiffly leaning against the wall. Her face looked old and crumpled.

At last the wardress could not resist poking her nose into the peep-hole.

"What's the matter with you?" she asked, staring at Murka.

"Bring some valerian drops," I said, still pacing up and down the cell. It was the only medicine that could be had on demand.

She went away, angrily slamming the peep-hole shutter. Wardresses are inquisitive and like to be talked to, though it is forbidden.

Murka sat in silence in a stiff, strained attitude. I walked six paces one way and six another, counting my steps: 230, 231, 232. . . . When I had counted 598 the wardress came back, opened the peep-hole and thrust in the medicine glass. I gave it to Murka. She swallowed the drops.

"Tell them I must see the doctor," she said to the wardress, who was expectantly gazing through the peep-hole waiting for the glass to be returned to her.

It is not allowed to leave glass objects in the cell lest

the prisoners should break and eat the glass; this is done sometimes, especially by common criminals. 'Intellectuals' prefer to sever their veins with the glass.

The wardress went away. Murka sat as though turned to stone, staring past me at the wall. I was walking up and down the cell, counting my steps. Seeing a doctor was a complicated business, and I had counted more than a thousand when the key rattled in the lock. Murka went out without a glance at me. Her suitcase lay on the bed till the evening when the wardress came to take it away. In prison no explanations are given, so I did not waste words asking where my neighbour had been transferred. And why, indeed, should I care to know what became of Murka? In the conditions of Soviet life her fate is by no means an exception.

SONYA

It was the First of May, 1931. On the eve of that day I lay peacefully on my prison bed, half asleep, reflecting with an extraordinary sense of comfort how nice it was to be alone in the cell. I had been sharing it with a woman who was seriously ill and she had just been removed. I was thinking that on May 1 the examining officers would be busy attending meetings and, like everybody else, be marching 'in serried ranks' or keeping watch over the behaviour of free citizens, and that consequently we in prison would be left in peace for a day. But nearly at midnight the light was switched on in my cell and the key rattled in the lock. The 'noseless' wardress came in. This woman with her sunken-in nose and nasal voice seemed to be always after me.

"Pack up," she said in a whisper. "No, not going home," she added humanely, understanding that a holiday night like this might inspire me with a sudden hope in proletarian mercy.

It was a nuisance to turn out of the cell to which I had grown used. I knew when the sun came into it, when the shadows began to fall on the wall opposite; I had washed the floor in it, the walls, the window-sill, the wash-basin—all this means a great deal in prison.

I was taken to a damp cell downstairs which had obviously been occupied by a man: the cell was disgustingly dirty and recking of tobacco.

As soon as the door closed after me I heard noise and stamping on the stairs. Someone had been brought in, a frightened and pitiful woman's voice was heard, and the wardress's 'sh-sh!' A key rattled, and there were more footsteps on the stairs. As they drew nearer I could tell there were two men, both drunk. Their feet caught at every step and they stumbled backwards. "Let go, you ——" swore one of them in choicest language. "Leave me alone." Another voice interrupted him, speaking thickly, "Do you think I'm drunk? Drunk? You think I've been abusing the Soviets? You think you can do what you like with a drunken man? he asked defiantly, and then, changing his tone, went on: "My dear fellow, comrade, citizen, do you hear, I am a working man. God is my witness, I'm a workman, a proletarian . . ."

It was clear they had been celebrating the First of May and using strong language about the Soviet Government. Evidently the G.P.U. officials did not relax their vigilance even on holidays.

It was disgusting to listen to their swearing, to lie on the filthy mattress, to think that in Soviet life one could not have an hour's respite.

The following morning there was a disturbance during the walk. The warder was taking us out in larger batches than usual so as to finish with the job the sooner. When he let me out on to the gallery and went up to the next floor to fetch another prisoner, a woman, followed by a sentry, ran up the staircase from the floor below, screaming. When the sentry tried to seize her she threw herself on the floor and leaning back against the wall began to kick. A wardress rushed up to her, the warder who was taking me out ran up to me shouting,

"Go back!" but before he had had time to lock me up I had a good look at the 'fresher.' The type was unfamiliar to me. Young and thin, she looked like a girl in her teens; her hair, waved in small curls, was dishevelled; she was wearing a silk dress of a particularly crude shade of green, a lilac shawl, pink stockings and cream-coloured shoes.

I could not tell by the sounds what became of her. When I was led out of my cell again there was a dead stillness all round. The warders were very clever at covering up all traces of any disturbance.

Some three weeks passed by. It was evening. The sun was setting. I could see the red glow on the windows of the prison wing opposite. The sun scarcely came at all into the cell that I was in. I was slowly collecting my washing, thinking of my boy who would come the following day to the prison to fetch it and bring me things which would be to me a token of his care and affection. The key rattled in the lock—but again my hopes were dashed to the ground!

The girl whom I saw on the First of May was pushed into my cell. She was again sobbing, screaming, banging her head against the bed and kicking with her feet in the cream-coloured shoes. The shoes were the last word of fashion, with high heels, pointed toes and ornamental stitching. They must have cost at least 250 roubles. But they were all that was left of her once smart attire: the dress looked shabby and bedraggled, the stockings were torn. She wore a red cotton kerchief on her head.

"Would you like a drink of tea? I have some cold tea left," I offered by way of soothing her.

"Much do I care for tea, and cold tea at that!" she

shouted, sitting up on the bed and staring at me inso-
lently with tears still flowing from her eyes. "Nice sort
of neighbours they give one! In hospital I had no peace
from the likes of you. I am sick of your politeness,
damnation take you all, you——" and she flung a
stream of abuse at me.

She certainly had a rich vocabulary.

"Locking me up with an old woman!" she went on
hysterically. "I'll die of boredom! Prison is bad
enough, and to have neighbours like that into the
bargain! There's no end of you here, you damned
intellectuals. Not a living soul to talk to."

She threw herself on the bed again, burying her face
in the tiny parcel of her belongings.

I sat opposite her thinking that it was rather unexpected, but that it was probably only fair that
she should loathe my presence quite as much as I
did hers. And there certainly was something loathsome
about her.

Young, rather pretty but sickly looking, slightly
crooked, with rotten teeth and an unclean smell about
her she somehow suggested a bit of garbage.

"Why don't you say anything?" she shouted at me
again.

"Why should I talk to you if you swear at me?" I
answered, understanding that it was no use being nice
to her.

"I like swearing — I've done it all my life," she
answered in a more friendly voice.

"Not a very long life, is it?"

"Twenty years, but I expect I've seen more than you
have. In the old days you people were as good as kept
in cold storage.

"Not a bad way of putting it," I thought, and said smiling, "Anyway, I've preserved my teeth."

"Your teeth? That's because you haven't been starved as a child. And I grew up in the famine years. Don't you remember what it was like in 1920? I had two teeth pulled out while I was in prison and those that are left are all rickety," she said, thrusting her dirty fingers into her mouth and speaking in quite a friendly tone. "My life was very different from yours. My mother was a washerwoman. Do you know what it's like when you can hardly breathe for steam?"

"And what is she now?"

"She is a washerwoman still. But she doesn't earn anything like what she used to, and the firewood is so dear now. And there is no soap."

"Have you had any schooling?"

"Schooling, indeed! Not much good in that when one is hungry all the time. Mother did send me to school, but I stayed away. It was so cold there and uninteresting. I did go in sometimes during the break to play with the boys. And I went to school dances too, but not to any of their meetings. Sheer waste of time."

She stood up, stretched herself and sang scarcely audibly in a clear and musical voice.

"A pussy-cat has four legs
And a long tail behind . . . "

"What's that?" I asked, surprised at the change in her moods.

"I can dance the foxtrot, too. Can you?"

"No."

"You don't know the foxtrot! What's the good of

letting you out of here when you know nothing? Prison is the place for you. Miserable old woman, that's what you are, rotten gentry!" She grew spiteful again.

"Who is rotten?" I asked, not grasping the full implications of the word.

"Well, what if I am? Yes, I've got syphilis right enough. Are you frightened? You'll see plenty more like me in prison. There are five of us and we are all ill with it. It's that cursed Manka infected us all through our husbands."

"Are you married?"

"Yes, it's my third marriage. I'm simply crazy over my Mishka. My sweetie, my ducky, my lovely baby! He is quite a highbrow, you know; he can speak German. He is very clever," she said with conviction.

"Is he in prison, too?"

"Of course. It's through him we've all been nabbed."

"What for?"

"It's clear enough. For ration cards. We started a fine piece of business between us. Might have made our fortunes! We made a good fifteen thousand roubles a day or more," she boasted.

"That's a lot."

"Not at all. This was how it was: One evening we had nothing to do . . . and my Mishka thought it all out, clever lad that he is. You see, a friend of his, Karlushka, was a Government clerk and it was his job to carry freshly printed ration cards for clothes and manufactures from the printers to the office. So my Mishka said to him, no one counts those cards, you give me a packet or two. So they took the cards and wrote different names and addresses in them—looked them up in the telephone book. And of course they put

the names of the co-ops in which the card holders were
to get the goods. Then they kept watch on the different
co-ops to see which of them had any goods to sell, and
as soon as we found out we all went and took our places
in the queue. We got whatever was being sold—stockings, galoshes, overcoats, dress materials—and took it
straight away to the free market. At the co-op we paid
80 copecks or a rouble for a pair of stockings and we
sold them for 10 or 12 roubles. For an overcoat we
paid 100 roubles and we sold it for 500. People were
only too glad to buy."

"How long did you carry on?"

"For two months. An American gave us away."

"What American?"

"Don't you understand?" she laughed. "An American is a man who does all sorts of clever business. And
that one was a G.P.U. agent as well. He gave us all
away. He did it on the First of May, just when new
goods are sent to the co-ops and people are more likely
to buy. My Mishka was so hard worked that he sometimes did not come home at night. But we did have
some fun, too! As soon as we had any cash, off we went
to the Hotel Europe. Have you been there?"

"No."

"Why, you know nothing, nothing at all! Absurd
that you should have got into prison. We at any rate
have seen something of life. We did some foxtrotting
anyway! It was lovely fun. Such luxury! Palms,
flowers. Waiters serve at table, and so polite, too—not
like in common dining-rooms. And such a lot of
foreigners! I danced with one. He wasn't very young,
but ever so smart. He was an Englishman, I believe, or
perhaps a German."

I wondered what his impression of Russian women could have been after that.

"When we had finished dancing he took me to his room and showed me his little daughter sleeping there. Pretty like a doll she was! Mishka and I also took a room there once or twice. Such luxury, carpets, mirrors, and everything so clean. They give you scented soap. Foreign make, I believe. I could not resist stealing a piece and Mishka laughed and said that in the old days one could have bought a truckload of soap for the price of our room and supper. They simply fleece one there. But anyway, it's life, and a bookworm like you knows nothing about it."

The girl and I spent more than two months in the same cell. At first not a day passed without her flying at me with abuse, but afterwards I learned to manage her. She told me with relish her whole life story. First came the dances at which she used to secure the best partners—hooligans like herself or young University students, especially those fresh from the country. Then came her marriages. Her first husband was a hairdresser who won her heart by his skill at doing ladies' hair 'like a picture,' inserting eyelashes and shaving armpits. But he turned out to be jealous and a drunkard, so that she had to have her hair done by others. "It did not pay at all," she said seriously, summing up her first marriage.

After that she had casual connections, her chief requirement being that the man should dance well, take her out to dances and not be jealous. One of her admirers took her to a dining-room where they made friends with the girl cashier; suddenly the cash desk was robbed and 'the wretch' was so angry with them that she gave them both away to the police and they had the greatest difficulty in getting off. With another man she used to sleep for the simple reason that he had a nice bed and a wardrobe with a mirror. But one day he missed some of his belongings and drove her away, "though what had I to do with it?"—she remarked; "there were plenty of lodgers in the flat."

She tried to work in a factory but was not strong enough and it was difficult to get up in time for the buzzer after dancing all night. Once she got a job in a confectioner's shop. She liked it very much because she could eat sweets ("though if one is hungry, one can't eat many, it makes one sick," she explained) and weigh out generous portions for all her friends and relatives. But soon there were no sweets left, the shop was ordered to sell soap instead, and almost all the saleswomen were dismissed.

Almost every one of her stories ended in a sharp attack on me: she wanted to prove that she was a proletarian and a working woman, and I invariably pulled her up and pointed out that there was nothing 'proletarian' in her ideas and conduct.

"Fancy your sticking up for the working class!" she protested angrily. "In any case you are the old régime and I—the new. It wasn't for you that the revolution was made, so naturally you don't fit in. But me the Soviets have to reckon with, because I am what they made me."

"But here we are both in prison," I remarked ironically.

"There's nothing in that. The point is which of us will be let out."

There was a great deal of truth in her words. I do not

know what was the G.P.U. officer's idea in putting her into my cell, but she certainly made my prison life worse and taught me to understand many peculiarities of the Soviet system. She had been brought up to believe that in a socialistic state the right to live belonged to her because she had grown up since the revolution, because she was a washerwoman's daughter and had worked for a few weeks at a factory. It was of no consequence that she was morally worthless and utterly ruined by the régime which encourages the worst features of the young generation; her self-confidence was unbounded. She was certain that she could do anything with impunity. It was impossible to make her understand that one ought to have a sense of duty or at least an elementary conception of honesty. What for? In order to sit idly in prison? She had enough brains to grasp the absurd position of the 'intellectuals' whose behaviour was a living reproach to her.

If I had not had daily intercourse with this new type created by the revolution I could not have believed that such people existed. And however much she deceived me, got me into trouble with the warders, cheated me and stole from me, I could never keep pace with her ingenuity, for I still felt that she was a fellow-creature. But for her I was 'a bourgeois,' a 'class enemy,' whom she had been taught to regard with hatred and contempt. And just when I imagined that she could not take me in any more, she played some fresh trick upon me. This was what she did shortly before I was let out.

It happened in the evening, before the roll call. The wardresses who had been on duty for hours were tired and relaxed their vigilance. Distinct sounds of tapping came from the floor above: 4.2—3.4—3.3—6.3—Sonya,

Sonya. That was my neighbour's name. In the prison
alphabet each letter is represented by several knocks.
She was so utterly incapable of concentration that she
had not fathomed the alphabet, though it was scratched
in three places on the walls of our cell.

"Sonya, Sonya," the tapping went on nervously,
insistently. I did not know what to do. Perhaps it was
her husband tapping, perhaps he was in the cell above
us. If such happiness fell to my lot! One might go mad
with joy.

"Sonya, Sonya."

Should I tell her? She did not know how to tap; I
would have to help her and she would be sure to play
me some nasty trick afterwards.

The tapping grew so desperate that to me it sounded
like a scream. Sonya, who did not understand any of it
was alarmed.

"What is it? Who is knocking?"

"The knocking means 'Sonya,'" I could not resist
saying.

"That's Mishka! That's my Mishka knocking! For
God's sake, dear, precious one, knock, tell him that I
am here, quick!"

I hesitated. I was angry with her because she had
just torn off a corner of the red binding of Herzen's
My Past and Thoughts in order to rouge her lips with it,
and I had said that as a punishment I would not speak
to her for the next twenty-four hours. One had to have
some means of keeping her in order.

At any other time she would have snapped her fingers
at my pedagogic measures, but now she stood in desperate need of me. She gazed at the wall from which
the knocking came like one spellbound, and, instantly

deciding that I must open that wall for her, she threw
herself at my feet and began kissing my knees, my dress.
My hands I wisely hid behind my back.

"Knock! I will do everything for you! Make haste
and knock! I will do everything, scrub the floor, wash
your clothes! You needn't speak to me for a week if you
don't want to, but knock now!"

"Sonya is here," I tapped.

A rapid succession of taps came by way of an answer.

"Can you make it out? What is he saying, what?"

"Sit down. Be quiet and listen."

"Sonya," I translated with intervals as though to
dictation, counting the knocks with strained attention.
"The case is finished—I've got five years—Very good—
Don't worry—They may let you out—Don't babble—
I confessed—I am going to the penal camp—Don't be
sad—Goodbye—How are you?"

"Tell him, ask him, where is his watch? A platinum
watch. Did they take it away from him? Ask, quick!"

"Sonya is well," I tapped in reply, repeating the
words aloud to her.

"His watch, ask him where is his watch?" she pes-
tered me. "Will they take it from him? Ask him at
once."

I was disgusted. The man was going to penal servitude, he was saying goodbye to her, and she had not a
good word to say to him!

"Where is your watch?" I tapped.

"Watch?" he repeated, evidently not grasping what
was meant. Then he understood and answered:

"When I return I'll get my own back—Goodbye—
Kisses—Don't knock any more—Goodbye—Take care
of yourself—Kisses."

The tapping ceased.

"He didn't say what became of his watch?" she pounced on me. "Knock again! Ask him! Such an expensive watch! What could he have done with it?"

"I mustn't knock any more. Don't you hear that the wardresses are changing?"

"Oh, you won't knock, you are funking it, you mangy devil! You stuck up beast! You won't take the trouble to knock! You damned prig! Very well, I'll do without you."

She began knocking senselessly, mixing up the figures, making no intervals, stupidly imitating what she had just heard. It was impossible to understand her knocking.

A wardress who had just come on duty, one of the worst ones we had, was walking up and down the corridor. Mishka hastily tapped "Be quiet!" I translated it to her, hoping it would bring her to reason.

"Oh, indeed! 'Be quiet!' When he knocks I've got to listen, and when I want to speak he shuts me up," she muttered, going on with her tapping.

"You will get us all into trouble. Stop!" I begged her, though I was not very hopeful. But there was nothing for it. She did not listen. I sat down at the table with my back to the wall so that the wardress could not tell by my face, as she peeped in, that I had been expecting her look of malicious triumph.

There it was: the spy-hole opened. A horrid hissing voice trained to be toneless asked:

"What are you doing?"

Sonya turned round. She was beside herself with agitation, anger and disappointment.

"You were tapping?" the wardress asked hypocritically, pressing her foxy face to the opening. "To whom? You won't answer? Very well, you'll speak to the head warder."

She shut down the spy-hole with an ominous click and went away. Sonya sat utterly bewildered, not knowing on whom to vent her resentment. She had not the slightest sense of being in the wrong. It would have been useless to ask her not to give me away.

The wardress returned with the head warder in an astonishingly short time. It was her opportunity to distinguish herself and to prove her vigilance.

The head warder stalked menacingly into the cell. His boots were polished brightly and he reeked of cheap scent.

"Who was tapping?" he asked, turning to Sonya.

"She was," she squeaked, pointing at me with her finger.

"You?" the head warder asked still more angrily turning to me.

"Yes."

"To whom?"

Sonya fidgeted on her bed. She understood that she could not put the whole thing down to me and was quaking with fear.

"I say, I didn't mean to, forgive me, I did it just for a lark, I don't know how to do it properly."

"Then it was you who tapped?" the head warder turned to her again.

"Not really, I didn't mean to, I just wanted to try," she faltered.

"Who taught you? she asked in a tone that gave her a hope of mercy.

"She did," Sonya brought out immediately, pointing at me. He knew perfectly well that Sonya's husband was in the cell above. The incident was of small interest to him: my doing a service to a common criminal— to the so-called 'socially-near element' could not be much of a charge against me. For me the whole question was, would he punish me by forbidding parcels from home. If he did it would frighten and grieve my boy. To think that I had exposed him to it for the sake of that woman!

"Three days without a walk for both," he said indifferently, and sharply turning on his heels walked out of the cell.

The wardress pursed up her lips: she had hoped for more. I was glad: I was ready to put up with anything in prison so long as my son did not know of it. The walk did not matter in the least.

Cheered up, I decided to explain to Sonya how badly she had behaved.

"Tell me, have I done you a service?" I asked her ironically.

"Well, what if you have?"

"Why, then, did you try to get me into trouble?"

"And what of it? You didn't expect me to take the blame on myself, did you? You've said yourself it's wrong to tell lies."

"But whose affair is it all, yours or mine?"

"You leave me alone! Sticking to one like a leech! Much it matters—the lady has been left without her walk, if you please! As though I cared a damn about you! Preaching at me, you ——."

And she went on pouring out torrents of abuse at me. As I listened to her vile language I reflected with dismay that so far from being the only one, she was merely a sample of the new type produced by the revolution.

A POLITICAL PRISONER

ONE of the peculiarities of the Soviet régime is the Government's love of change. They enjoy altering names and moving their offices from one place to another. A special Re-naming Committee had to be formed which provided food for numberless anecdotes. When Petrograd was changed to Leningrad various institutions were re-named accordingly, and Petrographic Institute became Leninographic Institute, because it had not occurred to the authorities that petrography, the science of stones, had nothing to do with Peter the Great. The Voznesensky Prospect had no sooner been re-named Mayorov Street than Mayorov proved to be an *agent provocateur*. Vladimirsky Prospect was changed to Nahimson's Street, and tram conductors called out at the stopping place by the church 'Nahimson's church.' A Communist member of the Re-naming Committee told me that some of the proposals they had to consider were even more picturesque. Thus it was suggested that the Tchernigov Cold Storage Depot should be renamed 'Cold Storage of the Proletarian Dictatorship.'

Various institutions were continually moved from place to place, though it was very difficult to find fresh accommodation. When this proved utterly impossible, the authorities had to be content with shifting the different departments. I remember, at the Hermitage,

we wasted several months in rearranging all the study
rooms and most of the special subjects' libraries and
belongings; bookcases purposely fitted to the walls a
hundred years before had to be broken down, and the
result of it all was that many of the study rooms
proved to be within half an hour's walk from the
picture galleries.

I was very much surprised to find that this law of
change applied to prison also. I had thought that
solitary confinement meant being thoroughly wedded
to one's cell. But not a month passed without the
prisoners being shifted from one cell to another. Those
from the common cell were put into the solitary
confinement cells or vice versa. Sometimes it was done
by the examining officer, but for the most part by
head warders who were changed every month so as
not to have time to get into touch with the prisoners.
Each new man thought it necessary to show his energy
and to re-shift the prisoners. It was always done at
night, in a fearful hurry, with shouts, jeers and a
certain amount of swearing if we were not instantly
ready, though all it amounted to was moving to another
floor. The way it was done was always insulting and
humiliating and brought home to us afresh our utter
helplessness and dependence upon somebody else's
arbitrary whim; but the actual change was a good
thing, for it introduced us to new neighbours and
widened our prison horizon. Besides, every change
inevitably resulted in a muddle: we received other
prisoners' parcels by mistake, were called up to be
examined instead of some other person, and in this
way each time we learned something new which was
a little distraction in the deadly prison existence.

And so it happened that after being in a cell by

myself I was transferred to one which had another occupant. She was none too pleased by my arrival.

"Damn it all, they bring people in the night as though day was not long enough!" she grumbled. "It's never been done in any decent prison before. Now they'll be sure to mix you up with somebody else and wake us at nights for nothing for the next fortnight. Do they often call you up?"

"Not once for the last two months," I answered reassuringly.

"Well, that's so much to the good. Make haste and go to bed while the light is on. I'm certainly not going to talk to you at night," she announced firmly, though I had not opened my mouth. "There will be time enough for that. We aren't likely to come out of here soon, it isn't a Tsarist prison for you. I may not come out at all until they carry me out head foremost."

At that moment the light was switched off and we were left in complete darkness. I covered the dirty mattress with my sheet as best I could, curled myself up under my overcoat and tried to lie still so as not to annoy my angry neighbour. Her breath was coming in quick gasps. When twenty minutes later the light was switched on again for checking the prisoners, she threw off her dirty faded blanket with a quick, business-like movement, picked up a newspaper from the stool, wrapped up her feet in it, put another newspaper round her shoulders and covered herself with the blanket once more.

"It's for warmth," she said. "It's a good plan if one has cold feet. Those devils arrested me by fraud, strictly speaking. It's the first time I'm in prison without any belongings. I haven't a toothbrush even. I shiver like a dog under their rag of a blanket. And I am feverish, too."

When at seven in the morning the wardress thrust a broom into the cell, and I got up to sweep the floor I was struck by my neighbour's yellowish pallor. In the night she had not struck me as being particularly thin but that was because she was of broad, proletarian build. In the dim light of the morning she looked so worn out that with her eyes closed she might be taken for a corpse.

"You must forgive my not getting up to sweep the cell, but in the mornings I feel particularly rotten."

"I'll sweep it, that's nothing, but what's wrong with you?"

"I'm in consumption. It seems to have got much worse in prison. But it's not in an infectious form— —so far as that's possible, anyway," she added sarcastically. "In any case, I'll try to be careful about you. Though I can't understand why they should have thrust you into my cell. I made a row once already when they put a young girl here who might easily get infected. They took her away, but now they've sent you. I'm going to write a protest to-day."

"Don't bother. I am not afraid of infection, certainly not in your case. I've been in the same cell with a syphilitic."

"How disgusting! But you did protest, didn't you?"

"I did nothing of the kind."

"Why not?" she asked crossly.

"Because it's no use. They won't change their methods, anyway," I answered indifferently, vainly struggling to sweep the hardened dust off the old, rusty looking asphalt floor.

"There you are! Non-resistance! Just like the

intelligentsia!" she exclaimed indignantly. "Why could
we struggle against the Tsarist methods in prisons, and
you cannot struggle against the Soviet? Gaolers are
always gaolers, it's their profession. If you acted as
an organised body as we used to under the Tsars,
prison régime would be better instead of being infinitely
worse."

"Acted as an organised body!" I repeated angrily,
pushing the broom out of the door which the wardress
immediately locked. "Under Tsarism you were arrested
for organised actions, for belonging to a party which
struggled against the Government; there was a definite
charge against you, but why are we in prison now?
Because the Government arrests people wholesale, to
terrorise now one section of the population and now
another, because it knows that there are no secret
societies, no organised opposition, and makes up for
this by mass-arrests, using the argument of quantity
when it cannot find qualitatively important enemies."

At that moment the wardress thrust into the spy-hole
in the door two slices of black bread, and, to my surprise,
a pinch of tea and an ounce of sugar wrapped in paper.

"Why such luxury?" I asked.

"That's for me! I am a 'political,' " she laughed.

"But surely so am I?"

"No, my dear, you are a 'counter-revolutionary.'
You come under the Criminal Code. Only those who
belonged to revolutionary parties before the revolution
are reckoned as 'politicals.' You'll see, they'll bring
me soup with meat in it for dinner and porridge with
oil for supper. They show us some respect, you know!"

"And are there many of you?" I asked, smiling.

"A good few, it seems. Former anarchists, left-wing
Social-Revolutionaries, so called Trotskists. I've lost

touch with that set. I am afraid in prison they aren't 'organised' either."

"I confess I can't make out why they put in prison those who helped them to make the revolution."

"You are wrong there. A few of us still remember what we once believed in and have some critical thought left. The mystery is why they arrest people like you—former aristocrats, priests, tradespeople and above all intellectuals, who can offer no real opposition to the Government and are in no sense a danger to it. Prison fare is simply wasted on you."

"What about yourself?" I asked laughing.

"It's wasted on me, too," she answered with a sad smile. I liked this woman. She was a typical old Nihilist, with decisive opinions, rude speech, and curt manners. I liked her attitude towards prison. She hated and despised it, but it left her completely unconcerned, though it was obviously robbing her of what little strength she had left.

It appeared she had belonged to the bolshevik party before the revolution, but when her comrades seized the power she did not forthwith conclude that all her ideals were achieved, or regard the decisions of the Party's Central Committee as infallible. Extremely carefully and conscientiously she compared Soviet achievements with pre-revolutionary life, weighing one thing against another and invariably coming to the conclusion that victory was the worst calamity that could befall a political party.

"If you only knew what splendid people there used to be among us!" she said. "And now I feel like one lost in a forest—a forest where a scoundrel or a bandit is hiding behind every tree."

"I hope you don't say this to your examining

magistrate?" I teased her. We were always arguing or making fun of each other.

"Of course I do. I give him a regular dressing down each time he favours me with an interview."

"What for? Do you want to end your days here?"

"It's all the same where to die. It may be simpler in prison than out of it, where I have no one and nothing belonging to me, by the way. And perhaps he may remember my words one day, after all. That wretched boy would suffer from swelled head if one didn't put him in his place."

I very much wanted to know who she was and why she was in prison, but I was afraid to upset her by my questions. Her health was giving way so rapidly that she refused to go out for walks.

"What do I care about your walks?" she grumbled when I tried to persuade her to get up. "In the old days at any rate it was an hour's walk and in the Kiev prison two hours', and in the summer we were allowed to work in the kitchen-garden. And here, even if I do manage to go down for the sake of those cursed ten minutes, I'll never be able to walk up the stairs again."

One evening she was lying down and I was walking up and down the cell—six steps one way and six steps back. She was feeling better, and I asked what she had been imprisoned for before the revolution.

"For many things." She had evidently not made up her mind whether she would tell me. The habits of an old conspirator were very strong in her. "The first time I was arrested for spreading seditious literature."

"Yes?"

"Well, that's nothing interesting, everyone begins by it. I was fifteen. I came of a working-class family.

I happened to go to a secret political meeting one
day. I was fascinated by speeches about freedom
of conscience, of speech, of meetings, of the Press,
about the freedom and happiness of the people. Such
rot. . . . I was filled with hatred for the tyrants, the
oppressors, the gendarmes, the Tsar's minions and so
on, and so on. I longed to lay down my life for the
good of the people. And so one of the older comrades
commissioned me to take a parcel of proclamations to
a factory town. The papers were packed in a basket
among my text-books and copy-books, and I was to
pretend that I was going home for a holiday. I was
fearfully thrilled. My one regret was that it wasn't
bombs I was carrying. I grew quite clever at it and
smuggled in a lot till a peasant woman tracked me out.
She hated me because I was whispering with the men
and trying to cause a strike."

"Were you arrested?"

"Yes. But I wasn't even imprisoned. I was handed
over to my parents on bail. I wonder what my
comrades would do now?"

"Not long ago a number of schoolchildren have been
imprisoned for belonging to a perfectly harmless school
circle. The eldest was sixteen."

"Scoundrels. Putting children in prison makes
revolutionaries of them. That's what happened to
me when I was arrested a second time."

"What was that for?"

"I was asked to give a list of flats at the Party's
disposal to a certain member of the Party, and she
turned out to be in the service of the Secret Police.
A horrid old woman. She is still living."

"What was your sentence?" I asked with interest.

"Oh, I got off easily. I was kept at the Butyrki

prison for a bit, where, so to speak, I got my schooling:
the cells were not locked in the day-time and we used
to meet together, talk, read and argue. It was a
regular political university. After the trial I was
exiled to Viatka, not very far. What would it have
been now?"

"I doubt if there are any secret parties nowadays,
but if they suspected the least trace of one the leaders
would of course be shot and the rest sentenced to ten
years' penal servitude."

"Cruel life."

"It's a case of 'The very thing we struggled for
has proved a stumbling block.' "

Whenever we came to that point in our conversations
there was a long silence. The methods used by 'the
revolution' were a painful subject, especially to those
who whole-heartedly believed in revolutionary ideas
but condemned bolshevik practice.

When we both felt a little better I asked her:

"But that wasn't the end of your revolutionary
experience, was it?"

"Of course not. That sort of thing gets hold of one
for life. The passion for revolt, the longing for freedom,
equality and fraternity, the simple logic of oppression
being bad for the oppressors themselves—all that
becomes part of one's nature. One can't shake it off
suddenly and settle down to the humdrum existence
of ordinary people. While still in exile I picked up
the threads, and a year later I had a secret printing
press in my house. I had a notice board saying 'Dress-
making,' a sewing machine and a stand in the front
room, but in the kitchen I had a rotator hidden by a
washtub and in the cellar a printing press. When

they came to arrest me everything was found, the machine, the press, the proclamations. It was no use disclaiming it."

"Did someone give you away?" I asked.

"Perhaps, though in those days people seldom informed against us. But a revolutionary is bound to be caught sooner or later. After all, there was a secret police, poor as it was. And what is it like now?"

"Their method is different: they arrest hundreds at once and sort them out afterwards, in prison."

"That's stupid. Only two or three people were arrested with me, and they managed to get off."

"And you?"

"You know, it was all so ordinary and prosaic that it almost bores me to talk of it. I was brought here, to this very Shpalerka prison. I sat here, read books, and peacefully waited for my trial and sentence. I knew what it would be: the legal penalty was five years in the fortress; there were no extenuating circumstances, the death penalty was only applied to terrorists. And five years they gave me. My comrades provided me, as usual, with a counsel for defence, but I asked him not to waste his eloquence at the trial. The only thing he did was to give me a piece of good advice: not to answer any questions at the trial."

"How do you mean?"

"Why, Tsarist laws allowed the accused not to answer questions if they didn't want to. Isn't it the same now?"

"I don't know," I could not help laughing: old-fashioned respect for the law seemed so incongruous with the practice of the G.P.U. "I don't think anyone has ventured to try the method."

"Do you mean, they would force one to speak?"

"Perhaps—they wouldn't stand on ceremony. But the point is that if you have really committed a crime, silence may help you to conceal something—but if you haven't done anything and have to prove that there has been nothing, absolutely nothing suspicious in any of your actions, what's the sense of not speaking?"

"That's true," she agreed.

"Tell me, why did you refuse to answer at your trial?"

"You see, it would have been ridiculous to try and justify myself when all the evidence was there. But if I began to answer the judges' questions I might easily be trapped into saying something about my 'accomplices.' The only thing I could do was not to put them on anybody else's track."

"And they allowed you to be silent?"

"Why, how could they have made me speak?" she retorted indignantly. "By putting down in the protocol that the accused refused to answer? Well, they did put it down—twenty times over. As though that made any difference!"

"What was your sentence?"

"Five years in the fortress. Isn't that enough to your mind? Five years for a miserable little printing press! They were afraid of free speech, the bloated cowards!" she thundered.

"Believe me, now they would have shot you, and not you alone," I observed coldly.

"Perhaps." Her voice fell.

I understood that it was cruel of me to force those comparisons upon her. She suffered from them far more than I did. She had sacrificed her youth for the revolution and here she was imprisoned by her own comrades.

"Well, and what happened then?" I asked, knowing

that all who have been in prison love to talk about that heroic period of their lives.

"I prepared to go to the fortress, but my comrades decided to arrange my escape."

"From the Shpalerka?" I cried excitedly. I always thought this was impossible, for the prison consists of four big blocks forming a closed square.

"No, of course not," she answered, laughing at my ignorance. "No one has ever escaped from here. It was all much simpler. A friend came to see me . . ."

"Now only relatives are allowed to come, and then only in exceptional cases or before the prisoners are sent to concentration camps," I could not resist saying.

"In Tsarist days we had visitors every week, or else one's counsel for defence would make a row."

"We have no counsels for defence."

"I am sorry. I understand that all these details touch you on the raw, but I can't get rid of the idea that if one is in the same prison the prison routine must be the same."

"Alas, it isn't."

"I know. But you must see that I don't find it easy to get used to the new ways. We'd better drop the subject before we have quarrelled."

"Forgive me, I won't interrupt you any more. I really want to know how you escaped."

"I assure you there was nothing romantic about it. My friend told me to be ready and to ask, before being transferred to the fortress, to be allowed to say goodbye to my mother who could not get up from her bed of sickness."

"Was that true?"

"No. She was perfectly well, but for my sake spent

a fortnight in bed and also sent in a tearful petition. A doctor-friend gave her a suitable certificate. In short, we wangled it. The Party paid bail for me; I believe it was 2,000 roubles."

"That's not much."

"It was a great deal because it was Party money. I was against it, but, after all, five years in the fortress is no joke. Well, that was all, really. I was allowed to go and see my mother under the escort of a gendarme, a big sleepy fellow. He took me to the house, peeped into my mother's room, was abashed at the sight of an old woman in bed, and sat down to wait for me in the passage. I went out by another door, crossed the courtyard into the street, a sledge driven by one of my comrades was waiting for me and took me to the station. I was just in time for the train. For appearances' sake I was given a bouquet and a box of sweets, to say nothing of a suitcase, a passport, money and addresses of friends abroad."

"What was done to the gendarme?"

"I have no idea. We didn't bother about such people."

"And to your mother?"

"To my mother?" she repeated in surprise. "Nothing, of course. She couldn't be held responsible for me."

"Nowadays she would have answered for helping you to escape, for not informing against you and simply for being your mother."

"Nowadays the whole thing would have been impossible. Why, free citizens have more difficulty in leaving the country than prisoners like me had in the old days," she said sadly.

"Excuse me, but why are you in prison now?"

"If I tell you, I am afraid you'll say it serves me

right. I am here for my own foolishness which has nothing to do with my convictions or with politics."

"Do tell me!" I insisted, half jokingly.

"I felt home-sick abroad. I ought to have left there straight after the revolution, but I missed the right moment. You know, in bourgeois countries there are so many things to hold one. I could not very well throw up my work; then there was famine in Russia, then I was tempted to go and have a look at Italy, and in this way I lingered on till 1930."

"So you have only just returned?" I asked in surprise.

"A few months ago."

"Why, how did you manage to get into trouble so soon?"

"Now you begin to ask naïve questions like me. Don't you think it suspicious that an independent woman like me who had enough to eat, decent clothes to wear and a permanent job abroad should feel home-sick and want to become a Soviet citizen? You must admit it's queer."

"You haven't got over your youthful idealism?"

"No, I haven't. But everyone else has. And here I am in the same Shpalerka prison again. I might be enjoying my memories of it were it not for your sarcastic remarks."

"But what does the examining officer want of you?"

"He wants me to show what *real* inducement I had to return to my unlucky native land."

After that conversation we grew more friendly than ever, teasing and pitying each other as before. But I pitied her more and more because she was visibly sinking. I tried to persuade her to apply to one of her former comrades, but she crossly and obstinately refused. She considered that they ought to know who she was without being told and should not disgrace themselves by letting her die in prison. I pointed out to her that the G.P.U. might not know the old revolutionaries at all and that Party men probably had no clear idea of what the G.P.U. were doing, so that she had better write a letter to someone in power. She was hurt by the idea that no one cared about her now and that her comrades had created a 'red gendarmerie' worse than the Tsarist, but it made no difference to her determination. She declared that she would rather end her days at Shpalerka than ask to be let out.

Her fate began at last to worry the prison authorities. Wardresses inquired every day about her health, the head warder came to ask if she wanted anything; one evening a prison guard came to call her to the examining officer. She decisively refused to go saying she was too ill to get up. The man went away not knowing what to do.

Two or three hours passed. It must have been midnight. The wardress cautiously opened the peep-hole and whispered, "Get your things ready."

"I won't go," my neighbour answered loudly.

The wardress shut the peep-hole. She was evidently feeling at a loss.

"Look here, they are letting you out, you are going home!" I said, delighted on her account.

"But I haven't the strength to get up."

"I'll help you. I'll put your things together."

"No. Not to-night. And where am I to go at midnight? I'll drop dead in the street."

We lay still, but the wardress did not turn off the light and we heard her whispering with someone. A few minutes later the key rattled in the lock and she let in the head warder.

"What's the matter with you, citizen?" he asked drily.

"I can't get up. Please leave me in peace."

"But, citizen, we have an order . . ."

"Damn your order. You keep one here for months and then make a fuss about a few extra hours. I won't damage your bed by lying on it."

The head warder was utterly nonplussed. It was certainly the first case of its kind in his practice. He could find no answer and went away distinctly embarrassed. The light was turned off.

I lay in silence but could not go to sleep. I was excited by the thought that my nieghbour could get up, walk out of the prison and be free. My heart was thumping. Good heavens, if it had been me! I would have been home by two in the morning, I would have rapped at the window, wakened up my boy . . . There was still such a thing as happiness in the world!...

"Can't you understand," I heard her broken whisper in the darkness, "that life holds nothing for me? The revolution has flung open the door which I've been struggling to unfasten, but how can one enter the land of the future when prison, the G.P.U., the dictatorship and all the rest of it bar the way?"

I did not know what to say and only repeated her words in my mind till they were so firmly fixed in my memory that I could not get rid of them.

In the early morning the wardress called again and asked my neighbour something in a whisper.

"Not before eleven o'clock," she answered calmly.

I got up, gave her some tea and collected her few

belongings into a little bundle. She was conscious that the order for her release placed us poles asunder: she was a free woman and I still a prisoner. I said nothing and she watched me in silence.

After a time I helped her to dress. She put on all her clothes, her coat and hat and lay down again, exhausted.

I had always been glad to hear of anyone being released from prison, but that morning I could not suppress the feeling that it was I who ought to have been released and not she. She had worked for the revolution, her comrades were keeping up and extending the system of spying, of prisons and penal camps, so let them try the experiment on themselves—how did I come in?

When the prisoners in solitary confinement cells had returned from their walks—it must have been about eleven o'clock in the morning—the head warder, the guard on duty and a wardress came to fetch her.

"Don't you worry, comrade," the head warder reassured her gallantly. "We'll take your luggage, help you down the stairs and deliver you home in a motor-car, safe and sound."

"Wait a minute," she said peremptorily. She came up to me, pressed me warmly by the hand and, kissing me, said, "I hope that your going away from here will be happier than mine."

But her hope was not justified. A few weeks later I was set free, it is true, which is a rare piece of luck, but on the eve of my release I learned that my husband had been sentenced to five years' penal servitude and sent to the North, My heart felt as heavy as though I were exchanging one prison for another.

A G.P.U. OFFICIAL

It was my last winter in the U.S.S.R. My husband was in a penal camp and I had to help him by sending him regularly parcels of food. My son was at school, but during the five months that I was in prison he had grown pale and thin, and it was essential to feed him up. Our clothes were in a pitiable state. Every night I went to sleep and every morning I woke up with the thought "How can I raise the funds for the next parcel? How can I buy the boy a pair of shoes?" Everything I had of value had already been sold, and I was hopelessly short of money.

I decided at last to go to Murmansk and ask to have my husband's belongings returned to me. I hoped I could make something by selling them. It was not very wise to go to the place where the G.P.U. had killed my husband's comrades and very nearly had him shot as well, but I thought I would chance it.

In the carriage I lay almost all the time on the top bunk looking out of the window, though there was nothing to see. Deep drifts of snow covered everything as far as the eye could reach, and only feeble, stunted fir trees showed here and there. All the good trees had been cut down and sold abroad. It was said that the forest wealth of Karelio had been destroyed for at least the next hundred years, as trees grow very slowly so far north. The few stations were for the most part solitary, weather-beaten log huts, with no villages near and no road leading to them. At one of those stations I saw a strange sight: three coffins, two large ones and one a little smaller, stood right by the railway line. Each had a man's name and his occupation written upon it, for instance: 'Ivan Metrèyev, signalman'; 'Pavel Nikonov, a mechanic.' What did it mean? Had they been killed in a railway accident? Why were they not buried? I asked the conductor, and he laughed.

"Haven't you heard?" he said. "There's been an order that if a man makes a mess of his work, a coffin with his name on it is to be put up for everyone to see."

"And what happens?"

"Why, nothing. The coffins just stand there." The Murmansk railway was, and I believe still is, famous for its accidents. It was hastily built during the war with the intention of rebuilding it as soon as peace was made. Allowing the least possible margin of safety on the bends and inclines, it was laid through an awkward locality where frozen marshes are intersected by steep mountain ridges. In Soviet times, owing to the shortage of engines, the trains were of enormous length. Before going up a hill two extra engines were attached to the train, one in front and one behind. Some hills were climbed by letting the train run at full speed; if it did not succeed in getting to the top, it was taken back and made to gather speed once more. The most dangerous parts of the line were the sharp bends; the trains, especially goods trains, often fell down the slope. These places of frequent accidents were well known. As the train approached them, the railway staff grew extremely talkative, the passengers rushed in excitement to the windows, and the very carriages showed signs of nervousness. The engine drivers had different methods of passing these danger spots: some slowed down so that the carriages jerked and jostled one another; others went at full speed, trusting to luck. Sometimes their trust was justified and sometimes not. I travelled on the Murmansk railway nine times and was very fortunate: each time there had been a collision just before. That made our train ten or fifteen hours late—once it was nearly twenty-four hours late, but the driver was particularly careful and we eventually arrived at our destination. I have heard that not a week passes without an accident on that railway. The last time I travelled on it there was a lively discussion among the passengers as to why the Soviets did not rebuild it, instead of digging the useless White Sea-Baltic Canal. "The work could be done by the prisoners of the G.P.U. who are digging the canal, so why not? There wouldn't be a perpetual risk of accidents, anyway." This was said by a Communist workman who was sent to Murmansk 'by way of Party discipline.'

"They've forgotten to ask your opinion, I see," a fat co-operator interrupted him contemptuously. "The Government knows what it's doing."

Yes, indeed. Take Mibiny, for instance. It is a station beyond the Arctic Circle, in wild mountains, but a large party of peasants alighted from the train there. The men, many of them in bark shoes, were dressed in thin, shabby coats; the women had children with them wrapped literally in rags.

"Where are they off to?" the same discontented workman asked in surprise.

"To the Appatites," the co-operator answered indifferently.

"What are Appatites?"

"Oh, it's where they work," the co-operator explained vaguely.

"We take no end of people there," the conductor joined in the conversation. "These have come of their own accord, from hunger. They've been promised a kilo of bread a day and felt boots, so they came. But all it will come to is that they'll lose their children. The cold in the barracks is simply deadly. People live in dug-outs. But not many come here freely, it's mostly convicts; we carry trainloads of them! They say in the papers Karelia's population is growing. It's getting to be one big graveyard, that's what it is."

No one said anything. I did not explain that appatites were a rare mineral which contained phosphorus and was therefore an excellent manure. I happened to know this because in academic circles Fersman's discovery had been much ridiculed. Appatites were discovered and described at the end of the nineteenth century, but they were not exploited, because the ground beyond the Arctic Circle was hard to work in and there was no railway there at the time. Besides, in those days there were plenty of cattle in Russia and no artificial manure was needed. Knowing the bolsheviks' passion for 'discoveries,' Fersman discovered the appatites afresh, bringing the research party straight to the spot and was praised up to the skies. The Soviets decided that they would provide the whole world with appatites, and foreign money would flow into the U.S.S.R. Unfortunately the Murmansk Railway could not export the goods, and men could not do the work in the awful climate, especially as the last thing the Government troubled about was to create tolerable conditions of life for them.

The journey was supposed to last less than forty-
eight hours, but it was only on the morning of the third
day that the train climbed the last hill. The bay of
Kola lay before us, its waters black against the frozen,
rocky shore. To the right, at the bottom of a steep hill,
was the town of Murmansk. I saw it first in 1929, and
now it was 1932. During the three years a few new
buildings had been put up, but the general appearance
was just the same: houses, sheds, barracks were scattered
on the snowy slope without any plan or visible order,
with no streets in between. There were hardly any
fences and the buildings looked like wooden boxes
scattered about at random. The train drew up as before,
by the station house, built of logs. The platform was so
short that from most of the carriages the passengers had
to jump straight into the snowdrifts. As before, the
hotel greeted us with a mixed stench in which the
smells of alcohol and rotten cabbage predominated.

But this time I was not admitted into the hotel.

"No room," a huge lad who was guarding the entry
announced menacingly.

"Where am I to go, then?"

"That's your own business," he answered unconcernedly. I called at the post office to ask where I
could put up for the night and to find out, by the way,
why I was not allowed into the hotel. Something extraordinary was going on at the post office: peasant
women were washing and scrubbing the floor which
could not have been swept for the last few years. The
officials rushed about, whispering together, listened to
nothing that was said to them and seemed utterly
distracted.

"What on earth has happened?" I asked of no one
in particular.

"Mikoyan is coming to-morrow, the Commissar for Food Industries," answered one of the public.

I knew that the frantic commotion caused by the arrival of a Soviet big official made my case almost hopeless; but still I had to find refuge somewhere. There probably were people in the town who remembered me and perhaps even felt sorry for me, but I could not go to any of them—I was a convict's wife.

I went to the Fisheries Trust where my husband had worked. It had been moved to a new house. It had two storeys and looked well built, but inside the stairs were already slanting, the doors did not shut properly, the floors were dirty, the walls were covered with placards and typewritten notices, and an intolerable stench came from the lavatory.

I called on some of the Trust chiefs, but they were ridiculously alarmed at the sight of me. At last the charwoman took me in, promising to make up a bed for me on two chairs and a stool.

"You've come at the wrong time," she said sympathetically. "To-morrow Comrade Mikoyan is expected. You won't get anything done now."

"I only want to find out where my husband's things are."

"The G.P.U. has taken them all. You wouldn't go there, would you?"

"Why not?"

"They might arrest you."

"But why should they?"

"You never know. They just might. Well, here's a newspaper for you, you read what's going on here! When I've finished serving teas I'll come and tell you more."

What was going on was certainly very sad. The new

trawlers, ordered in accordance with the Five Year Plan, were arriving, but the harbour was not ready for them and the new captains who were to take charge of them had not yet finished their training. The newspapers complained indignantly that there were neither captains nor mechanics, and at the same time announced a new tremendous case against 'wreckers,' and demanded that captains whose ships had been wrecked should be dealt with 'mercilessly.' And there was a perfect epidemic of shipwrecks. During the ten years between 1920 and 1930 only one old trawler was wrecked owing to leakage and damaged steering; it landed on to the rocks, but the crew was unhurt and managed to save all the nets and tackle and even their haul of fish. But now one trawler was wrecked after another. In 1931 the trawler *Dolphin* was smashed against the rocks in the Bay of Kola. It happened while the first mate, a Communist, was on the watch. After that the captain, who did not belong to the Party, was shot. Another new trawler built in Germany, *Kasatka*, was sent to the rescue of a Soviet ice-breaker which had grounded by Nova Zemlya. The Captain refused to go because he had no navigation map of those parts; they threatened to shoot him and sent a Commissar to his ship to control him. The trawler was wrecked on the rocks by Nova Zemlya and sunk; the captain survived and was sentenced to seven years' penal servitude. Two new trawlers built in Leningrad went on their trial trip with two newly trained captains, collided, and one of them was sunk. Another new trawler left Leningrad for Murmansk and managed to collide with a trawler going from Murmansk to Leningrad for repairs; both were wrecked. In the autumn of 1931 one of the best old trawlers, under the command of a newly trained captain, was sunk with all the crew. On January 31, 1932, two new trawlers—*Dysoti* and another one with a Soviet name—perished in a storm with their crews in the Sea of Barents because the mechanics were not used to the new machinery. During the same storm some twenty-five trawlers were anchored at seven landing-stages in the bay of Murmansk, for there was no room for them in the harbour. The fierce gale carried some of them out to sea, battered them against the rocks and one another, and fifteen of them were seriously damaged. By the beginning of March the G.P.U. had drawn up 'a case' and the following day the captains, first mates and mechanics of those trawlers were to be tried. According to law, they could not be shot for a shipwreck of this kind, and so the G.P.U. charged them with *banditry*. I do not remember how the *Polar Pravda* managed to interpret as 'banditry' the men's heroic attempts to save what they could of the trawlers' equipment in that awful gale.

Another article in the same paper triumphantly declared that 'owing to the enthusiasm of the shock brigade' the *fourteenth* trawler would soon be repaired and afloat. In 1930 when my husband and his friends were arrested the Fisheries Trust had *twenty-seven* trawlers. Two of the men who had created the Trust were shot because they considered it impossible to have five hundred trawlers at work by the end of the Five Year Plan. It was unnerving to read the newspaper's bombast and to think that I was lucky as compared with the wives of the captains who were to be tried the next day: my husband had already been sentenced to five years and their husbands were threatened with the death penalty. The next day those old experienced men might be 'finished off'—to further detriment of the Trust.

"Now I've done my work and can give you some tea," said the charwoman, returning to the tiny room where she lived, got teas ready and acted as door-keeper. "You look much older," she remarked, scrutinising me sympathetically, "or is it the journey? Though of course prison doesn't improve one's looks. How long did they keep you?" she asked with a peasant woman's interest in gruesome subjects.

"Five months."

"Five months! In prison! Were you kept together with thieves?"

"I was with a thief for a time, but mostly it was with women like myself."

"With ladies, yes, of course. Anyway, it's nicer being with one's own sort. Well, my dear, what's going on here I simply can't tell you! The *Osyotr* was wrecked and all the crew was lost, every one of them. Only the captain had the sense to tie himself to a door. The door of one of the cabins had come off, it appears. He was tossed about on the sea for days, but at last the waves brought him ashore at Teriberki."

"Was he alive?"

"No, of course not. How could he be! Think of the frost. He was covered with ice all over and so disfigured that there was no recognising him. But his brother did know him all the same. He brought the body to Murmansk to be buried, and caught such a cold on the way that he could hardly stand on his feet. He buried the captain, took to his bed and died. He was taken to be buried and in the cemetery his wife—or perhaps it was his brother's wife, I don't remember—dropped dead suddenly. People ran up to her thinking she had fainted, but she was dead—heart failure. The way the women carry on when a trawler puts out to sea! They set up a proper wail; it's as good as seeing the men go to their death. All the crew are drunk. They just manage to get away from the shore and stop in another bay till the men sleep it off. And they must always leave up to time—a captain was three hours late once and got three years' imprisonment. There are hardly any captains left. When those on trial are shot there will be none to put out to sea. People say Mikoyan will stand up for them, but I think the G.P.U. will have it their own way. Will you really venture there? You must ask for Batushkina; she examined your husband and is now taking the case against those captains. The shame of it! A woman working for the G.P.U."

"I must go there, that's what I have come for," I said with a heavy heart.

On the way to Murmansk my mind was wholly occupied with the problem of rescuing my husband's belongings, selling them and taking some back to Leningrad. Now I suddenly grasped that I would have to meet the woman who ruined my husband and caused two of his friends to be shot—though she may not have been the only person responsible for it. I felt that it would be hard for me to go to the house of the G.P.U. not merely because I could be arrested there— one could be arrested anywhere and at any time—but because two years ago my husband had been examined at that house, and now two shipwrecked captains were imprisoned there. I did not know their names and had never seen them, but they were scapegoats like my husband and his friends; they, too, belonged to the non-Party working masses which always have to pay for the foolhardiness, ignorance, mismanagement and other sins of the Party chiefs. And yet I was curious to see the woman who in 1930 disposed of all who had organised the Fisheries Trust and in 1932 was finishing off those who were still left to carry on the work.

The G.P.U. House stood by itself in a conspicuous place above the railway and was painted light blue. Everyone avoided going near it. A warm wind was blowing in from the sea and a huge pool had formed in front of the steps. Two rotten planks were thrown across it, but they were half sunk in the water. In the U.S.S.R. dirt and disorder show no respect of persons or of Government institutions!

There was no sentry at the door, so that one could walk straight into the entrance lobby. Behind a low partition two big hefty lads in long military coats were lounging on chairs.

"Citizen, where are you going? What do you want?" growled one of them, rushing forward menacingly, though I came in very modestly and quietly.

"I want Batushkina, the examining officer," I answered calmly.

"Well, you can't see her, she isn't here," he said crossly.

"If she isn't here, ring her up and find out when she is coming," I insisted firmly.

"Have you been called up, citizen? Then produce your summons," he went on aggressively, as all who are proud of their high position are wont to do in the U.S.S.R.

"I haven't been called up and I have no summons. I want to see Batushkina. Do you understand? On personal business." I added the usual Soviet phrase to set the dull-witted fellow's mind in the right direction.

"On personal business? I see," said the other young man, yawning and stretching himself. "Ring her up, then."

The first young man began turning the handle of an antedeluvian telephone which rang like mad under his hand but apparently made no impression at the other end.

"Hallo, hallo, hallo!" he shouted. There was no answer. He drew a breath and began ringing and shouting again.

"Perhaps you'll call another time, citizen?"

"No, I must see her now," I persisted. "I won't go away till you get an answer. That's what I've come for."

He began ringing once more, thinking aloud, "Perhaps she's gone home? Perhaps she's gone to the dining-room?"

It was two o'clock—a slack time at the G.P.U. They work at night and so it was difficult to find her.

I sat down and watched them. I wondered what was passing in the minds of those village lads, fattened on the G.P.U. rations and trained in idleness. Here they were telephoning at my request, though I was a perfect stranger to them, but had I come under convoy they would have equally zealously searched me and kept watch over me. Two years ago they kept watch over Shcherbakov who had created the wealth of the Fisheries Trust; a year ago they guarded Pivovarov, who, trusting his Communist colleagues, returned from London and was apparently shot straight away; now they were guarding the shipwrecked captains. Did they understand what they were doing? Did they obey any orders that came?

At that moment the front door was flung open. They

both drew themselves up. A thin, angular little woman walked up to them, throwing a side-glance at me. Her yellow ill-natured face showed unmistakable signs of nervous irritability. She looked at the lads sharply, and one of them immediately explained my presence, trying to look stern and efficient.

"The citizen here has been asking for you. I told her to wait here."

She turned to me sharply.

"I am Tchernavin's wife. I want to see you about . . ."

"Tchernavin's wife?" she repeated with interest and some new expression came for a moment into her hard, piercing eyes. "Please will you come to my room," she said almost amiably. "Write out a pass," she ordered one of the young men.

He rushed to the book and clumsily dipped the pen into an ink bottle.

"Be quiet!" she said peremptorily. He hurriedly began to write, but his pen made a hole in the paper.

"You can send the pass afterwards, the citizen will come with me," she said with annoyance.

She rapped on the door with her knuckles. A sentry opened the door, let us in and shut it again. We were in a narrow corridor. On the left was a wall without any windows in it, on the right the cell doors with 'peep-holes.' The uncanny prison silence that I knew so well reigned in the corridor. The air was bad; there were evidently no lavatories and no *parashas* were kept in the cells.

Knowing the prison etiquette I walked in front. When we had come to her office door she stopped me, slightly touching my sleeve. Unlocking the door she let

me in, came in after me, and offered me a chair. She
immediately produced her cigarette case.

"Do you smoke?"

"No." I felt such a loathing for her that I could not
bring myself to say "thank you."

She lit a cigarette and quickly swallowed the smoke.
The ash tray on her table was full of cigarette ends;
they were lying about on the floor as well, and there
was cigarette ash all round her chair.

The most prominent feature in her plain, narrow,
bony face was her large mouth with moist flabby lips that
twitched nervously. Her dark greasy hair was badly
combed and badly arranged. Her moist hands with
thin flat fingers were none too clean. A knitted coat of
some absurd unbecoming colour hung loosely on her
flat chest.

Who was she? Where did she come from? Could
there have been any love in her life? Could anyone
think of her as a woman? I recalled my examining
officer who looked like Smerdyakov and wondered how
those two would like each other. He boasted that he
had shot the prisoners himself. Did she do it? I heard
that both in Moscow and in Leningrad there were
women in the G.P.U. who specialised in it. Her hands
were weak and shaky, but they could hold a revolver
right enough—and as to signing a death sentence, that
was nothing to her.

"So you are Tchernavin's wife?" she asked again,
scrutinising me with as much curiosity as I did her.

"Yes. I have come for my husband's furniture. So
far as I know his sentence said nothing about confiscation of property."

"You see," she said almost apologetically, "the

furniture is in our keeping. We thought there was no one to claim it."

"Aha!" I thought, "so you had intended to dispose of us both."

"But we have a son," I observed.

"Oh, yes, a son. We didn't know it."

"She is lying," I thought disgustedly. I knew that she had used our son as an argument to make my husband 'confess.'

"But all your things are perfectly safe with us," she went on in an amiable tone, which somehow made me suspect her veracity once more.

"May I take them away?"

"Yes, certainly. Some time this week?"

"I should like to have them to-day if possible. I must hurry home."

"Perhaps to-morrow? I haven't time to-day."

I understood that our furniture would have to be collected from various places, but thought I might as well go through with it.

"Very well, to-morrow, but in the morning, please."

"Then you will have to write out a formal statement for us."

"What sort of statement?"

"Saying that you ask for your husband's property which was supposed to belong to no one, since you were both under arrest."

"I thought that prisoners retained the right to their property unless a sentence of confiscation was passed."

"That's true, but you see if you write the statement it will make it easier for us in view of certain formalities.

Then we'll be able to return the things to you without any delay."

"Perhaps you would be so kind as to dictate to me what I am to write."

"Just as you like," she said, somewhat annoyed, and proceeded to dictate to me a well-worded statement in perfectly good Russian.

She comes of the educated class, I thought. She has certainly finished in a secondary school and has had some legal training. What could have brought her into the G.P.U., I wondered. Was it lust of power? The temptation of feeling that other people's lives and deaths were in her hands? There may be some peculiar satisfaction in knowing that an insignificant, false and contemptible creature like oneself can ruin so many good, strong men whose work is indispensable to the country.

"When can I get my things, then?" I asked again.

"Perhaps to-morrow."

"What time?"

"Eleven o'clock. Will that suit you?"

"Yes, thank you."

"How is your husband?" she asked me amiably, evidently on the look out for any odd bit of information that might come her way.

"Thank you," I answered, not intending to say anything more.

"How is his health? I heard he was not at all well. You know, we value him very much and hope that he will return to work at Murmansk. We badly need men like him, you know. There are perfect idiots in the Trust now. Have you heard how many trawlers they've wrecked?"

"And whose fault is that?" I thought with hatred.

"Till to-morrow, then. I will see you out," she said, as though she were doing me a courtesy, but of course I could not have gone past the sentry without her.

She took me down the corridor and gave me her cold moist hand.

The following day I arrived punctually at eleven, but she was an hour and a half late. Her face looked more yellow than ever, and there were dark rings under her eyes. She evidently had been examining the prisoners during the night and had not slept.

"There is a list of your things. They are in our store-room and all is in order," she said almost ingratiatingly.

"Excellent," I replied, glancing at the list.

"Please verify it. This ought to include everything," she said in a business-like tone.

I looked through the list. There was not a half of the things in it, but it was no use arguing with her.

"That's all," I said firmly, to avoid further conversation.

"Then perhaps you'll sign this receipt. Our store-room keeper will hand over the things to you."

"That's a nice way of doing things," I thought. "If I tried to hand over somebody's property in that way I would be had up at once and receive five years of prison, but these people can do what they like."

When I had signed a paper saying that I received everything in good order and had no further claims, I was taken to the store-room. There, among hay, broken-down sledges, torn nets and other rubbish, I found our furniture which had obviously just been brought there. Everything was broken and spoiled; the upholstering was torn, soiled, covered with grease. It was a heap of rubbish and not the furniture that I had carefully selected two years before to create a semblance of comfort for my husband in this wild, dirty place. It is astonishing how destructive people can be with things acquired dishonestly.

"Will you check them?" the store-room keeper, who may have had his share of using our furniture, asked me disapprovingly.

"It's clear enough as it is," said I without concealing my disgust.

"When will you take them?"

"To-morrow."

That same evening I took the train back to Leningrad. Our broken furniture was only fit to be burnt.

. . . . .

The last thing I heard before leaving Murmansk were the agitated conversations between the employees of the Fisheries Trust after their meeting with Mīkoyan. They were particularly upset by his complaint that they had not in their Trust a single man with a head on his shoulders. "I don't mind whether it's an enemy and a counter-revolutionary, provided he has brains," he thundered. "I declare that I'll find the man and put him here to work!"

"He had better ask that woman," I thought, "what became of the men who had created the Trust. Two of them have been shot, three are doing penal servitude, and now the last experienced captains are on their trial."

Mīkoyan was clamouring for "men," and the G.P.U. was steadily removing them.